POCKET SIZE 3

THE MENACE OF
ALIA RELLAPOR, PART THREE
The Akiko Series, Issues 14~18

SIRIUS ENTERTAINMENT
UNADILLA, NEW YORK

This book is dedicated
to my mother & father

AKIKO POCKET SIZE 3 AUGUST, 2004.
FIRST PRINTING. PUBLISHED BY SIRIUS ENTERTAINMENT, INC.
LAWRENCE SALAMONE, PRESIDENT. ROBB HORAN, PUBLISHER.
KEITH DAVIDSEN, EDITOR. CORRESPONDENCE: P.O. BOX X, UNADILLA, NY 13849.
AKIKO AND ALL RELATED CHARACTERS ARE TM & © 2004 MARK CRILLEY. SIRIUS AND
THE DOGSTAR LOGO ARE ® SIRIUS ENTERTAINMENT, INC. ALL RIGHTS RESERVED. ANY
SIMILARITY TO PERSONS LIVING OR DEAD IS PURELY COINCIDENTAL.
PRINTED IN THE USA.

THE STORY SO FAR

Welcome to Pocket Size Three, the last of three trade paperbacks comprising Akiko's first epic-length adventure story, "The Menace of Alia Rellapor." For those who may have missed the first two volumes, here is a brief summary of what has occurred thusfar.

The concept behind the series is this: a young girl by the name of Akiko is taken off to a planet called Smoo, where she leads a crew of companions on a series of adventures. Her friends on Smoo include Spuckler (a rugged space-pirate), Gax (Spuckler's trusty robot), Mr. Beeba (a nervous academic), and Poog (an inscrutable floating alien). Smoo is ruled by a benevolent king named Froptoppit, a character who appears only briefly in this last part of the tale.

In Volume One, Akiko is put in charge of a mission to rescue King Froptoppit's son, the Prince of Smoo, who has been kidnapped by his own mother, a mysterious woman by the name of Alia Rellapor. The seemingly straightforward mission is beset with problems, however, as Akiko and her friends are thwarted at every turn by pirates, sea monsters, and other threats they encounter on their way to Alia Rellapor's castle.

In Volume Two our heroes continue their perilous

journey, and are confronted along the way by Loza Throck, Alia Rellapor's evil henchman. He warns them to turn back, but this of course only intensifies their resolve to complete the mission.

Climbing an ancient wall and crossing a seemingly endless bridge, they finally pass into the realm of Alia Rellapor. There they meet up with an old friend, P. Q. Goybi, who agrees to help them on the last leg of their journey, despite the fact that he and Alia Rellapor were once close friends.

In the sequence preceding the first page of this volume, Akiko and her friends have just caught their first spectacular view of Alia Rellapor's castle. Now that they've finally reached their destination, they know only too well that the most dangerous part of the mission has only just begun.

Can they enter the castle undetected? Are they destined to meet face to face with Alia Rellapor? Will they succeed in rescuing the Prince? All the answers lie within the following pages, so read on!

If you have any questions or comments, feel free to contact me directly by e-mail at the address below. I'd love to hear what you think, and will do my best to reply to you personally.

mark@markcrilley.com

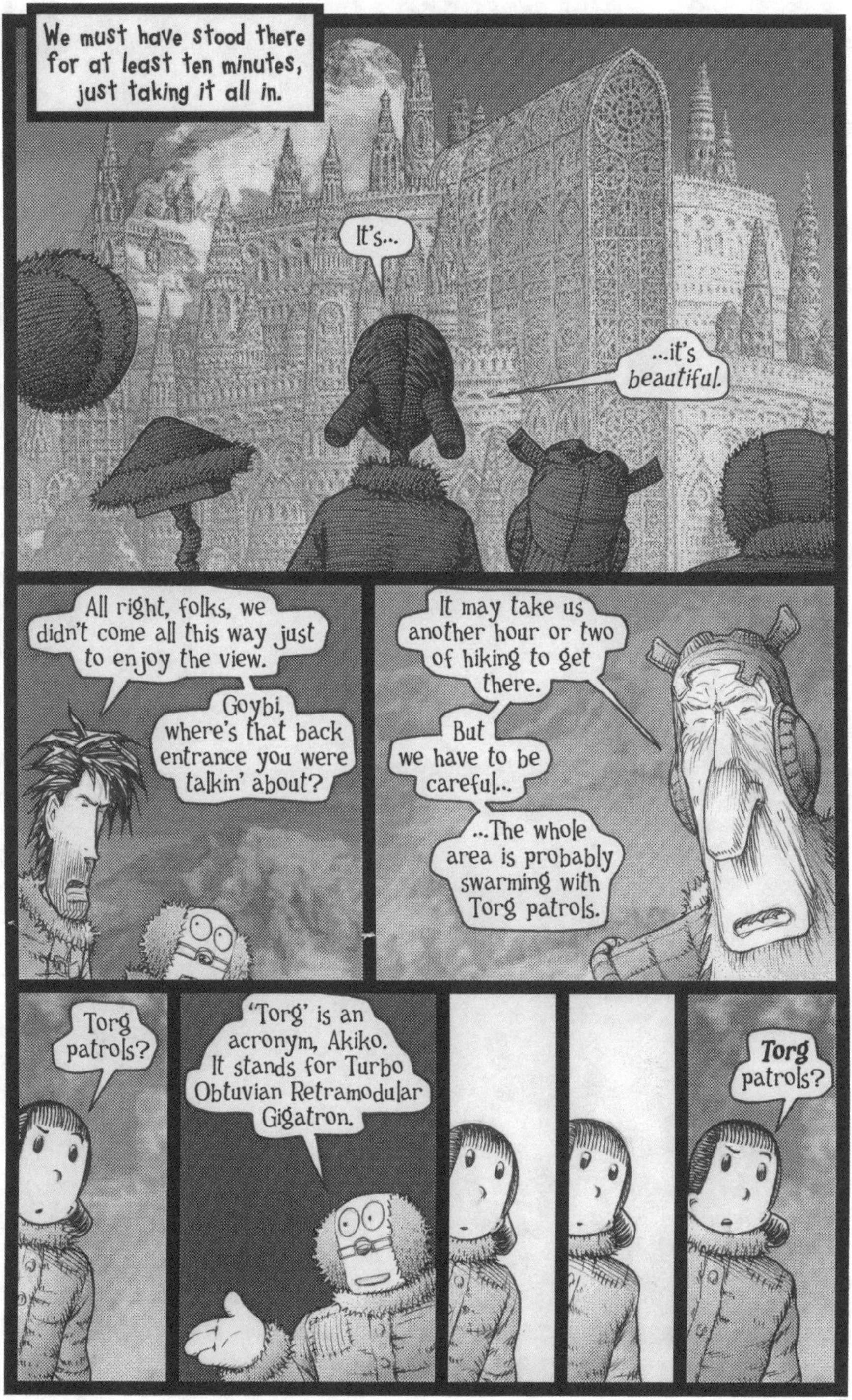
We must have stood there for at least ten minutes, just taking it all in.
It's...
...it's *beautiful.*
All right, folks, we didn't come all this way just to enjoy the view.
Goybi, where's that back entrance you were talkin' about?
It may take us another hour or two of hiking to get there.
But we have to be careful...
...The whole area is probably swarming with Torg patrols.
Torg patrols?
'Torg' is an acronym, Akiko. It stands for Turbo Obtuvian Retramodular Gigatron.
Torg patrols?

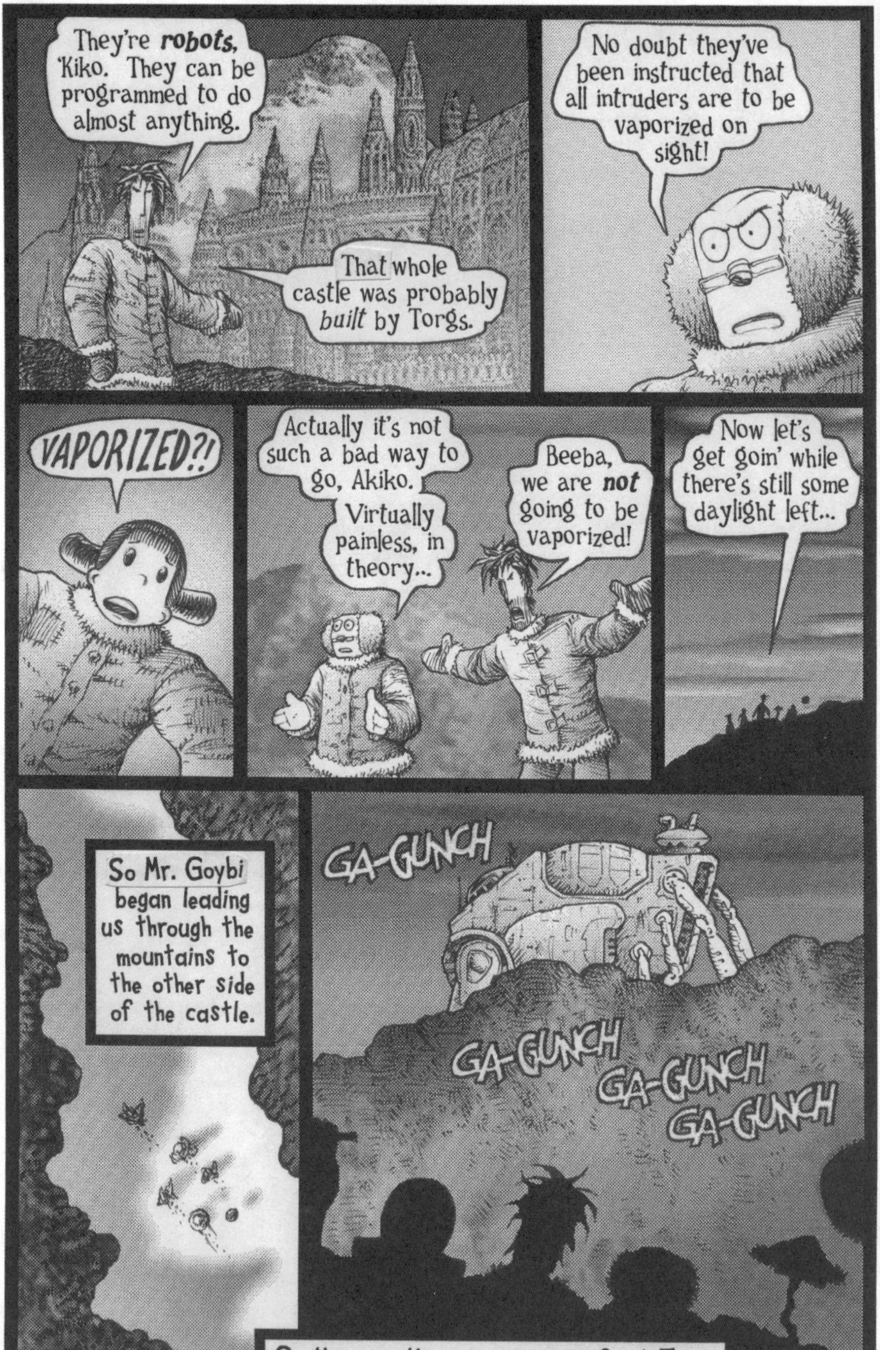
They're **robots**, 'Kiko. They can be programmed to do almost anything.
That whole castle was probably *built* by Torgs.
No doubt they've been instructed that all intruders are to be vaporized on sight!
VAPORIZED?!
Actually it's not such a bad way to go, Akiko.
Virtually painless, in theory...
Beeba, we are **not** going to be vaporized!
Now let's get goin' while there's still some daylight left...
So Mr. Goybi began leading us through the mountains to the other side of the castle.
GA-GUNCH
GA-GUNCH
GA-GUNCH
GA-GUNCH
On the way there we saw our first Torg.

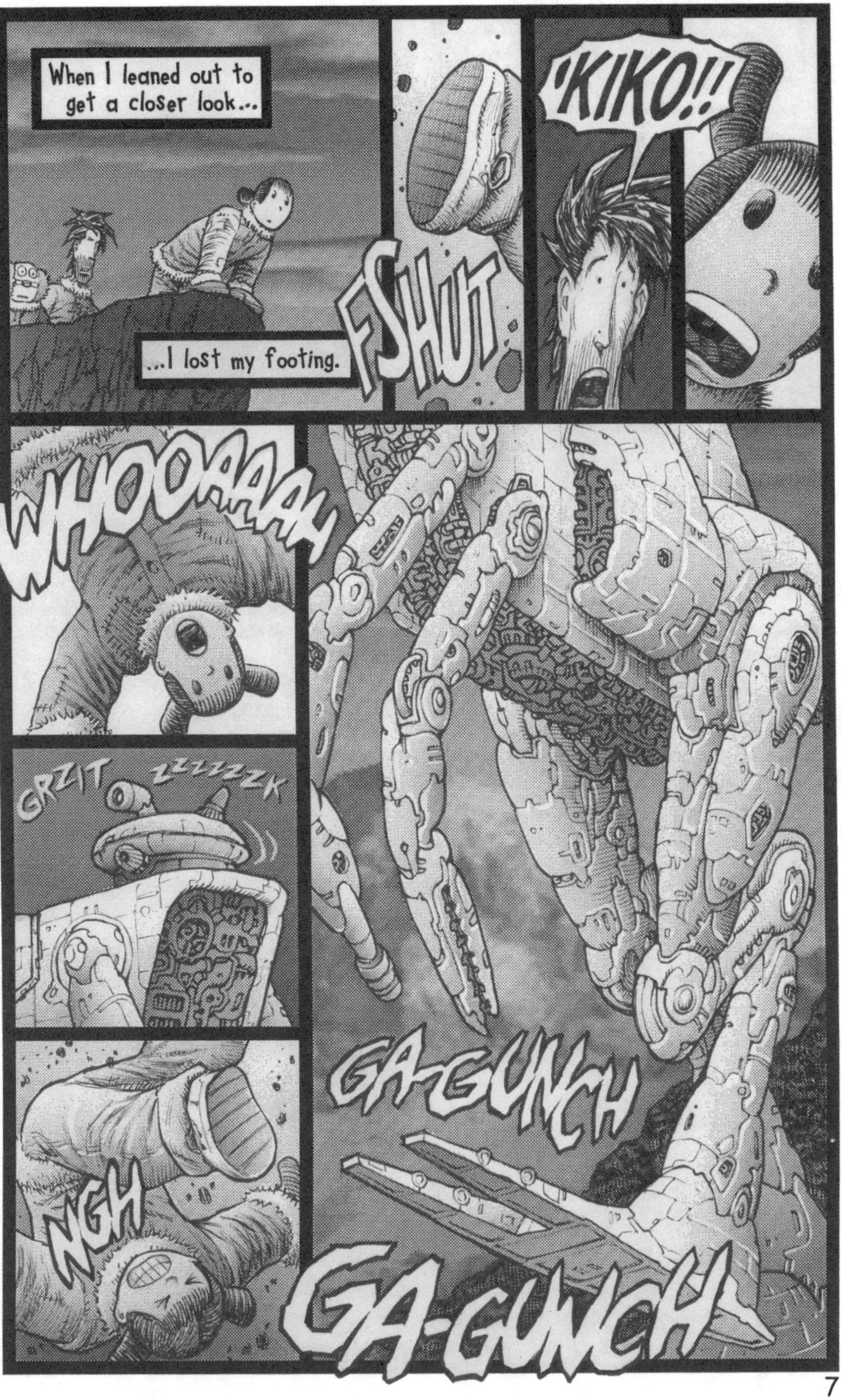
When I leaned out to get a closer look...
...I lost my footing.
FSHUT
KIKO!!
WHOOAAAH
GRZIT
ZZZZZZZK
NGH
GA-GUNCH
GA-GUNCH

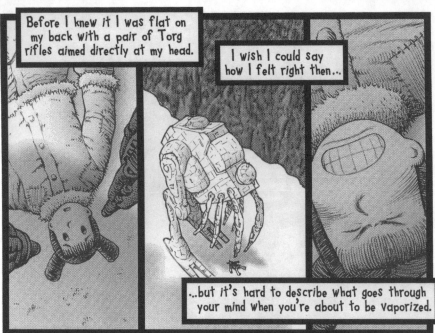

Before I knew *it* I was flat on my back with a pair of Torg rifles aimed directly at my head.

I wish I could say how I felt right then...

...but it's hard to describe what goes through your mind when you're about to be vaporized.

BLAAM

When I opened my eyes, the Torg stood motionless above me with a clean, little hole in *its* head.

Not bad, Goybi...

...not bad at all!

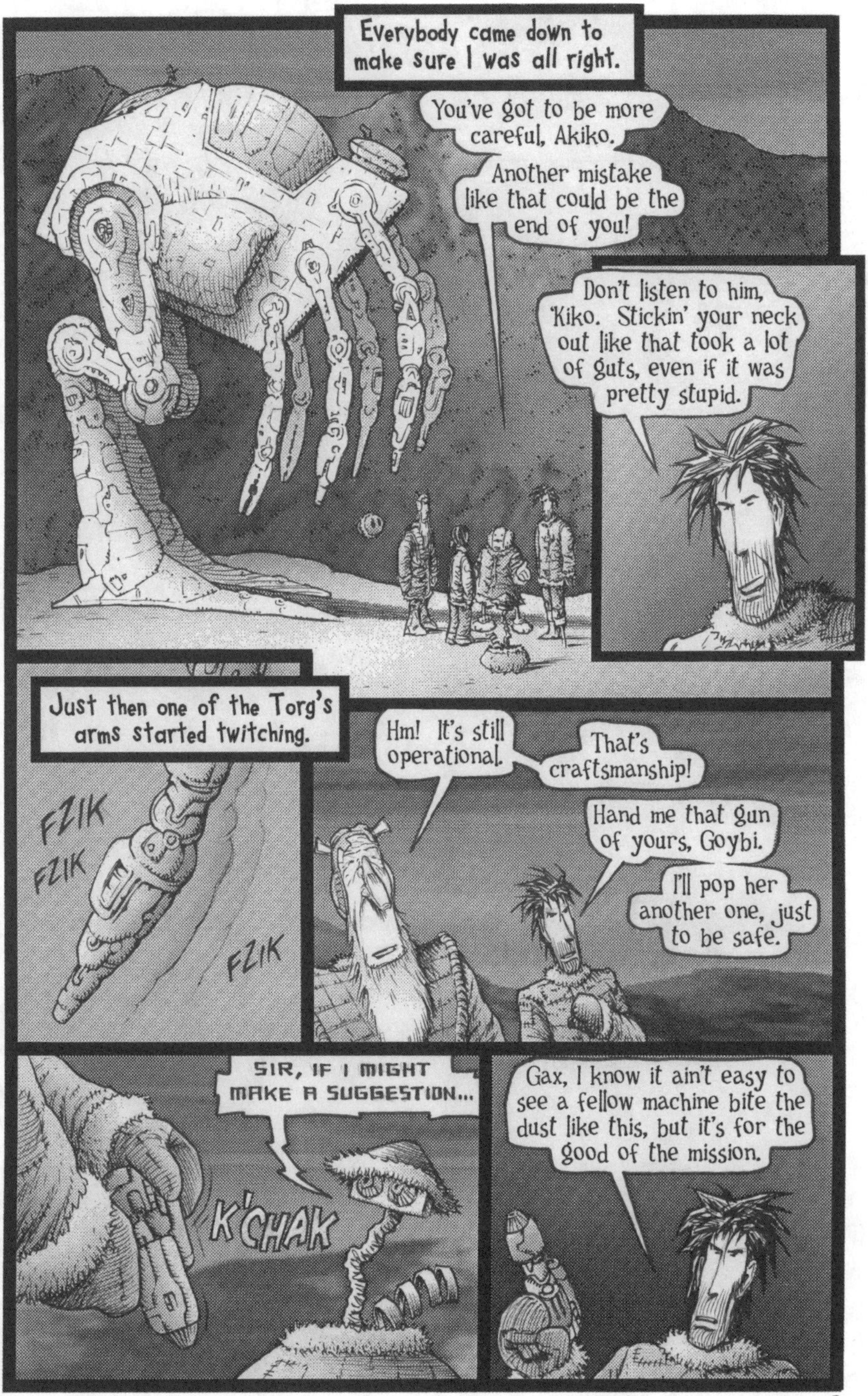
Everybody came down to make sure I was all right.
You've got to be more careful, Akiko.
Another mistake like that could be the end of you!
Don't listen to him, 'Kiko. Stickin' your neck out like that took a lot of guts, even if it was pretty stupid.
Just then one of the Torg's arms started twitching.
FZIK
FZIK
FZIK
Hm! It's still operational.
That's craftsmanship!
Hand me that gun of yours, Goybi.
I'll pop her another one, just to be safe.
SIR, IF I MIGHT MAKE A SUGGESTION...
K'CHAK
Gax, I know it ain't easy to see a fellow machine bite the dust like this, but it's for the good of the mission.

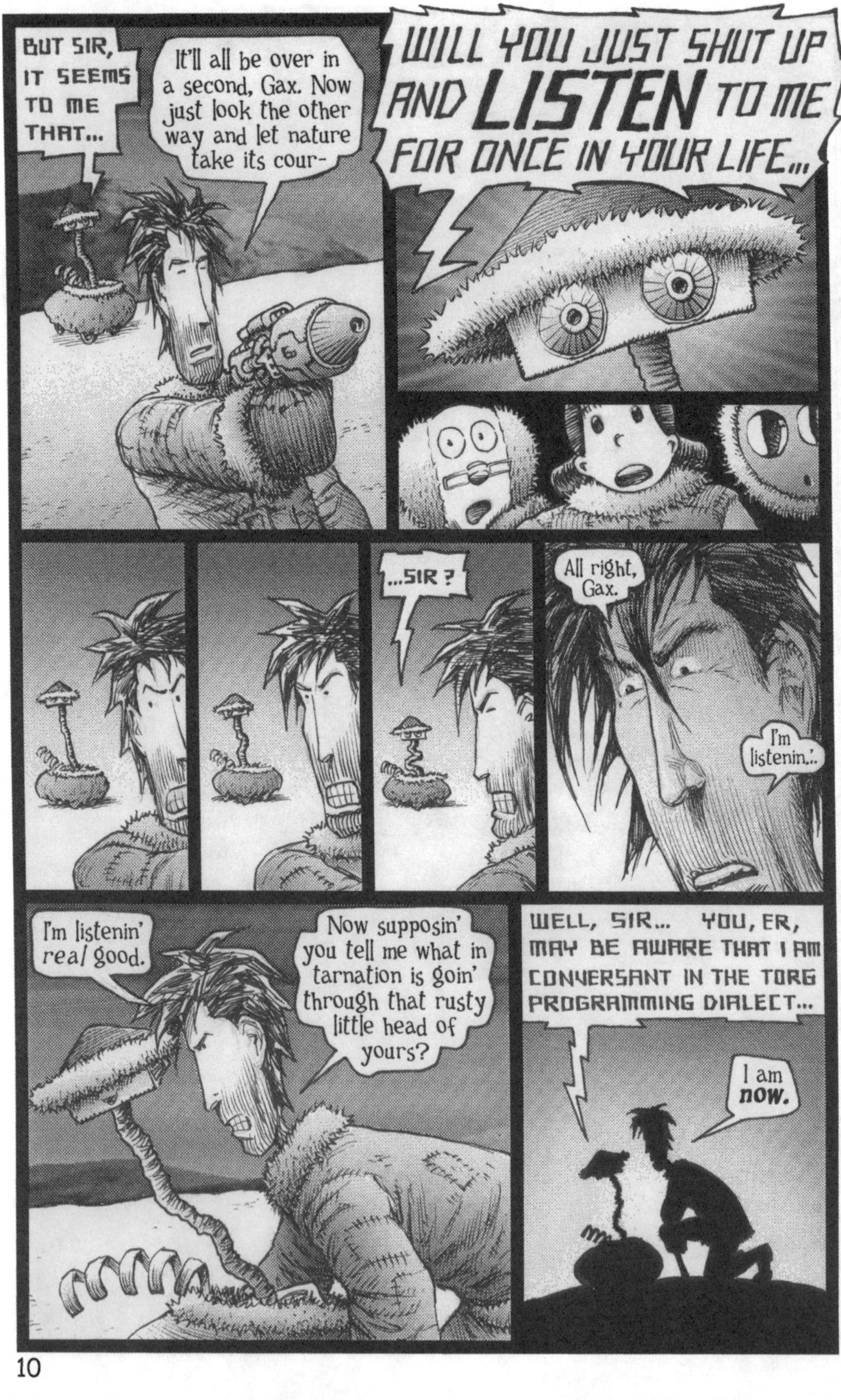
BUT SIR, IT SEEMS TO ME THAT...
It'll all be over in a second, Gax. Now just look the other way and let nature take its cour-
WILL YOU JUST SHUT UP AND LISTEN TO ME FOR ONCE IN YOUR LIFE...
...SIR ?
All right, Gax.
I'm listenin'...
I'm listenin' real good.
Now supposin' you tell me what in tarnation is goin' through that rusty little head of yours?
WELL, SIR... YOU, ER, MAY BE AWARE THAT I AM CONVERSANT IN THE TORG PROGRAMMING DIALECT...
I am now.

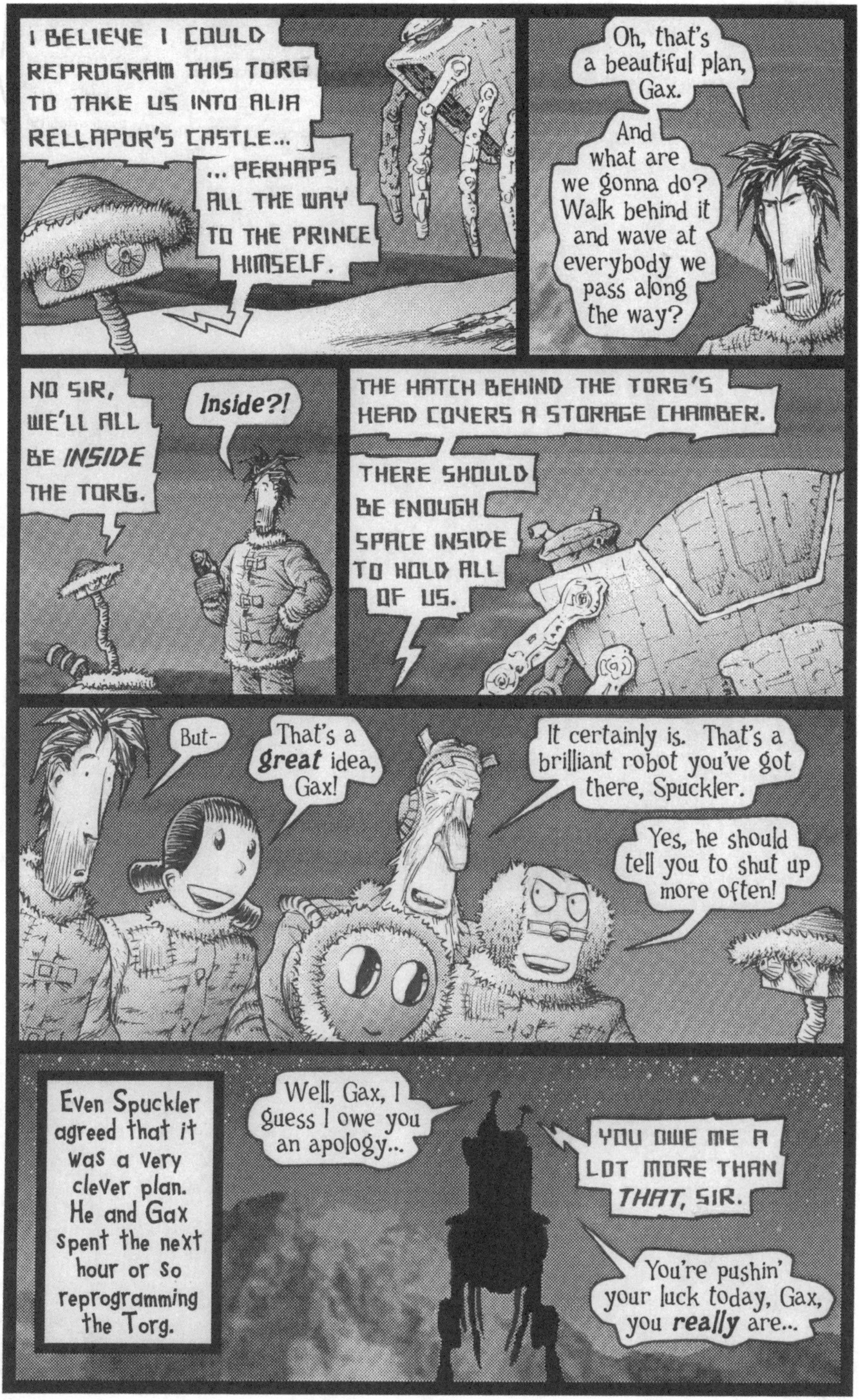
I BELIEVE I COULD REPROGRAM THIS TORG TO TAKE US INTO ALIA RELLAPOR'S CASTLE...
... PERHAPS ALL THE WAY TO THE PRINCE HIMSELF.
Oh, that's a beautiful plan, Gax.
And what are we gonna do? Walk behind it and wave at everybody we pass along the way?
NO SIR, WE'LL ALL BE *INSIDE* THE TORG.
Inside?!
THE HATCH BEHIND THE TORG'S HEAD COVERS A STORAGE CHAMBER.
THERE SHOULD BE ENOUGH SPACE INSIDE TO HOLD ALL OF US.
But-
That's a **great** idea, Gax!
It certainly is. That's a brilliant robot you've got there, Spuckler.
Yes, he should tell you to shut up more often!
Even Spuckler agreed that it was a very clever plan. He and Gax spent the next hour or so reprogramming the Torg.
Well, Gax, I guess I owe you an apology...
YOU OWE ME A LOT MORE THAN *THAT*, SIR.
You're pushin' your luck today, Gax, you **really** are...

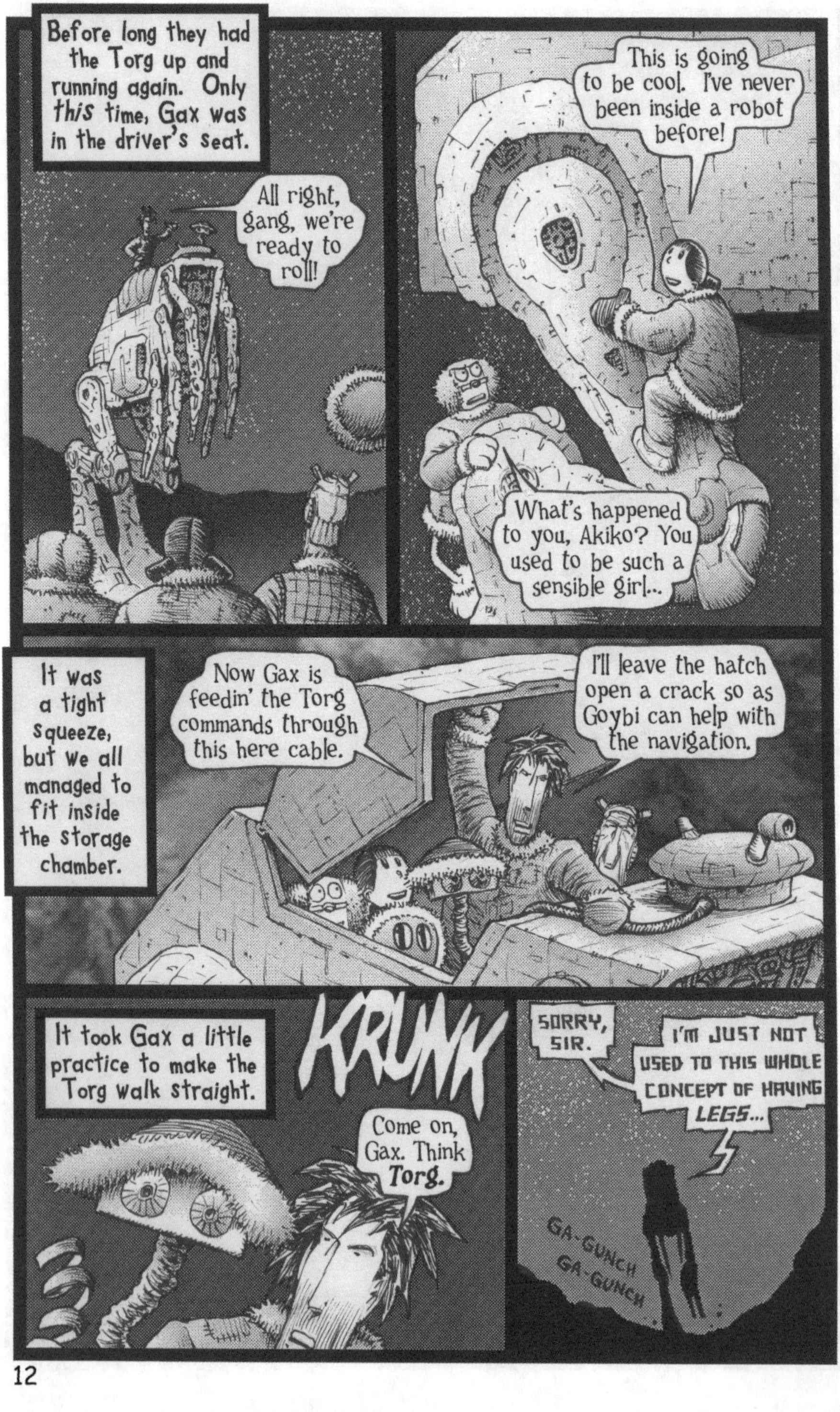
Before long they had the Torg up and running again. Only *this* time, Gax was in the driver's seat.
All right, gang, we're ready to roll!
This is going to be cool. I've never been inside a robot before!
What's happened to you, Akiko? You used to be such a sensible girl...
It was a tight squeeze, but we all managed to fit *inside* the storage chamber.
Now Gax is feedin' the Torg commands through this here cable.
I'll leave the hatch open a crack so as Goybi can help with the navigation.
It took Gax a little practice to make the Torg walk straight.
KRUNK
Come on, Gax. Think **Torg.**
SORRY, SIR.
I'M JUST NOT USED TO THIS WHOLE CONCEPT OF HAVING *LEGS*...
GA-GUNCH GA-GUNCH

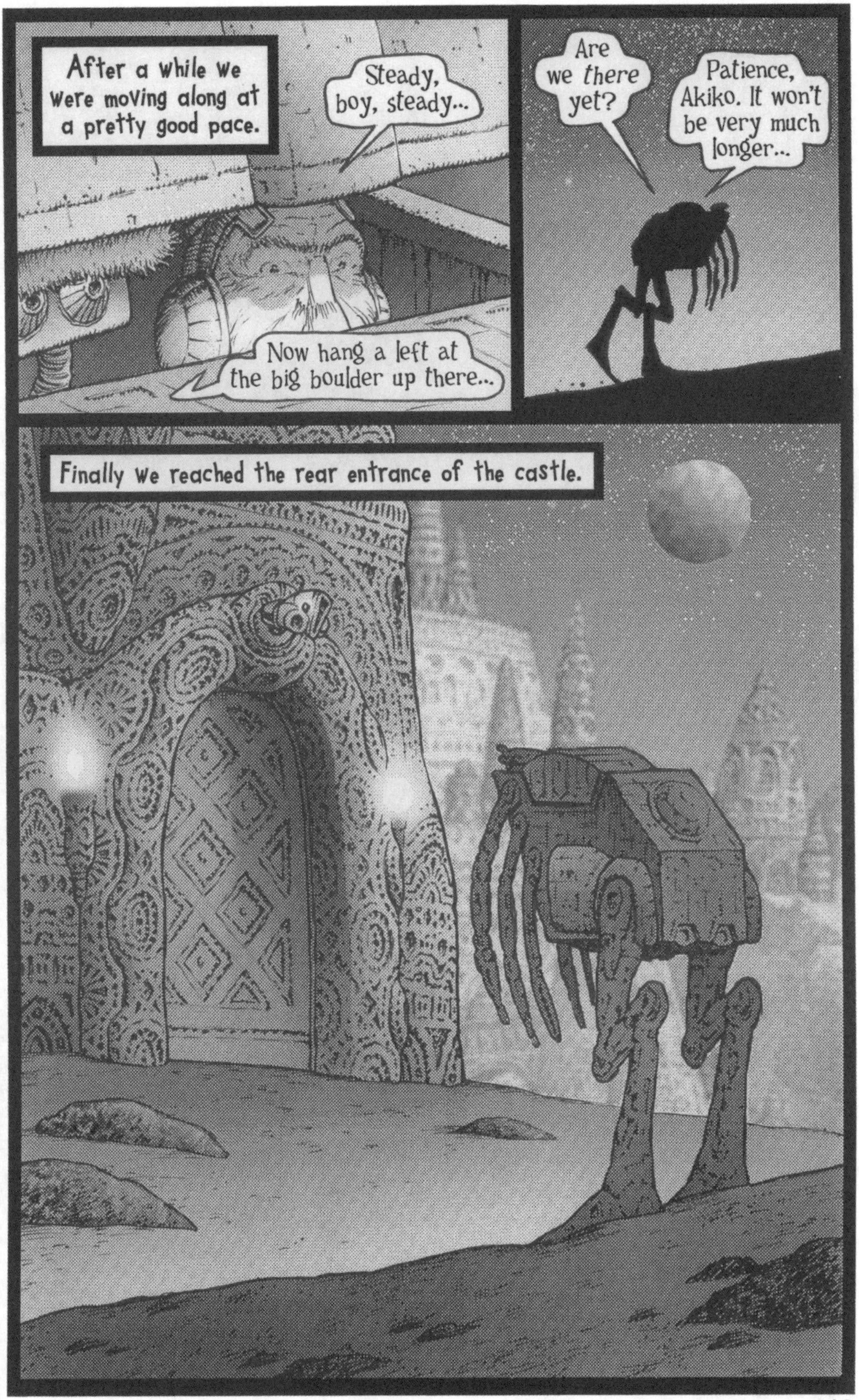
After a while we were moving along at a pretty good pace.
Steady, boy, steady...
Now hang a left at the big boulder up there...
Are we *there* yet?
Patience, Akiko. It won't be very much longer...
Finally we reached the rear entrance of the castle.

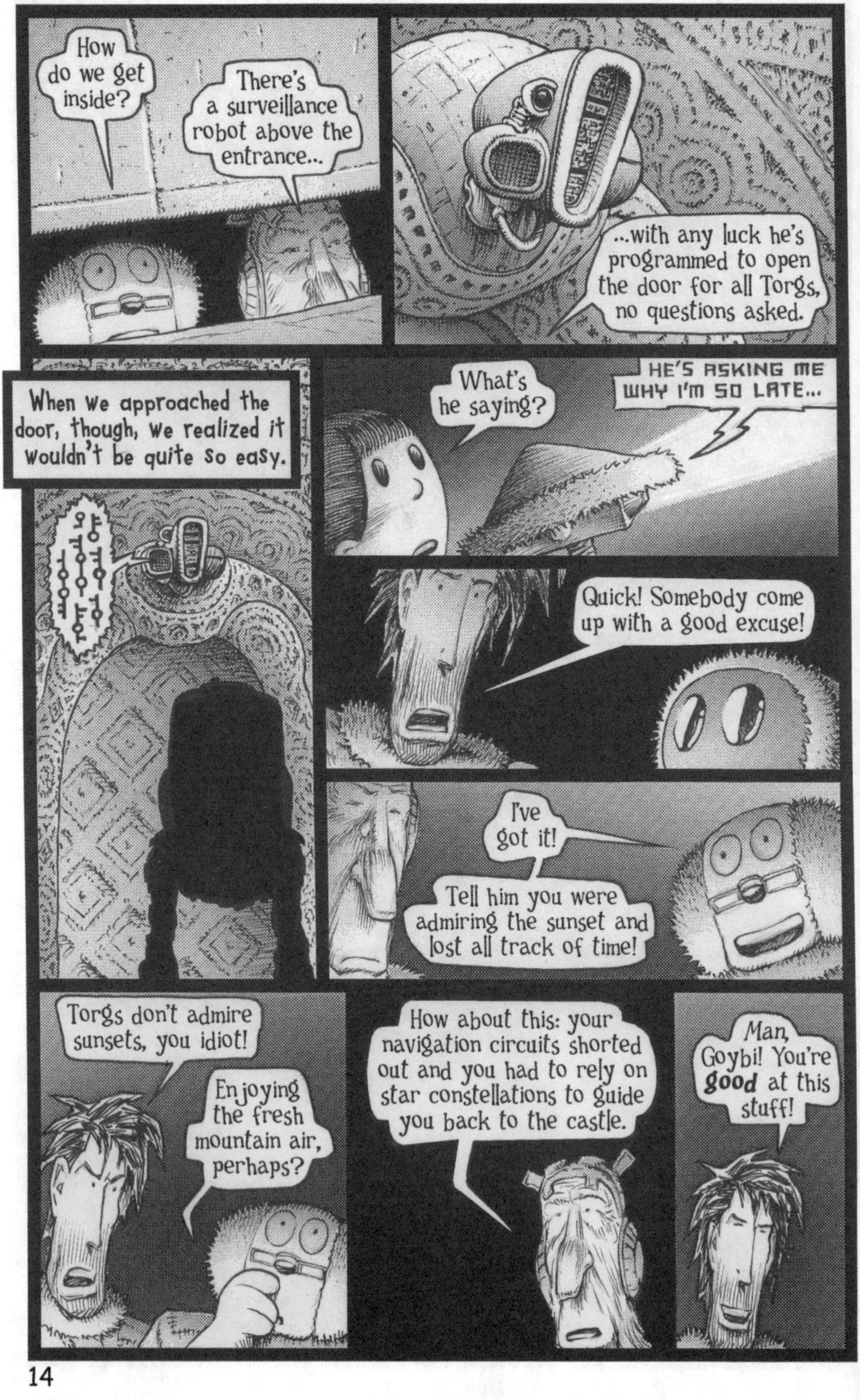

How do we get inside?
There's a surveillance robot above the entrance...
...with any luck he's programmed to open the door for all Torgs, no questions asked.
When we approached the door, though, we realized it wouldn't be quite so easy.
What's he saying?
HE'S ASKING ME WHY I'M SO LATE...
Quick! Somebody come up with a good excuse!
I've got it!
Tell him you were admiring the sunset and lost all track of time!
Torgs don't admire sunsets, you idiot!
Enjoying the fresh mountain air, perhaps?
How about this: your navigation circuits shorted out and you had to rely on star constellations to guide you back to the castle.
Man, Goybi! You're ***good*** at this stuff!

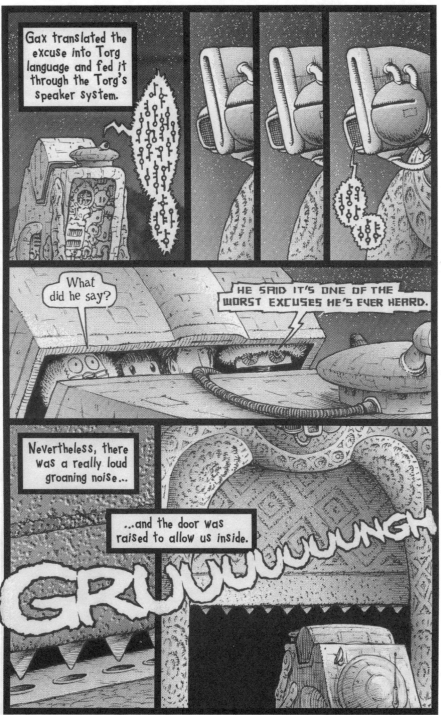

Gax translated the excuse into Torg language and fed it through the Torg's speaker system.

What did he say?

HE SAID IT'S ONE OF THE WORST EXCUSES HE'S EVER HEARD.

Nevertheless, there was a really loud groaning noise...

...and the door was raised to allow us inside.

GRUUUUUUUNGH

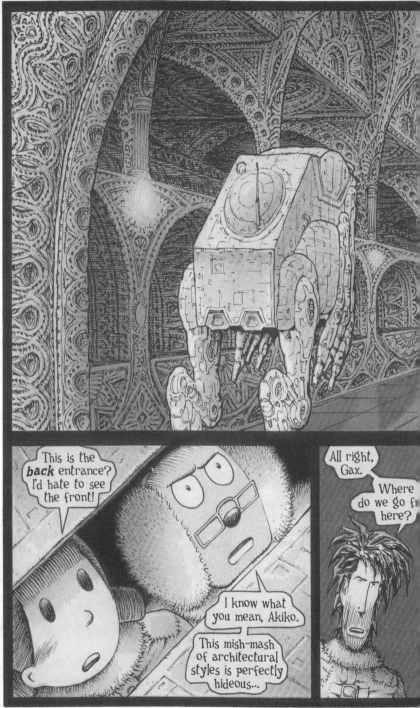

This is the **back** entrance? I'd hate to see the front!

I know what you mean, Akiko.

This mish-mash of architectural styles is perfectly hideous...

All right, Gax.

Where do we go f[r] here?

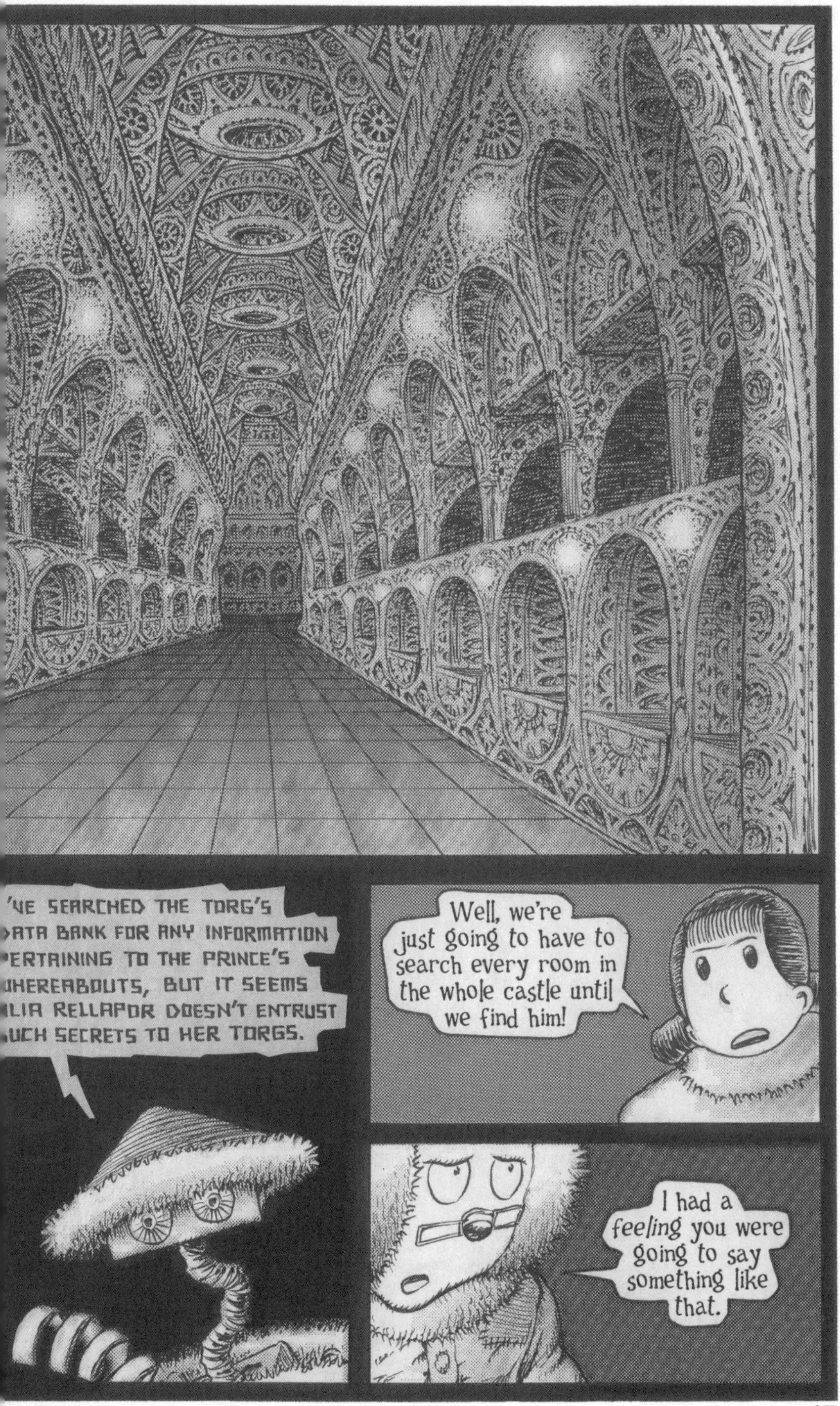
'VE SEARCHED THE TORG'S ATA BANK FOR ANY INFORMATION ERTAINING TO THE PRINCE'S HEREABOUTS, BUT IT SEEMS LIA RELLAPOR DOESN'T ENTRUST UCH SECRETS TO HER TORGS.
Well, we're just going to have to search every room in the whole castle until we find him!
I had a *feeling* you were going to say something like that.

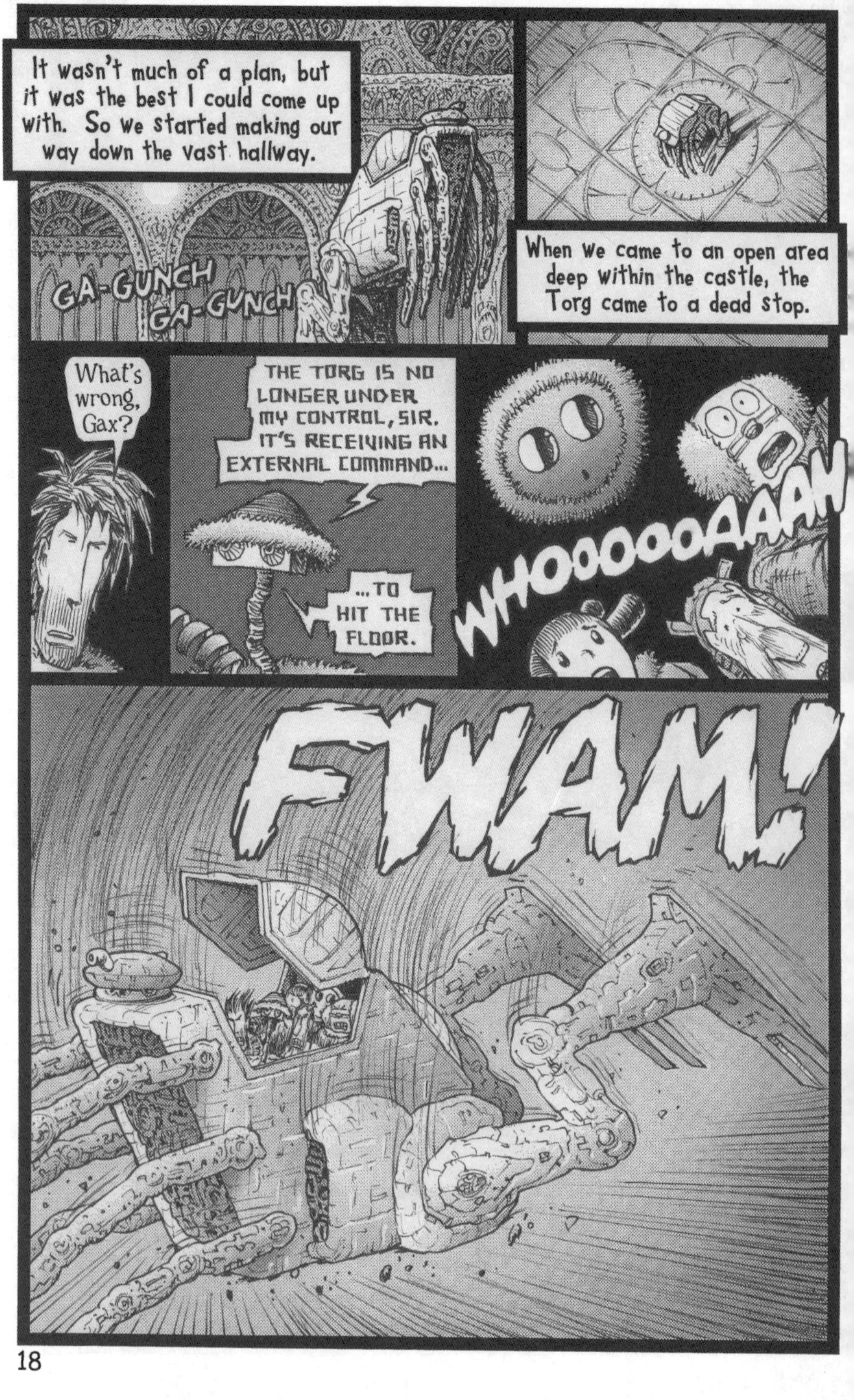
It wasn't much of a plan, but it was the best I could come up with. So we started making our way down the vast hallway.
GA-GUNCH
GA-GUNCH
When we came to an open area deep within the castle, the Torg came to a dead stop.
What's wrong, Gax?
THE TORG IS NO LONGER UNDER MY CONTROL, SIR. IT'S RECEIVING AN EXTERNAL COMMAND...
...TO HIT THE FLOOR.
WHOOOOOOAAAH
FWAM!

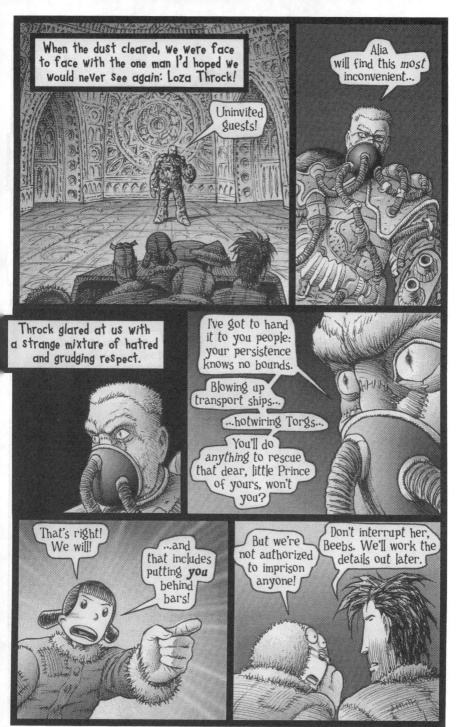

When the dust cleared, we were face to face with the one man I'd hoped we would never see again: Loza Throck!

Uninvited guests!

Alia will find this *most* inconvenient...

Throck glared at us with a strange mixture of hatred and grudging respect.

I've got to hand it to you people: your persistence knows no bounds.

Blowing up transport ships...

...hotwiring Torgs...

You'll do *anything* to rescue that dear, little Prince of yours, won't you?

That's right! We will!

...and that includes putting *you* behind bars!

But we're not authorized to imprison anyone!

Don't interrupt her, Beebs. We'll work the details out later.

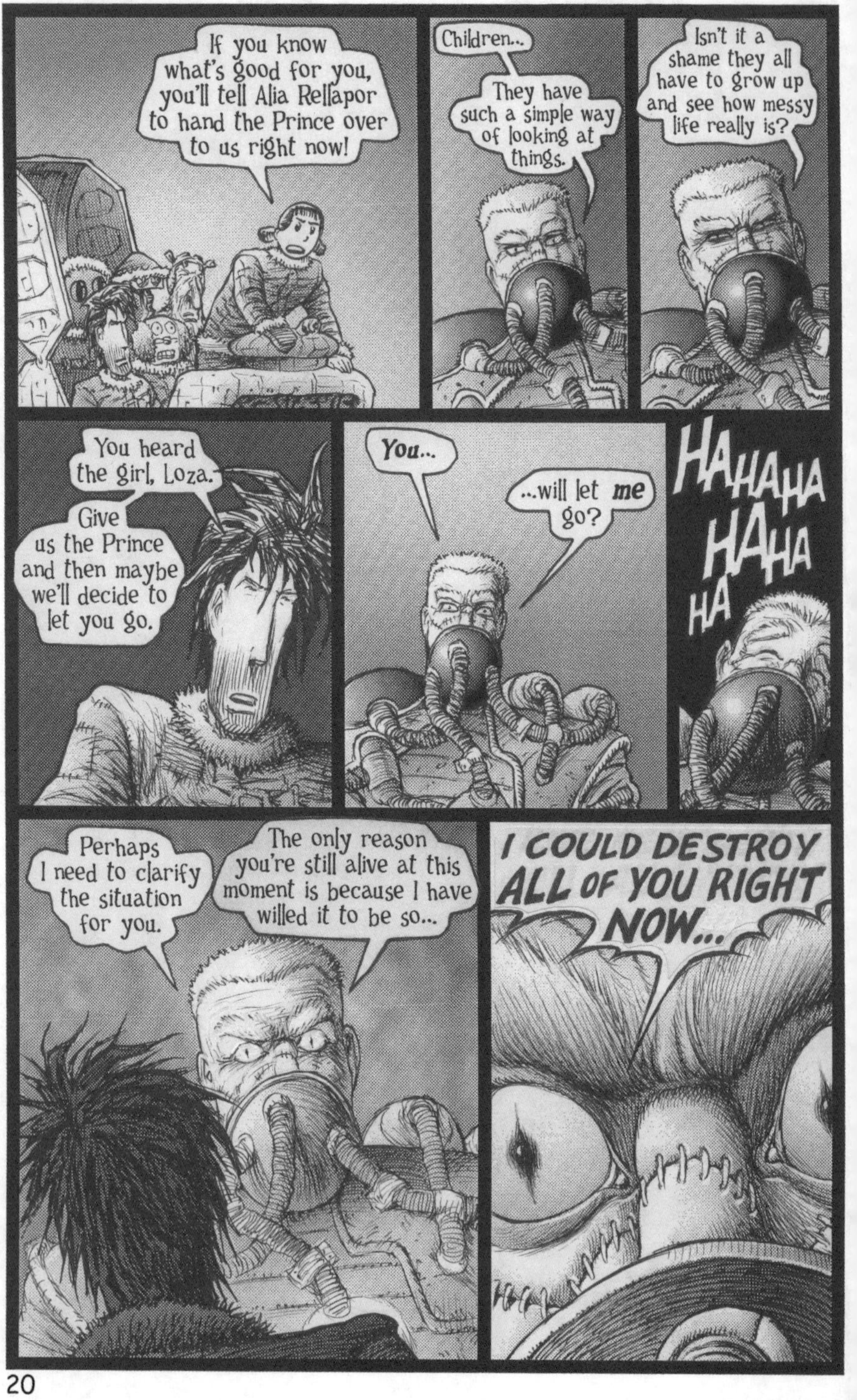
If you know what's good for you, you'll tell Alia Rellapor to hand the Prince over to us right now!
Children...
They have such a simple way of looking at things.
Isn't it a shame they all have to grow up and see how messy life really is?
You heard the girl, Loza.
Give us the Prince and then maybe we'll decide to let you go.
You...
...will let me go?
HAHAHA HAHAHA HA
Perhaps I need to clarify the situation for you.
The only reason you're still alive at this moment is because I have willed it to be so...
I COULD DESTROY ALL OF YOU RIGHT NOW...

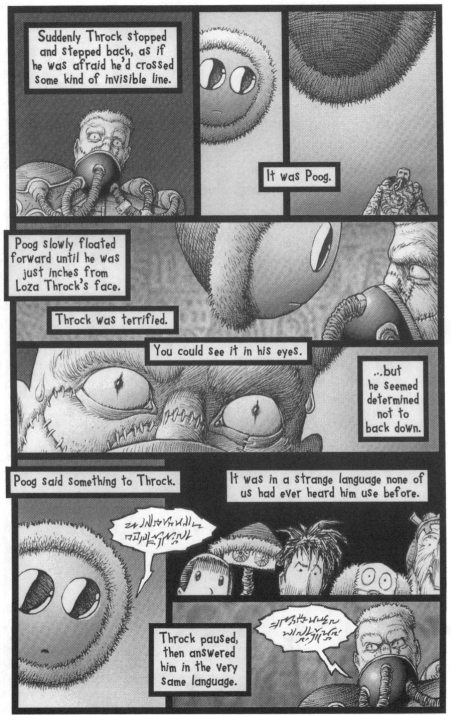

Suddenly Throck stopped and stepped back, as if he was afraid he'd crossed some kind of *invisible* line.

It was Poog.

Poog slowly floated forward until he was just inches from Loza Throck's face.

Throck was terrified.

You could see it in his eyes.

...but he seemed determined not to back down.

Poog said something to Throck.

It was in a strange language none of us had ever heard him use before.

Throck paused, then answered him in the very same language.

21

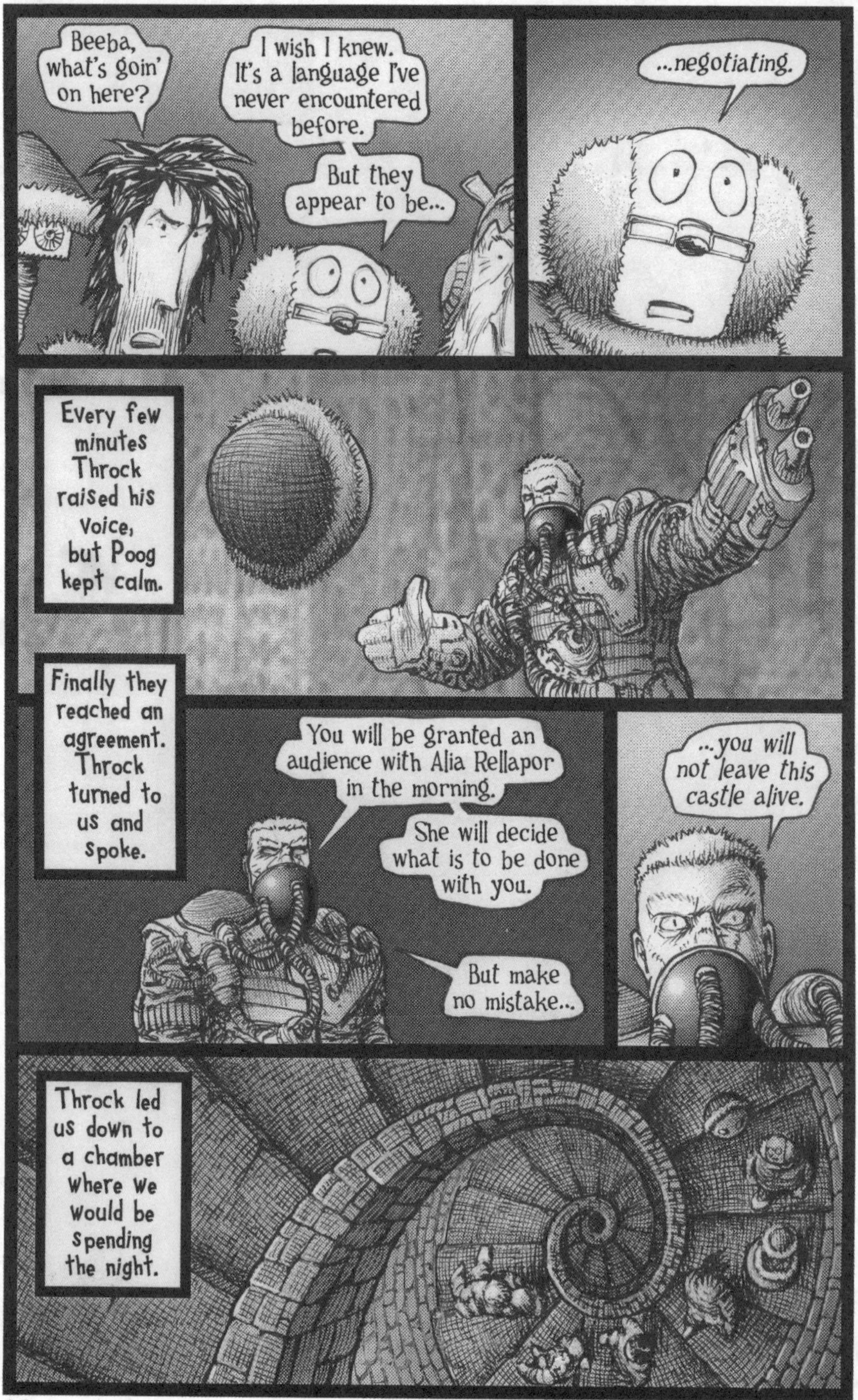
Beeba, what's goin' on here?
I wish I knew. It's a language I've never encountered before.
But they appear to be...
...negotiating.
Every few minutes Throck raised his voice, but Poog kept calm.
Finally they reached an agreement. Throck turned to us and spoke.
You will be granted an audience with Alia Rellapor in the morning.
She will decide what is to be done with you.
But make no mistake...
...you will not leave this castle alive.
Throck led us down to a chamber where we would be spending the night.

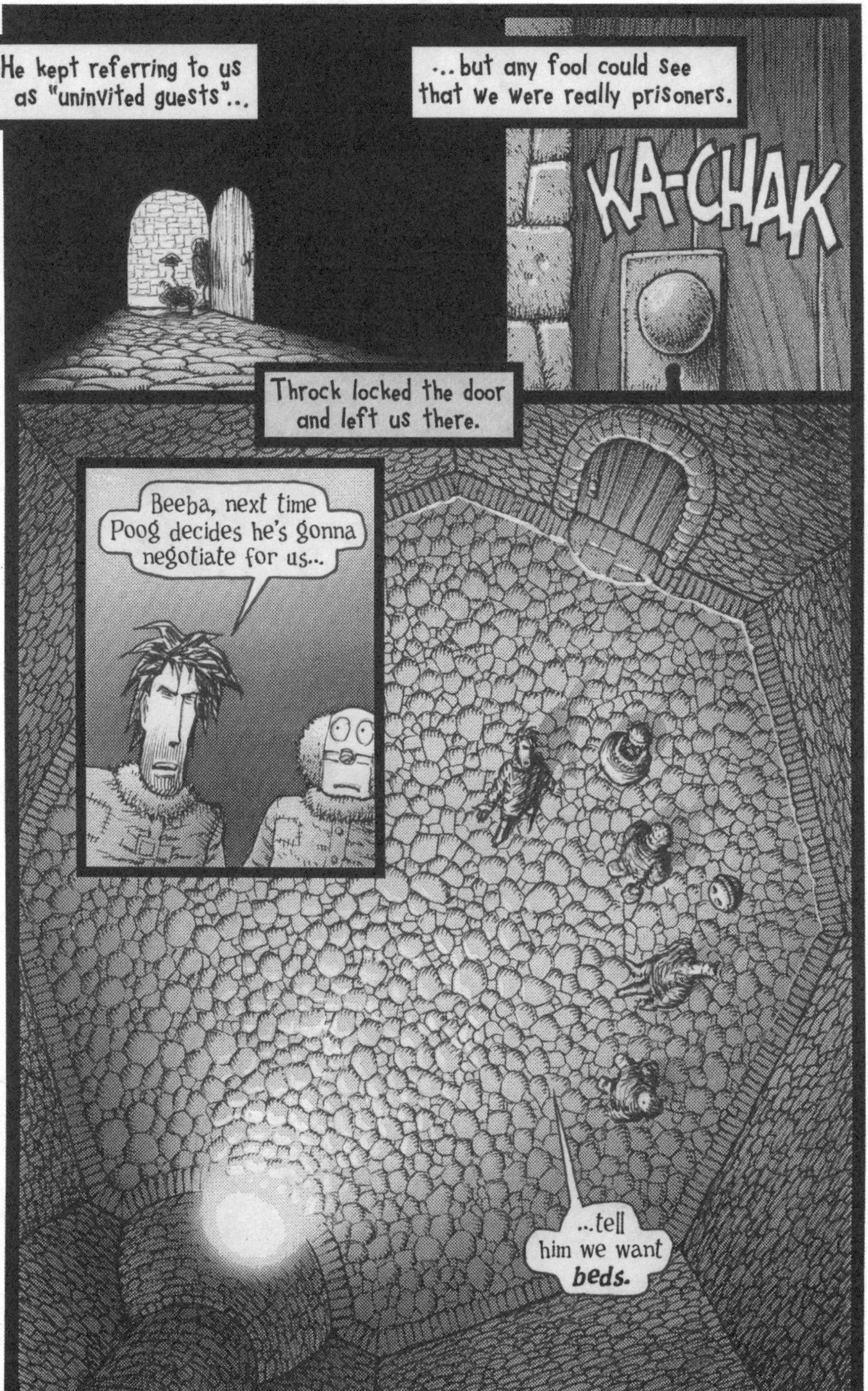

He kept referring to us as "uninvited guests"...
...but any fool could see that we were really prisoners.
KA-CHAK
Throck locked the door and left us there.
Beeba, next time Poog decides he's gonna negotiate for us...
...tell him we want *beds.*

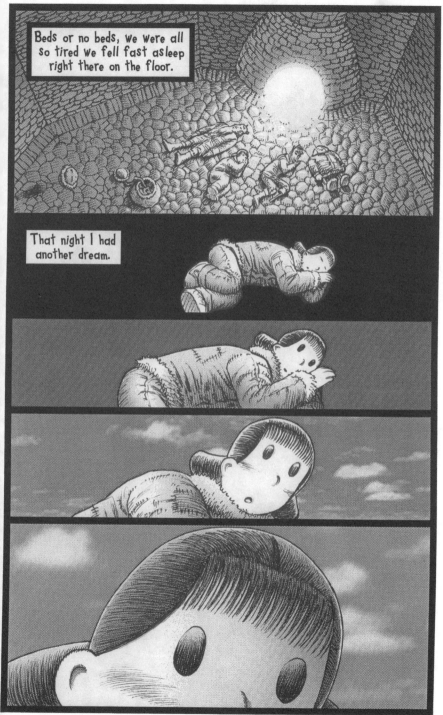

Beds or no beds, we were all so tired we fell fast asleep right there on the floor.

That night I had another dream.

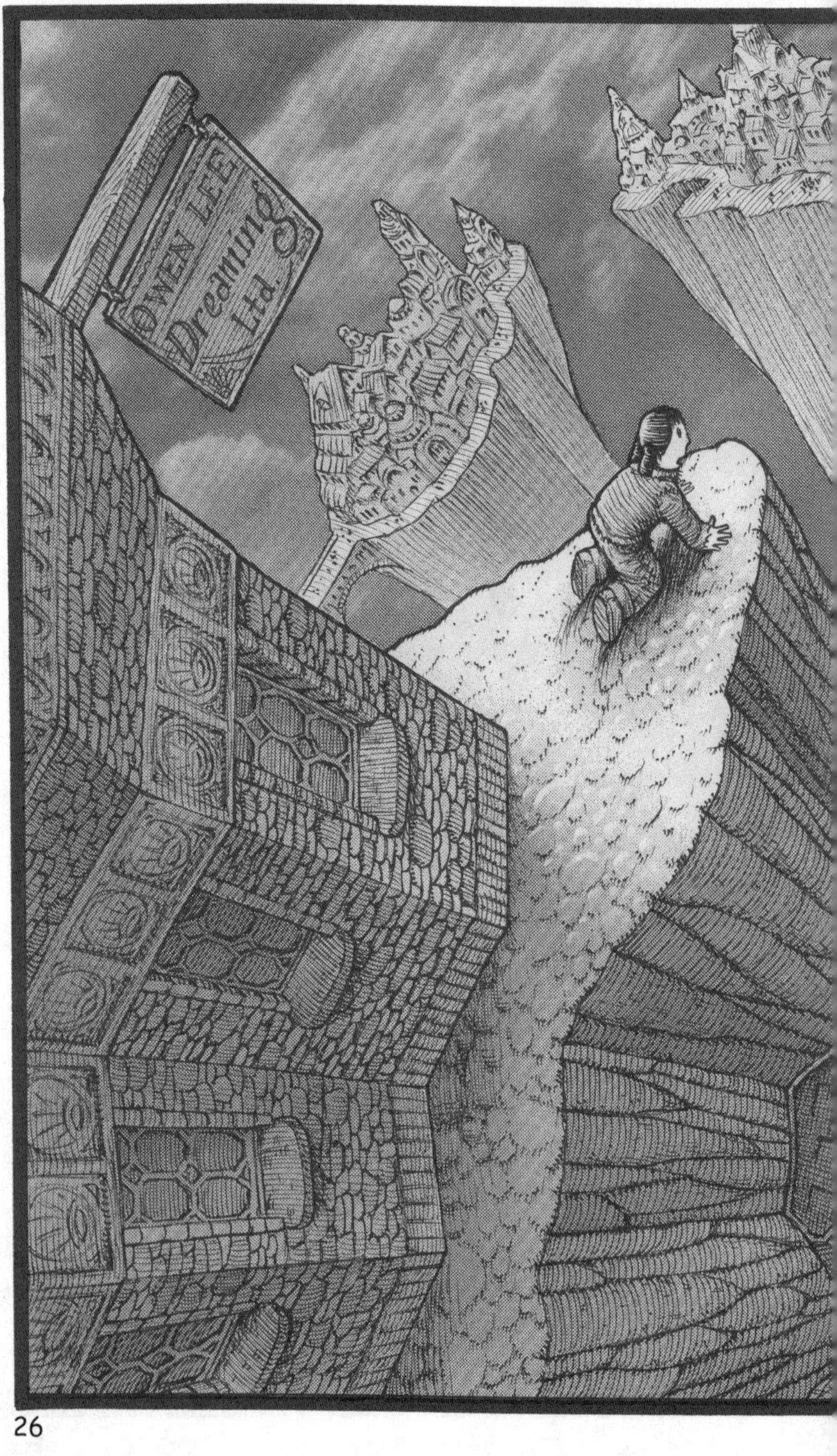
OWEN LEE
Dreaming
Ltd.

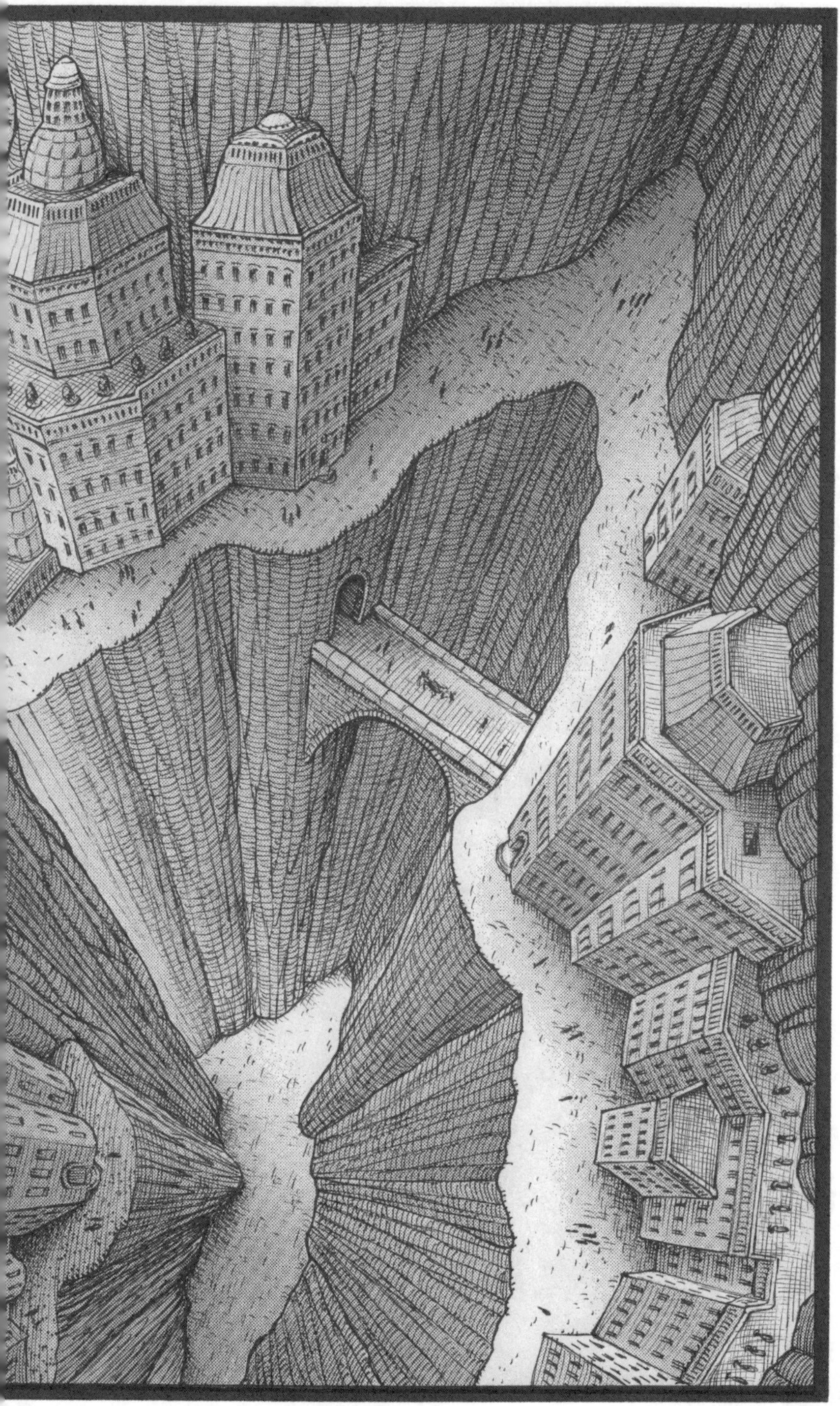

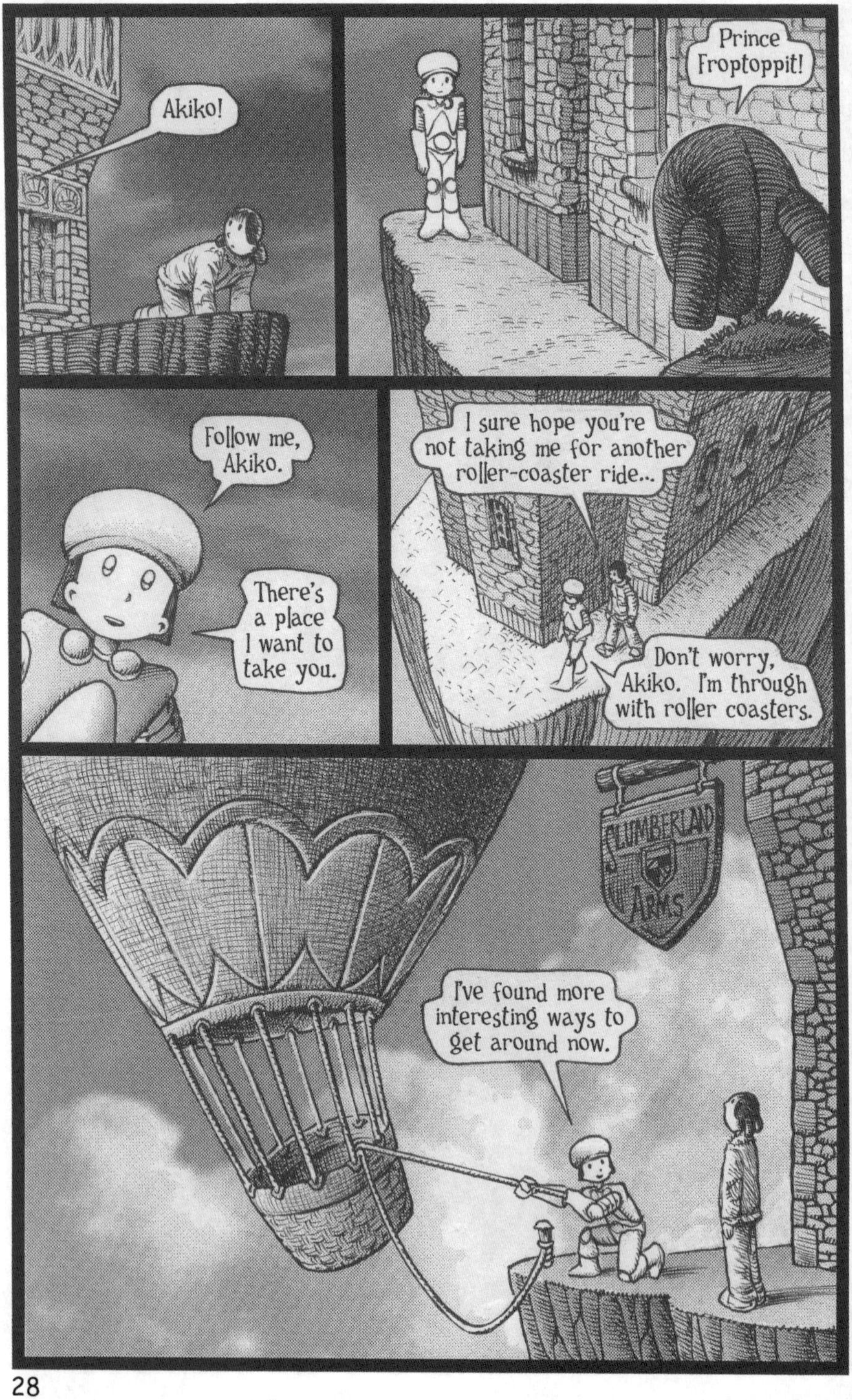
Akiko!
Prince Froptoppit!
Follow me, Akiko.
There's a place I want to take you.
I sure hope you're not taking me for another roller-coaster ride...
Don't worry, Akiko. I'm through with roller coasters.
SLUMBERLAND ARMS
I've found more interesting ways to get around now.

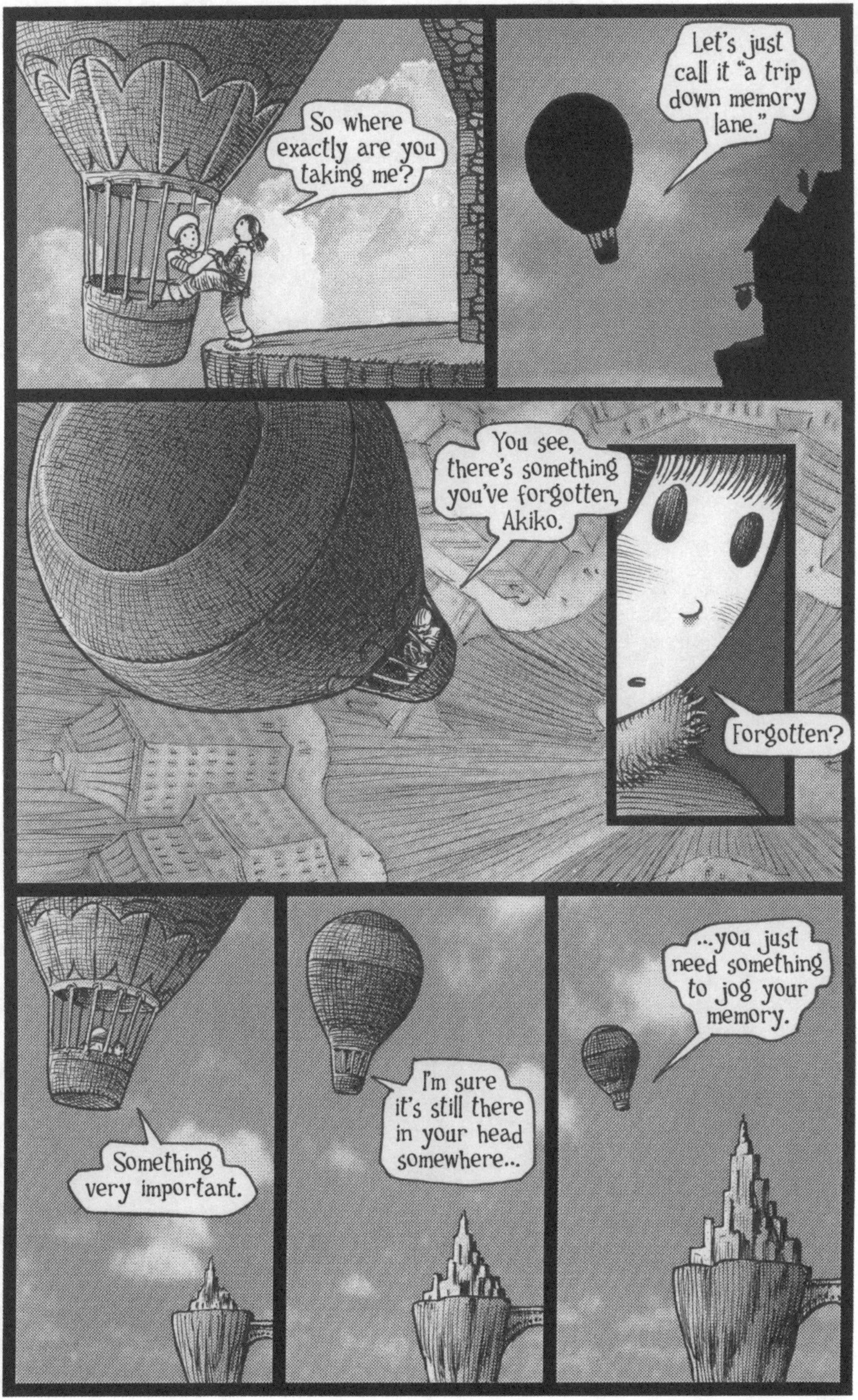
So where exactly are you taking me?
Let's just call it "a trip down memory lane."
You see, there's something you've forgotten, Akiko.
Forgotten?
Something very important.
I'm sure it's still there in your head somewhere...
...you just need something to jog your memory.

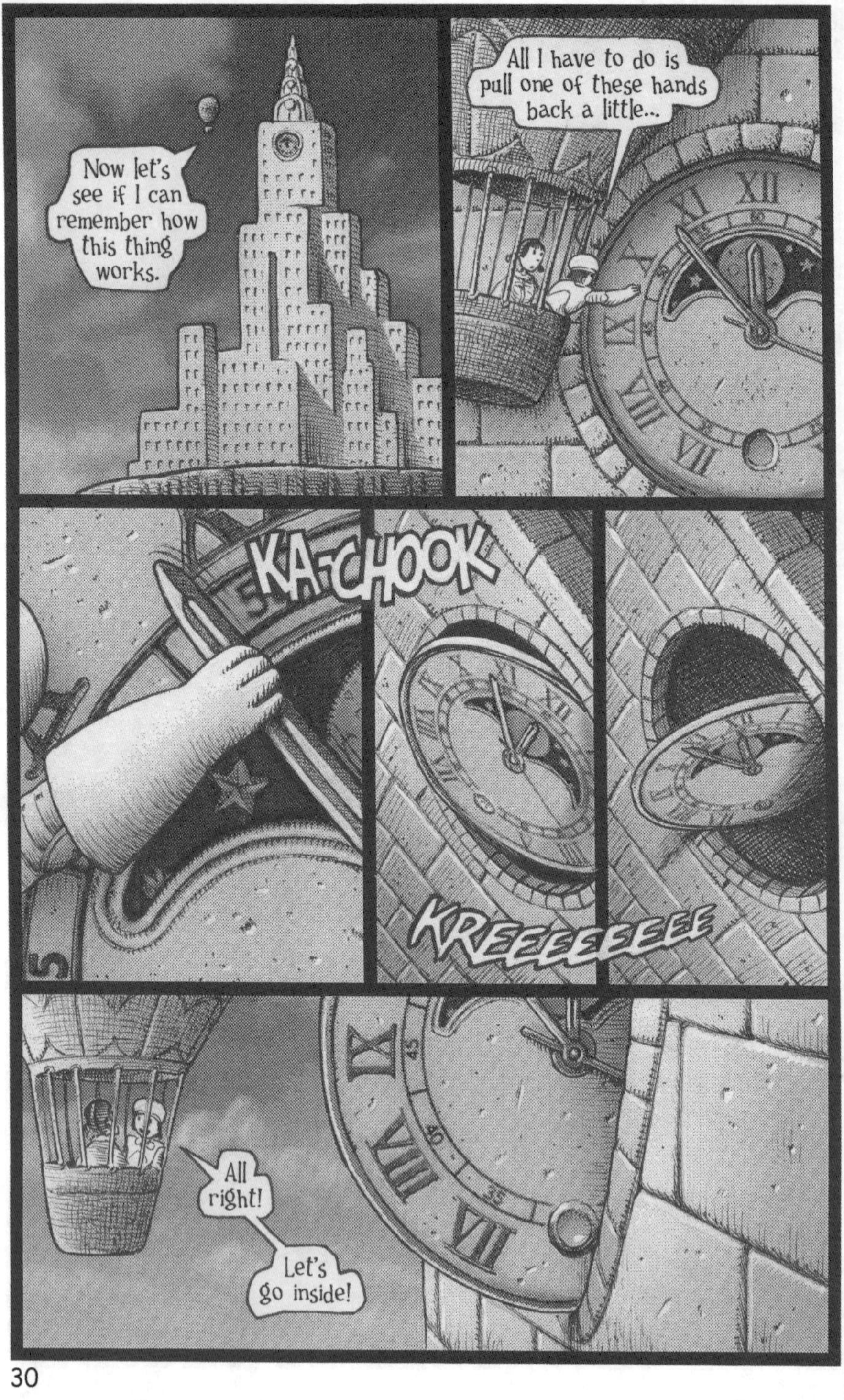
Now let's see if I can remember how this thing works.
All I have to do is pull one of these hands back a little...
KA-CHOOK
KREEEEEEEE
All right!
Let's go inside!

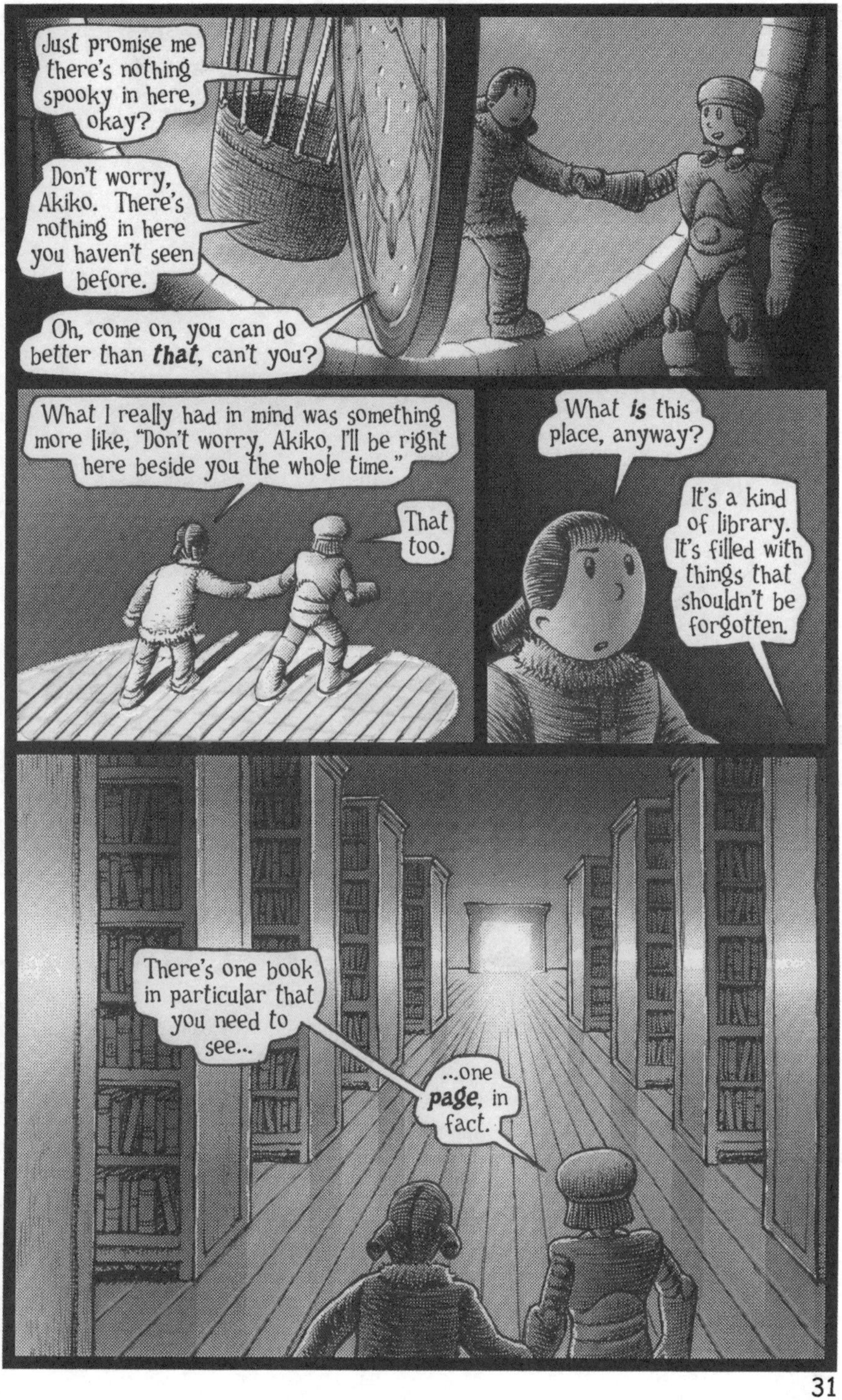

Just promise me there's nothing spooky in here, okay?
Don't worry, Akiko. There's nothing in here you haven't seen before.
Oh, come on, you can do better than ***that***, can't you?
What I really had in mind was something more like, "Don't worry, Akiko, I'll be right here beside you the whole time."
That too.
What ***is*** this place, anyway?
It's a kind of library. It's filled with things that shouldn't be forgotten.
There's one book in particular that you need to see...
...one ***page***, in fact.

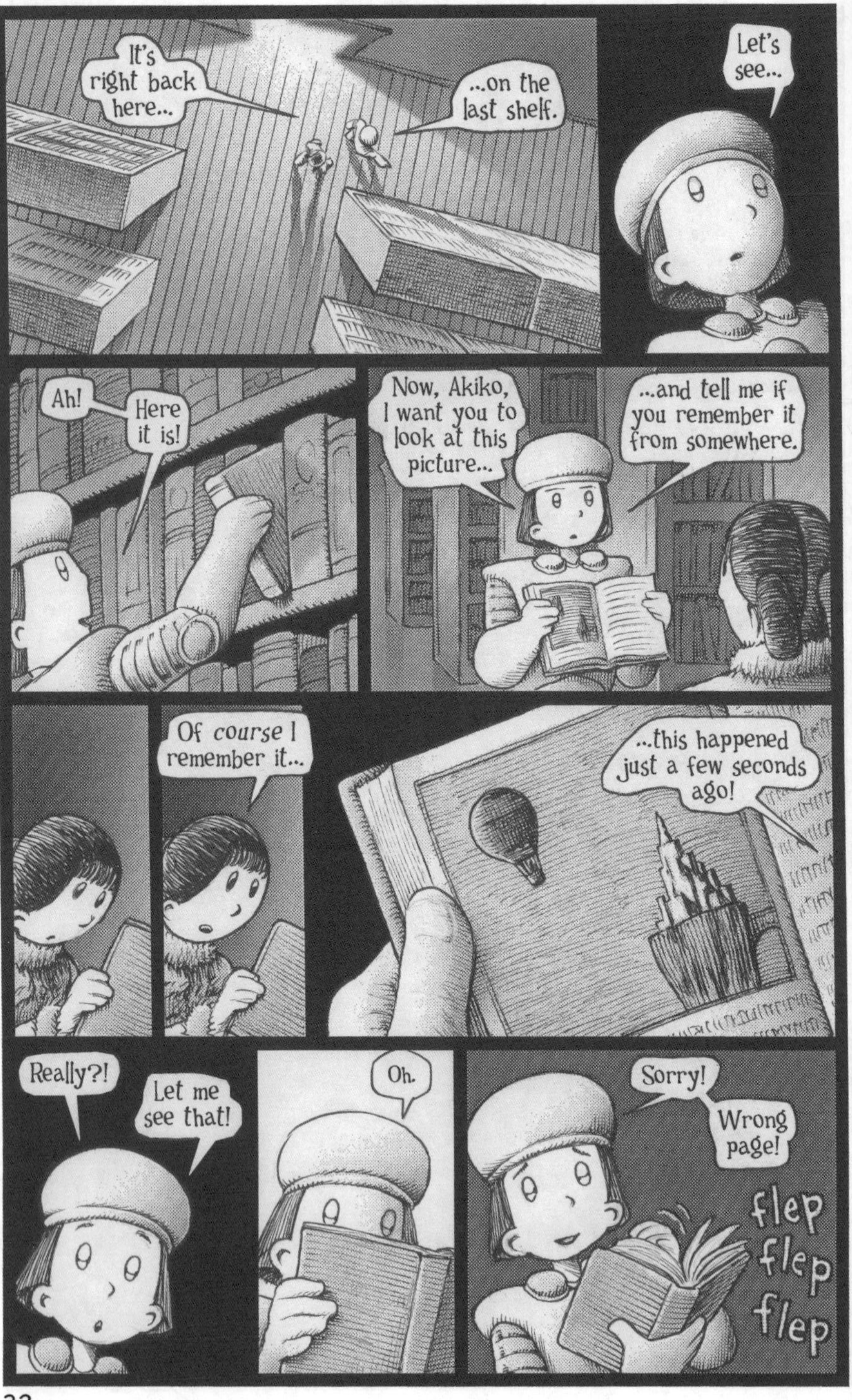

It's right back here...
...on the last shelf.
Let's see...
Ah!
Here it is!
Now, Akiko, I want you to look at this picture...
...and tell me if you remember it from somewhere.
Of *course* I remember it...
...this happened just a few seconds ago!
Really?!
Let me see that!
Oh.
Sorry!
Wrong page!
flep
flep
flep

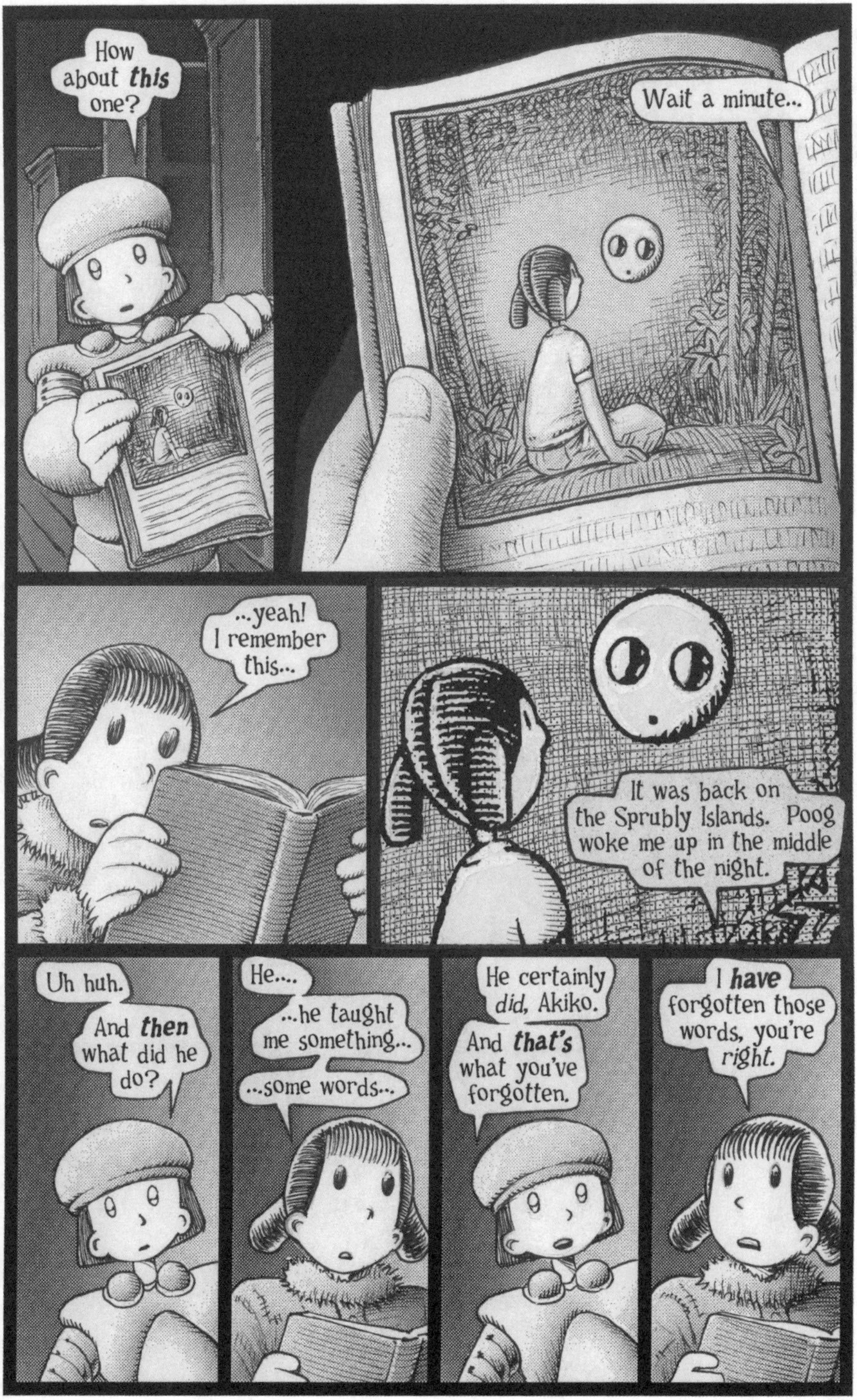
How about **this** one?
Wait a minute...
...yeah! I remember this...
It was back on the Sprubly Islands. Poog woke me up in the middle of the night.
Uh huh.
And **then** what did he do?
He....
...he taught me something...
...some words...
He certainly *did*, Akiko.
And **that's** what you've forgotten.
I **have** forgotten those words, you're *right.*

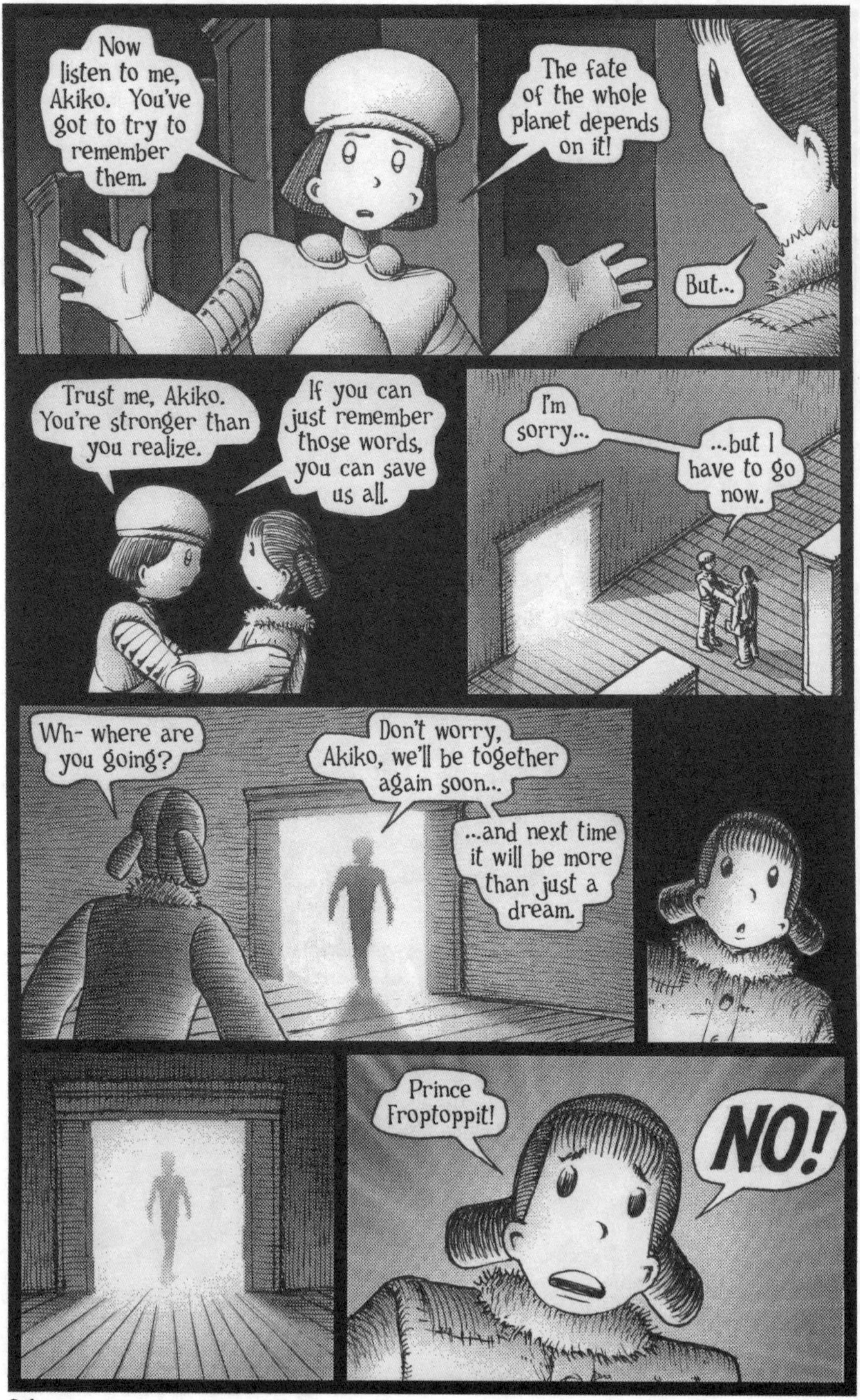
Now listen to me, Akiko. You've got to try to remember them.
The fate of the whole planet depends on it!
But...
Trust me, Akiko. You're stronger than you realize.
If you can just remember those words, you can save us all.
I'm sorry...
...but I have to go now.
Wh- where are you going?
Don't worry, Akiko, we'll be together again soon...
...and next time it will be more than just a dream.
Prince Froptoppit!
NO!

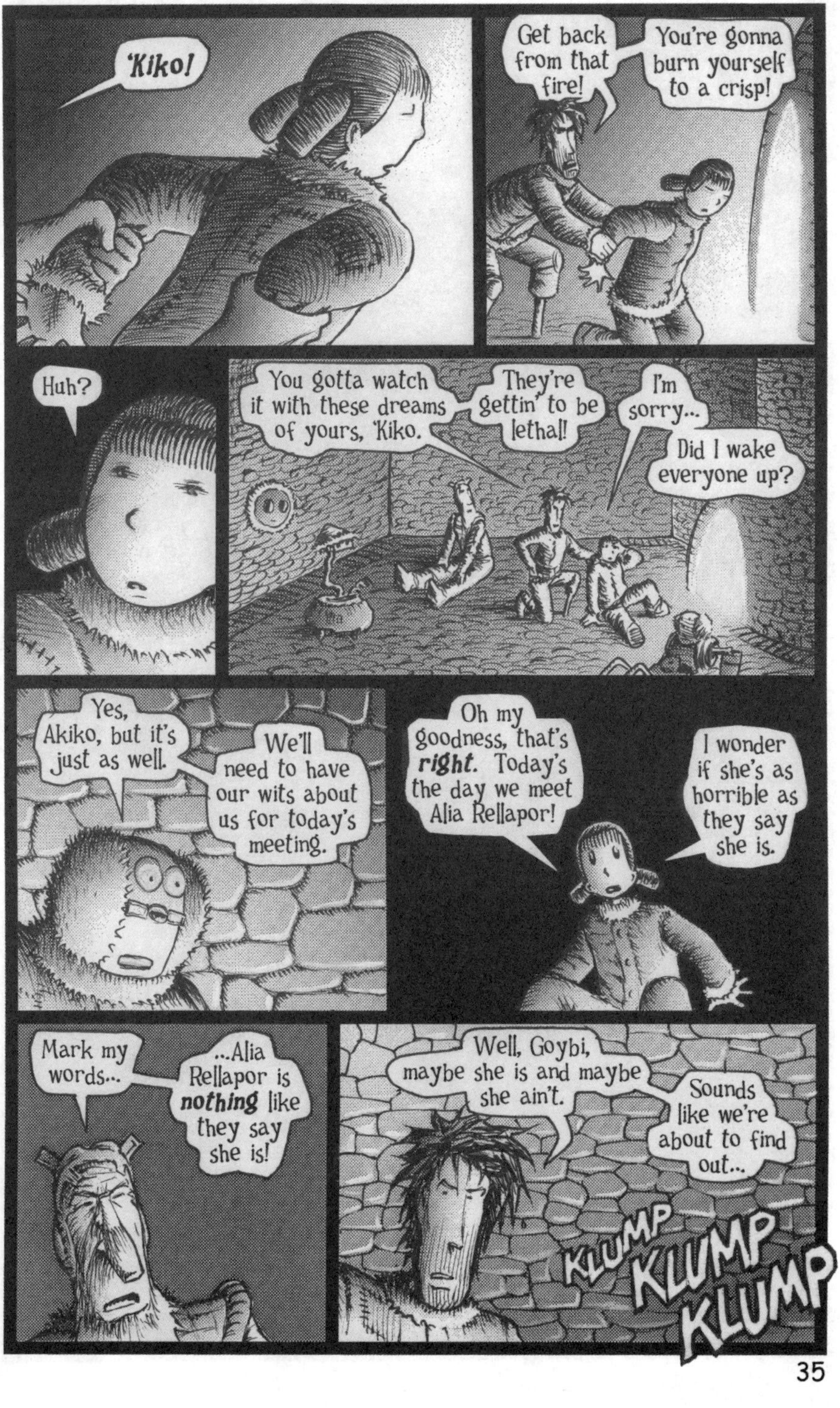
'Kiko!
Get back from that fire!
You're gonna burn yourself to a crisp!
Huh?
You gotta watch it with these dreams of yours, 'Kiko.
They're gettin' to be lethal!
I'm sorry...
Did I wake everyone up?
Yes, Akiko, but it's just as well.
We'll need to have our wits about us for today's meeting.
Oh my goodness, that's **right**. Today's the day we meet Alia Rellapor!
I wonder if she's as horrible as they say she is.
Mark my words...
...Alia Rellapor is **nothing** like they say she is!
Well, Goybi, maybe she is and maybe she ain't.
Sounds like we're about to find out...
KLUMP KLUMP KLUMP

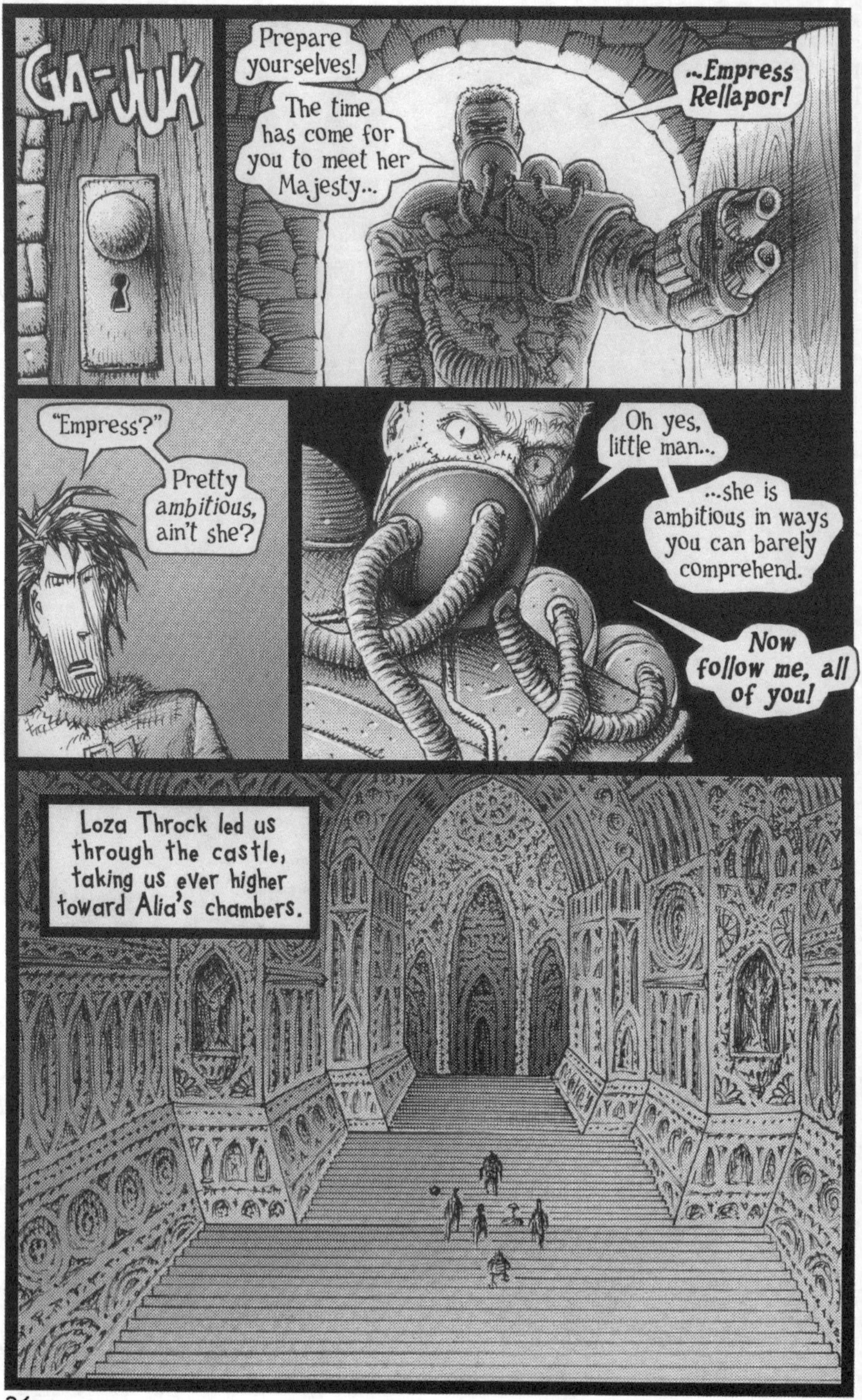
GA-JUK
Prepare yourselves!
The time has come for you to meet her Majesty...
...Empress Rellapor!
"Empress?"
Pretty ambitious, ain't she?
Oh yes, little man...
...she is ambitious in ways you can barely comprehend.
Now follow me, all of you!
Loza Throck led us through the castle, taking us ever higher toward Alia's chambers.

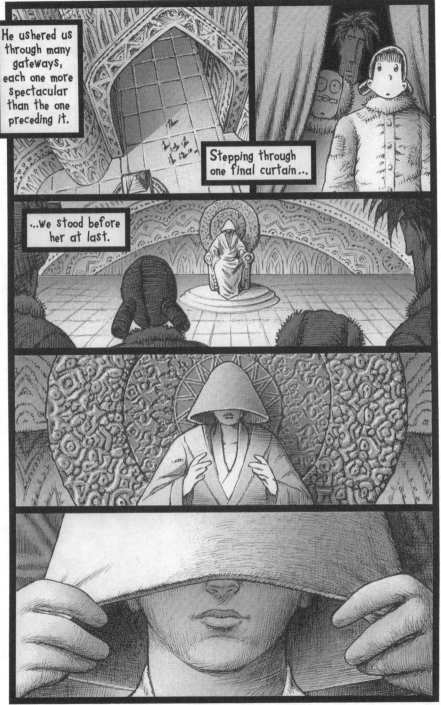

He ushered us through many gateways, each one more spectacular than the one preceding it.

Stepping through one final curtain...

...we stood before her at last.

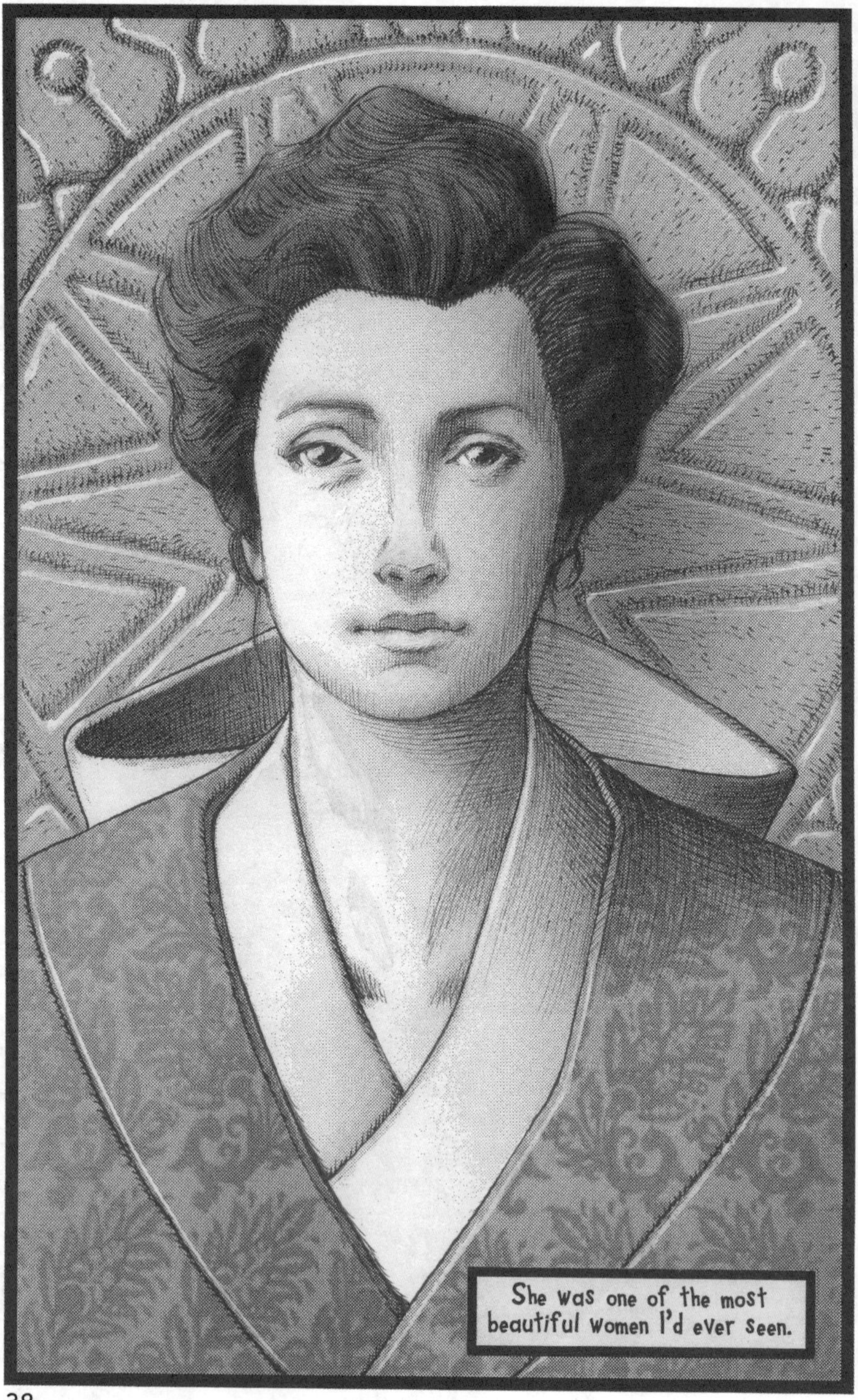
She was one of the most beautiful women I'd ever seen.

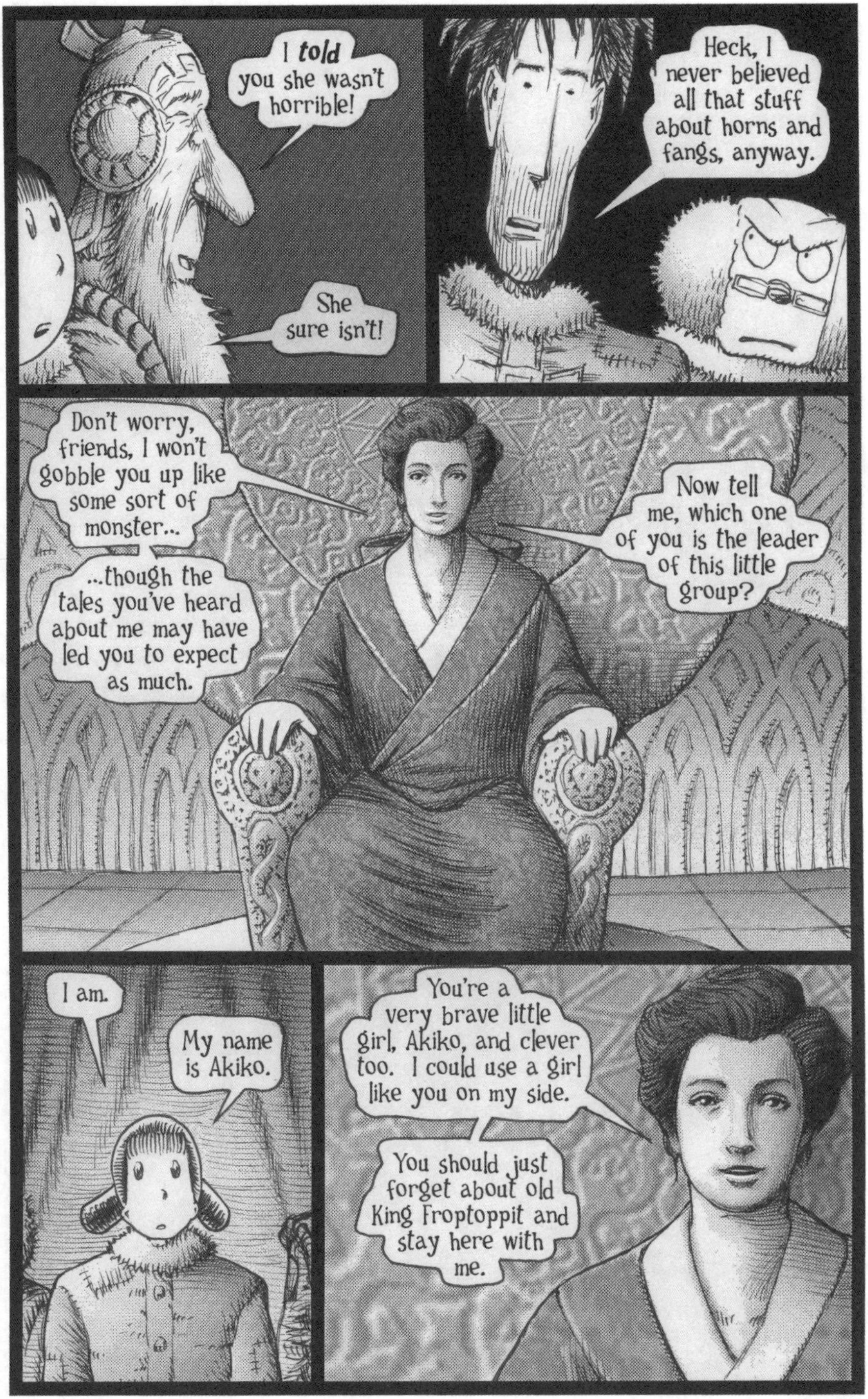
I *told* you she wasn't horrible!
She sure isn't!
Heck, I never believed all that stuff about horns and fangs, anyway.
Don't worry, friends, I won't gobble you up like some sort of monster...
...though the tales you've heard about me may have led you to expect as much.
Now tell me, which one of you is the leader of this little group?
I am.
My name is Akiko.
You're a very brave little girl, Akiko, and clever too. I could use a girl like you on my side.
You should just forget about old King Froptoppit and stay here with me.

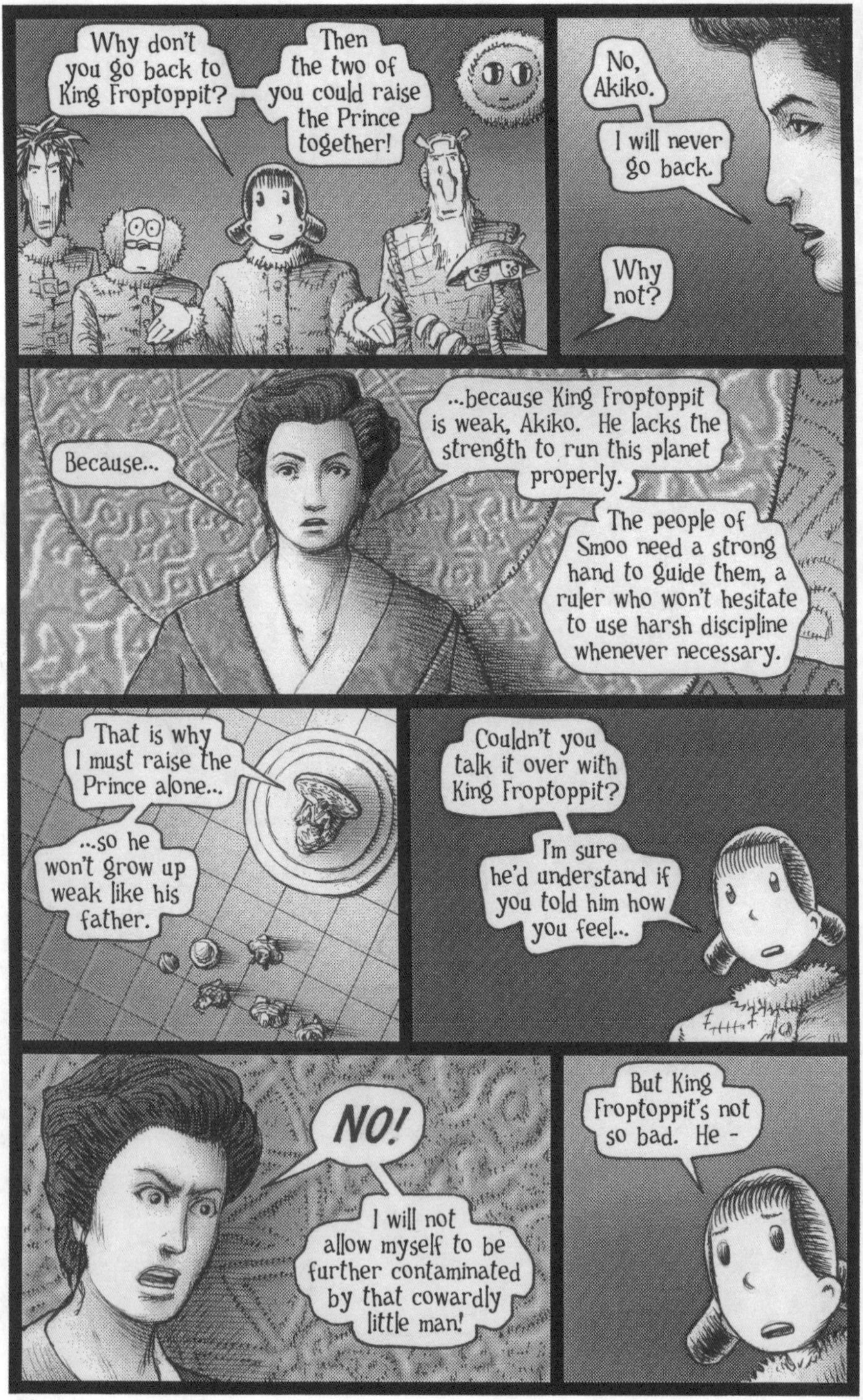

Why don't you go back to King Froptoppit?
Then the two of you could raise the Prince together!
No, Akiko.
I will never go back.
Why not?
Because...
...because King Froptoppit is weak, Akiko. He lacks the strength to run this planet properly.
The people of Smoo need a strong hand to guide them, a ruler who won't hesitate to use harsh discipline whenever necessary.
That is why I must raise the Prince alone...
...so he won't grow up weak like his father.
Couldn't you talk it over with King Froptoppit?
I'm sure he'd understand if you told him how you feel...
NO!
I will not allow myself to be further contaminated by that cowardly little man!
But King Froptoppit's not so bad. He -

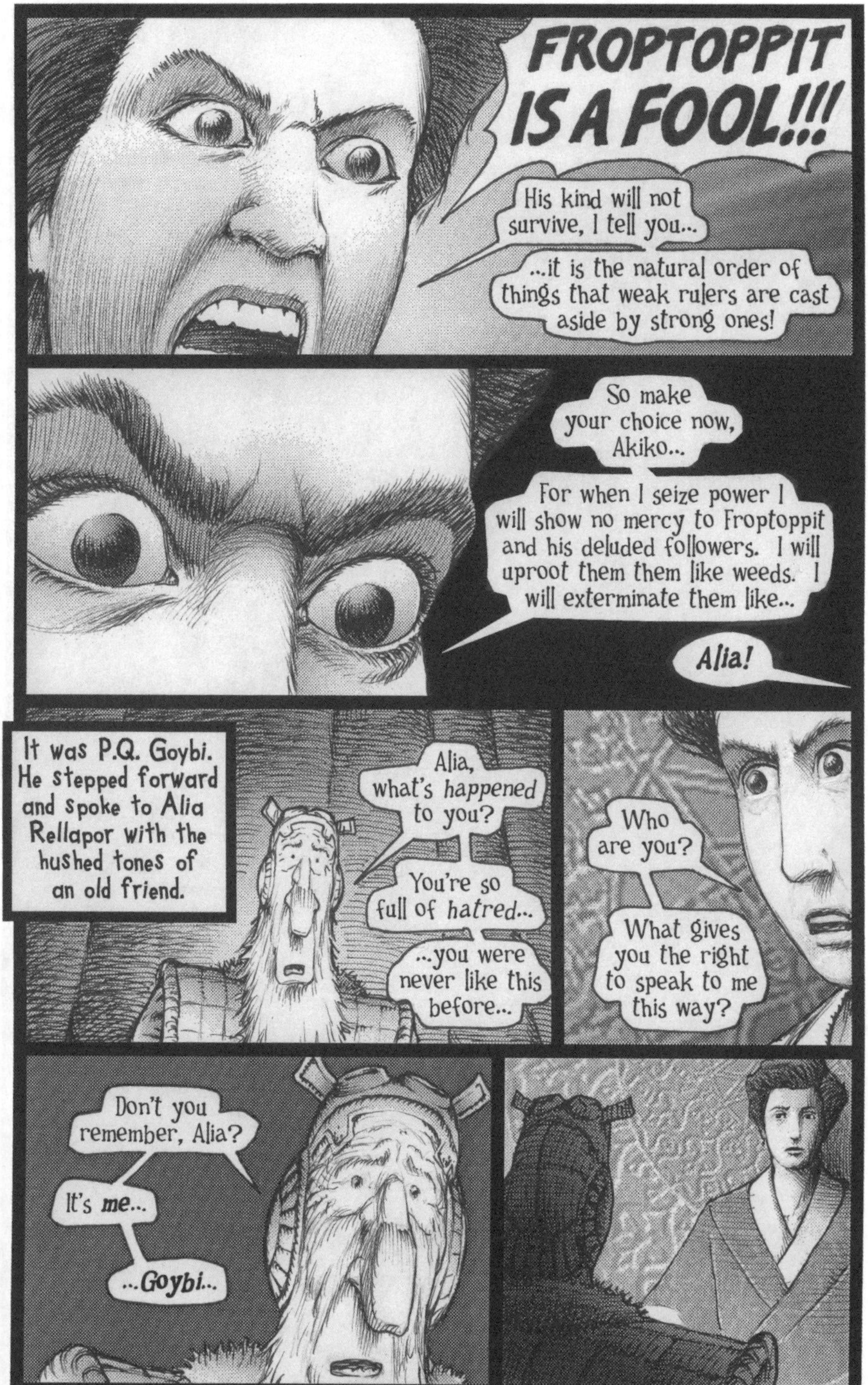
FROPTOPPIT IS A FOOL!!!
His kind will not survive, I tell you...
...it is the natural order of things that weak rulers are cast aside by strong ones!
So make your choice now, Akiko...
For when I seize power I will show no mercy to Froptoppit and his deluded followers. I will uproot them them like weeds. I will exterminate them like...
Alia!
It was P.Q. Goybi. He stepped forward and spoke to Alia Rellapor with the hushed tones of an old friend.
Alia, what's happened to you?
You're so full of hatred...
...you were never like this before...
Who are you?
What gives you the right to speak to me this way?
Don't you remember, Alia?
It's me...
...Goybi...

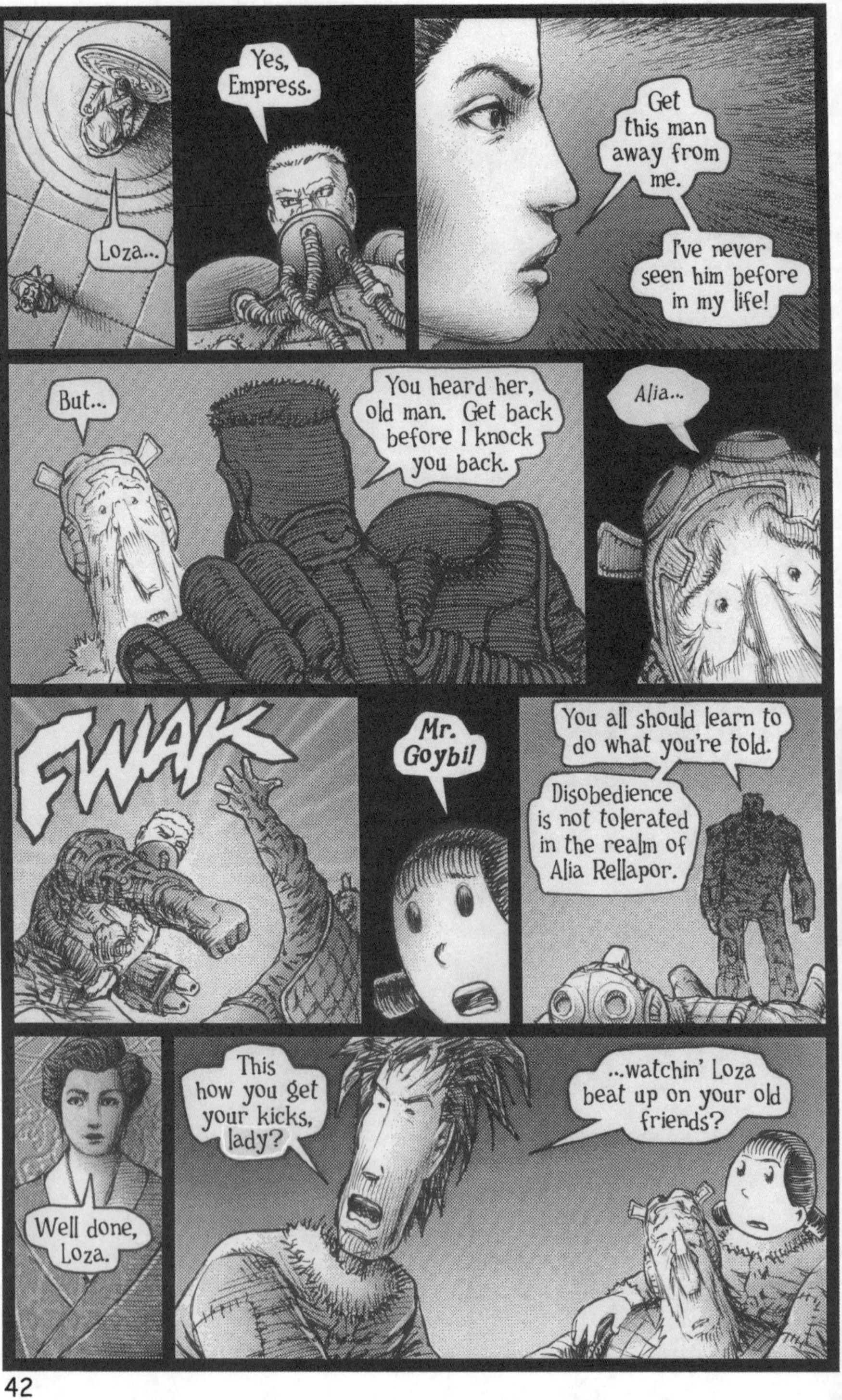
Loza...
Yes, Empress.
Get this man away from me.
I've never seen him before in my life!
But...
You heard her, old man. Get back before I knock you back.
Alia...
FWAK
Mr. Goybil
You all should learn to do what you're told.
Disobedience is not tolerated in the realm of Alia Rellapor.
Well done, Loza.
This how you get your kicks, lady?
...watchin' Loza beat up on your old friends?

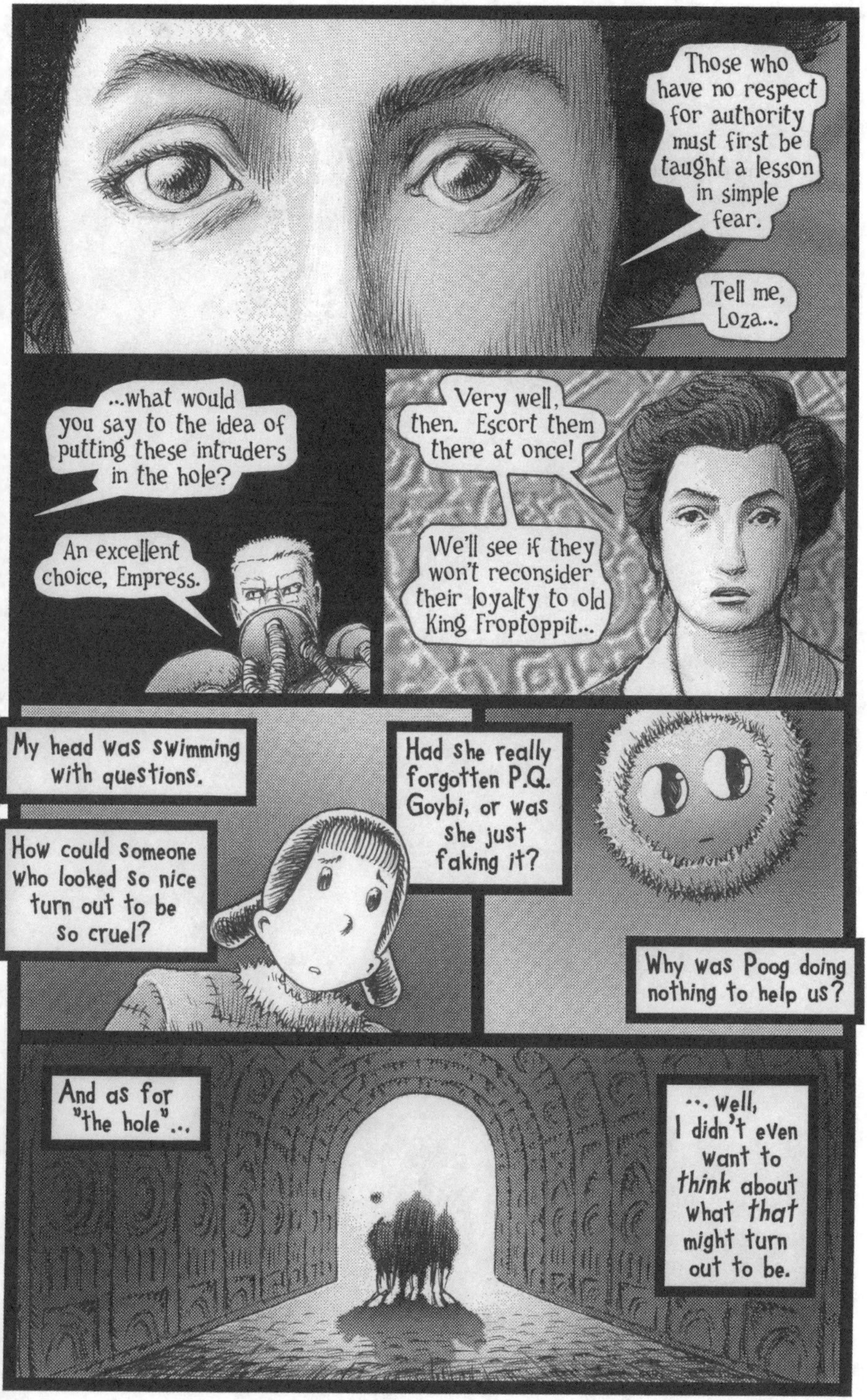
Those who have no respect for authority must first be taught a lesson in simple fear.
Tell me, Loza...
...what would you say to the idea of putting these intruders in the hole?
An excellent choice, Empress.
Very well, then. Escort them there at once!
We'll see if they won't reconsider their loyalty to old King Froptoppit...
My head was swimming with questions.
How could someone who looked so nice turn out to be so cruel?
Had she really forgotten P.Q. Goybi, or was she just faking it?
Why was Poog doing nothing to help us?
And as for "the hole"...
... Well, I didn't even want to think about what that might turn out to be.

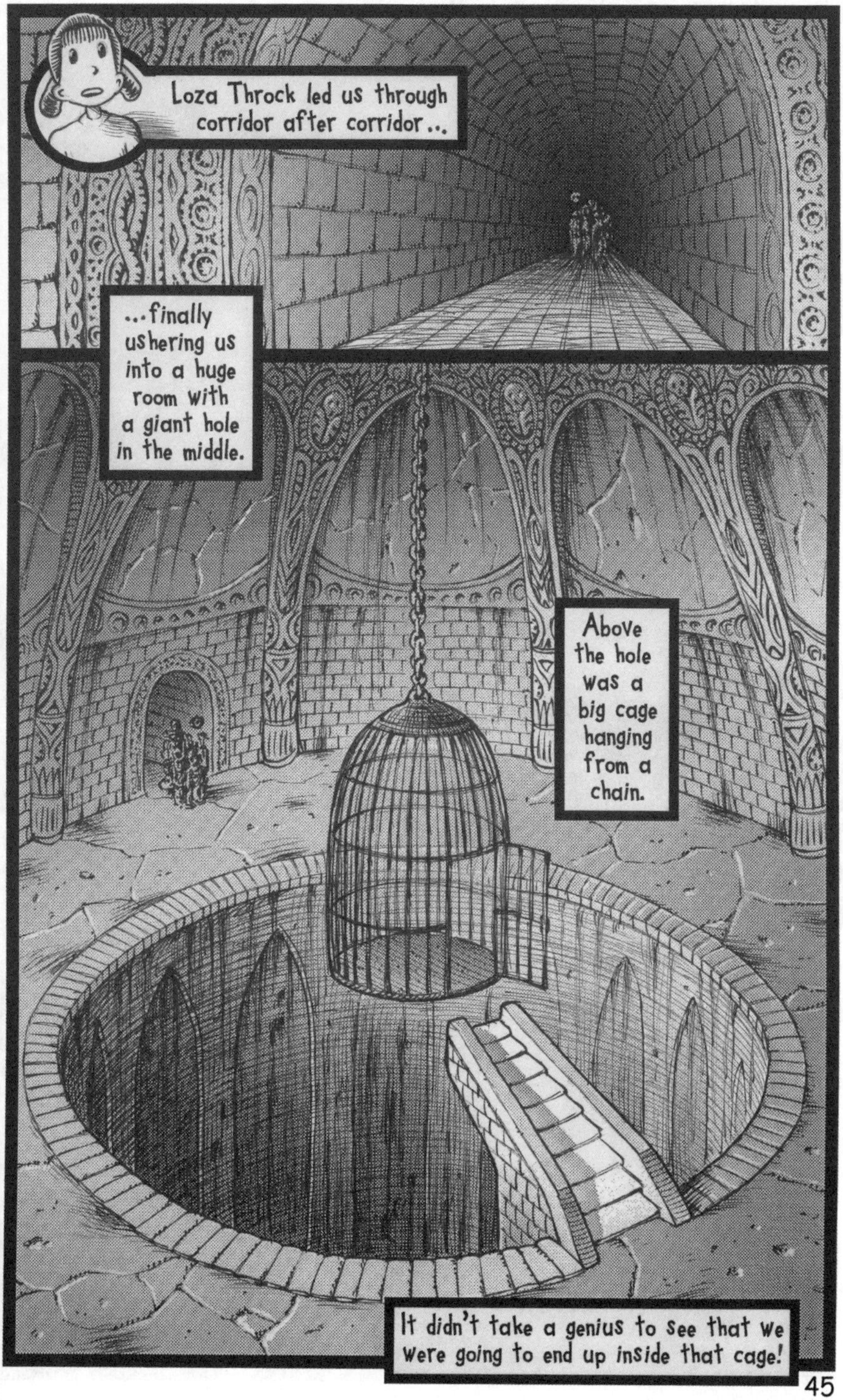
Loza Throck led us through corridor after corridor...
...finally ushering us into a huge room with a giant hole in the middle.
Above the hole was a big cage hanging from a chain.
It didn't take a genius to see that we were going to end up inside that cage!

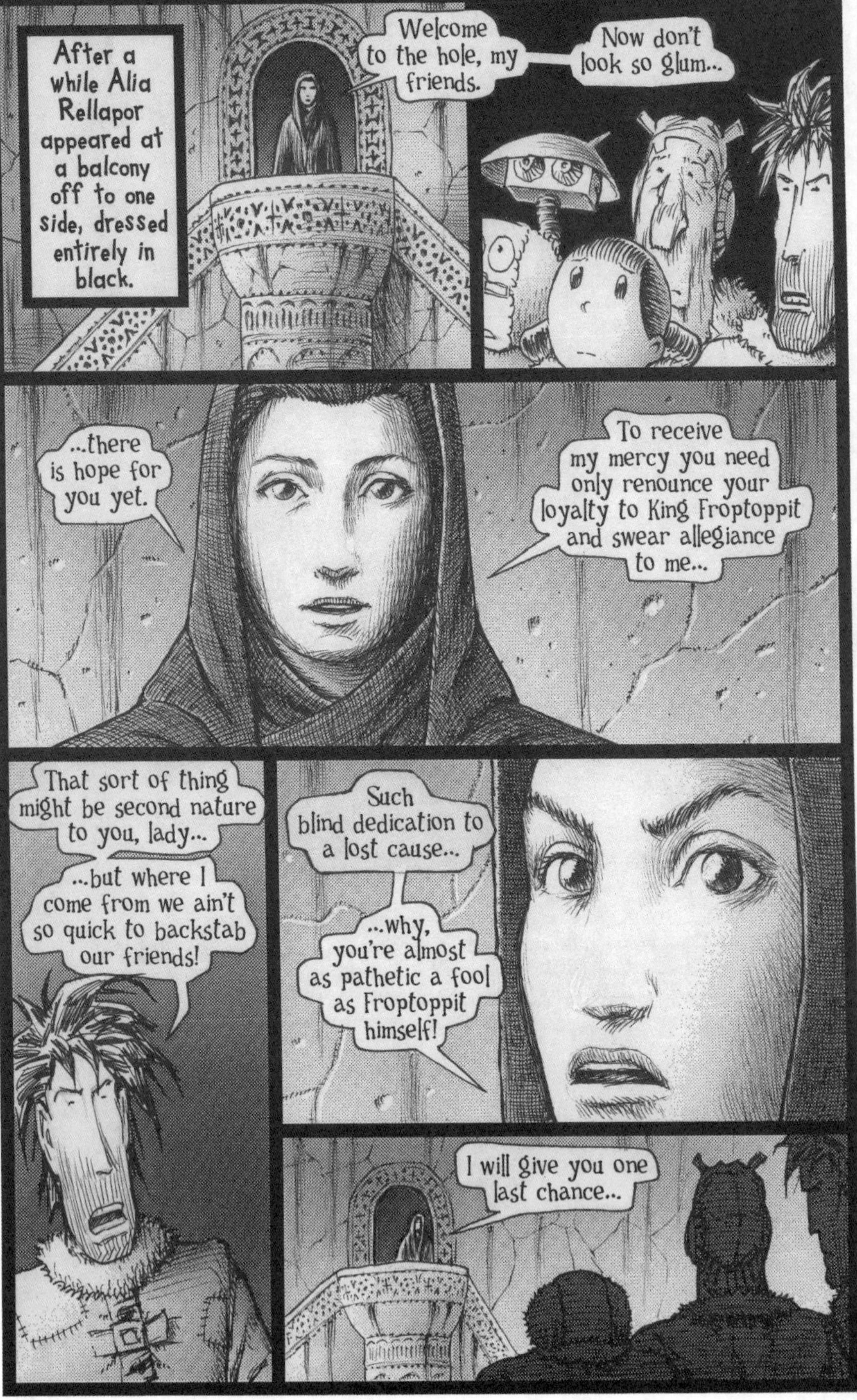
After a while Alia Rellapor appeared at a balcony off to one side, dressed entirely in black.
Welcome to the hole, my friends.
Now don't look so glum...
...there is hope for you yet.
To receive my mercy you need only renounce your loyalty to King Froptoppit and swear allegiance to me...
That sort of thing might be second nature to you, lady...
...but where I come from we ain't so quick to backstab our friends!
Such blind dedication to a lost cause...
...why, you're almost as pathetic a fool as Froptoppit himself!
I will give you one last chance...

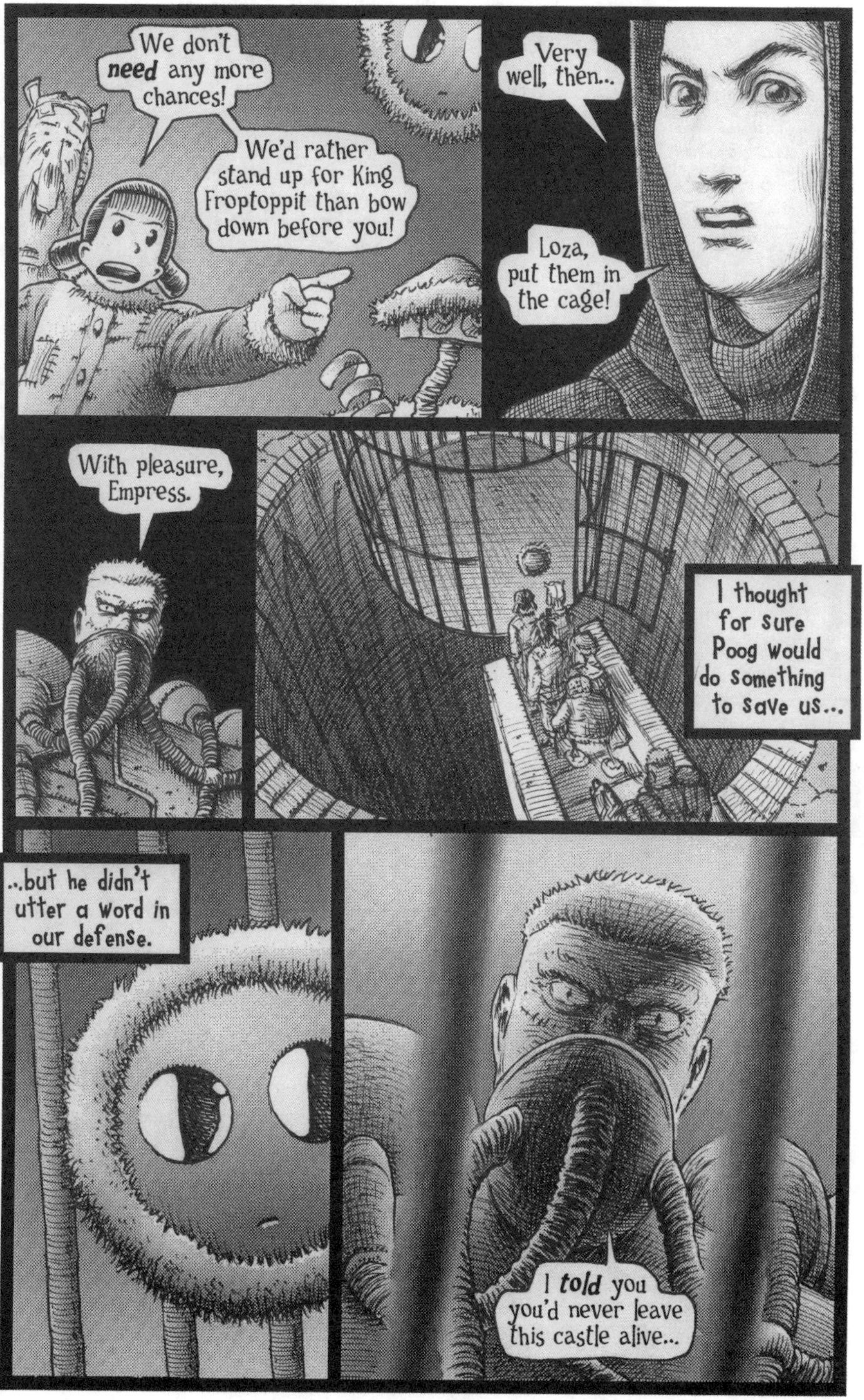
We don't **need** any more chances!
We'd rather stand up for King Froptoppit than bow down before you!
Very well, then...
Loza, put them in the cage!
With pleasure, Empress.
I thought for sure Poog would do something to save us...
...but he didn't utter a word in our defense.
I **told** you you'd never leave this castle alive...

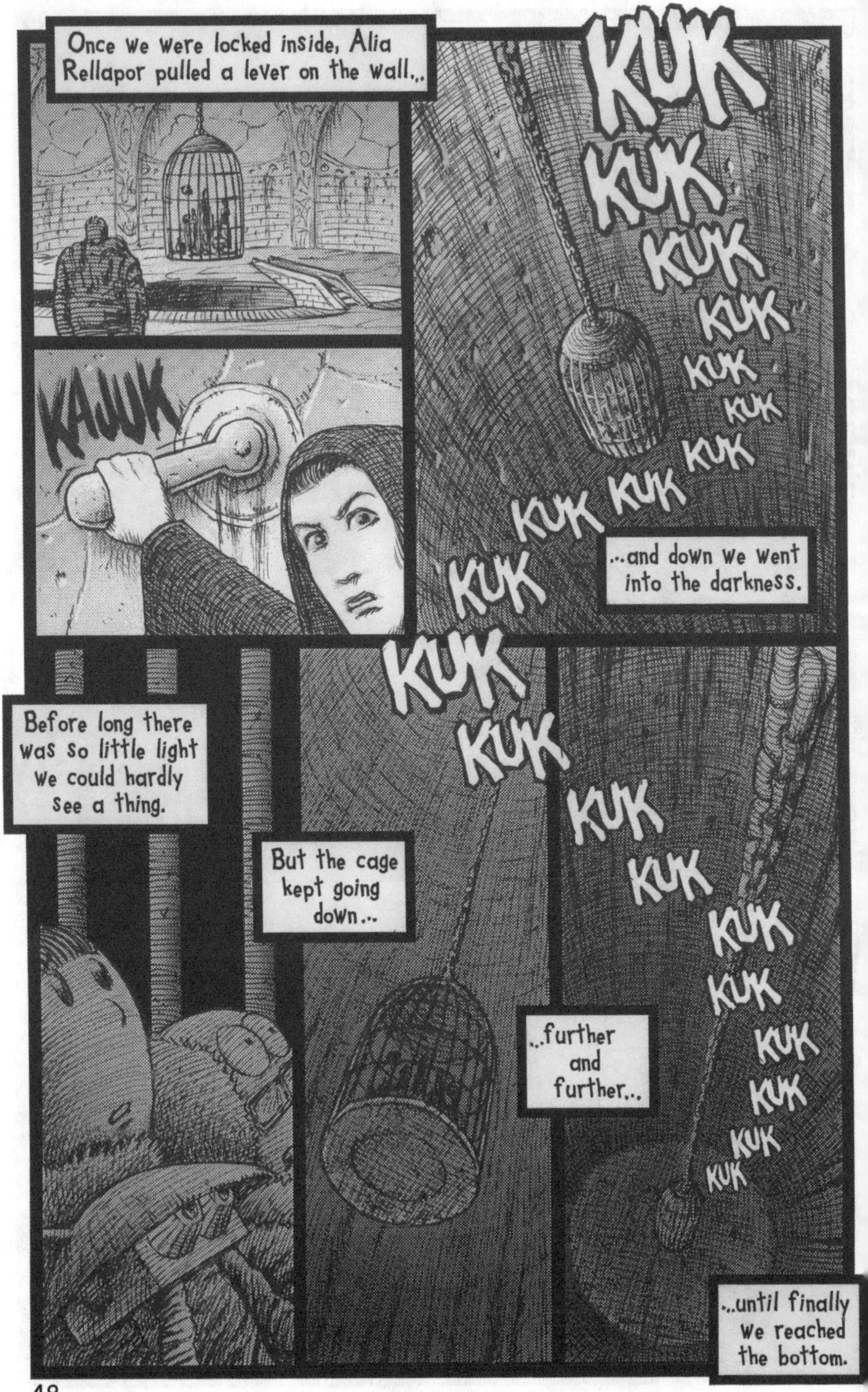
Once we were locked inside, Alia Rellapor pulled a lever on the wall...
KAJUUK
KUK KUK KUK KUK KUK KUK KUK KUK KUK KUK
...and down we went into the darkness.
Before long there was so little light we could hardly see a thing.
But the cage kept going down...
KUK KUK KUK KUK KUK KUK KUK KUK KUK KUK
...further and further...
...until finally we reached the bottom.

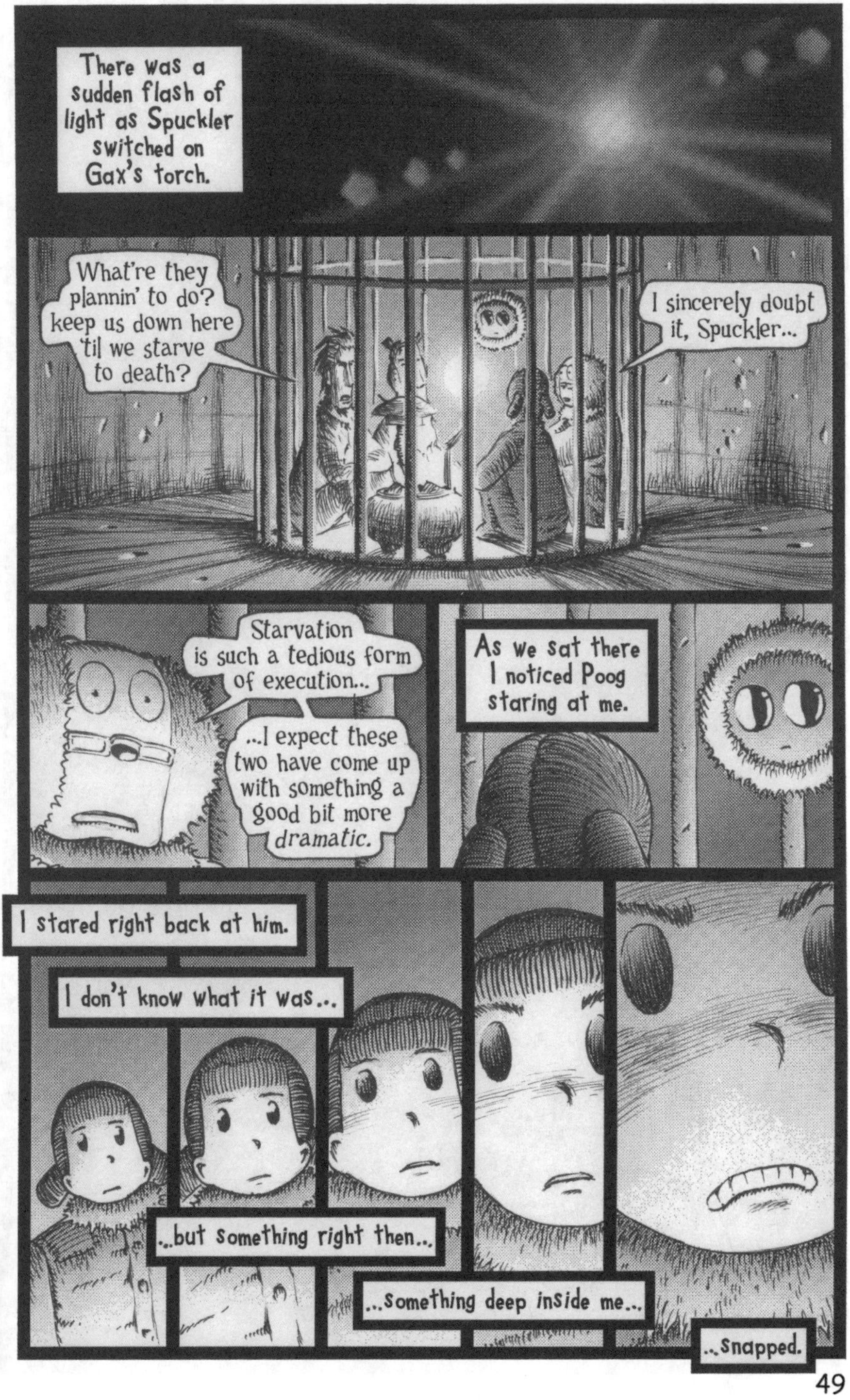
There was a sudden flash of light as Spuckler switched on Gax's torch.
What're they plannin' to do? keep us down here 'til we starve to death?
I sincerely doubt it, Spuckler...
Starvation is such a tedious form of execution...
...I expect these two have come up with something a good bit more *dramatic.*
As we sat there I noticed Poog staring at me.
I stared right back at him.
I don't know what it was...
...but something right then...
...something deep inside me...
...snapped.

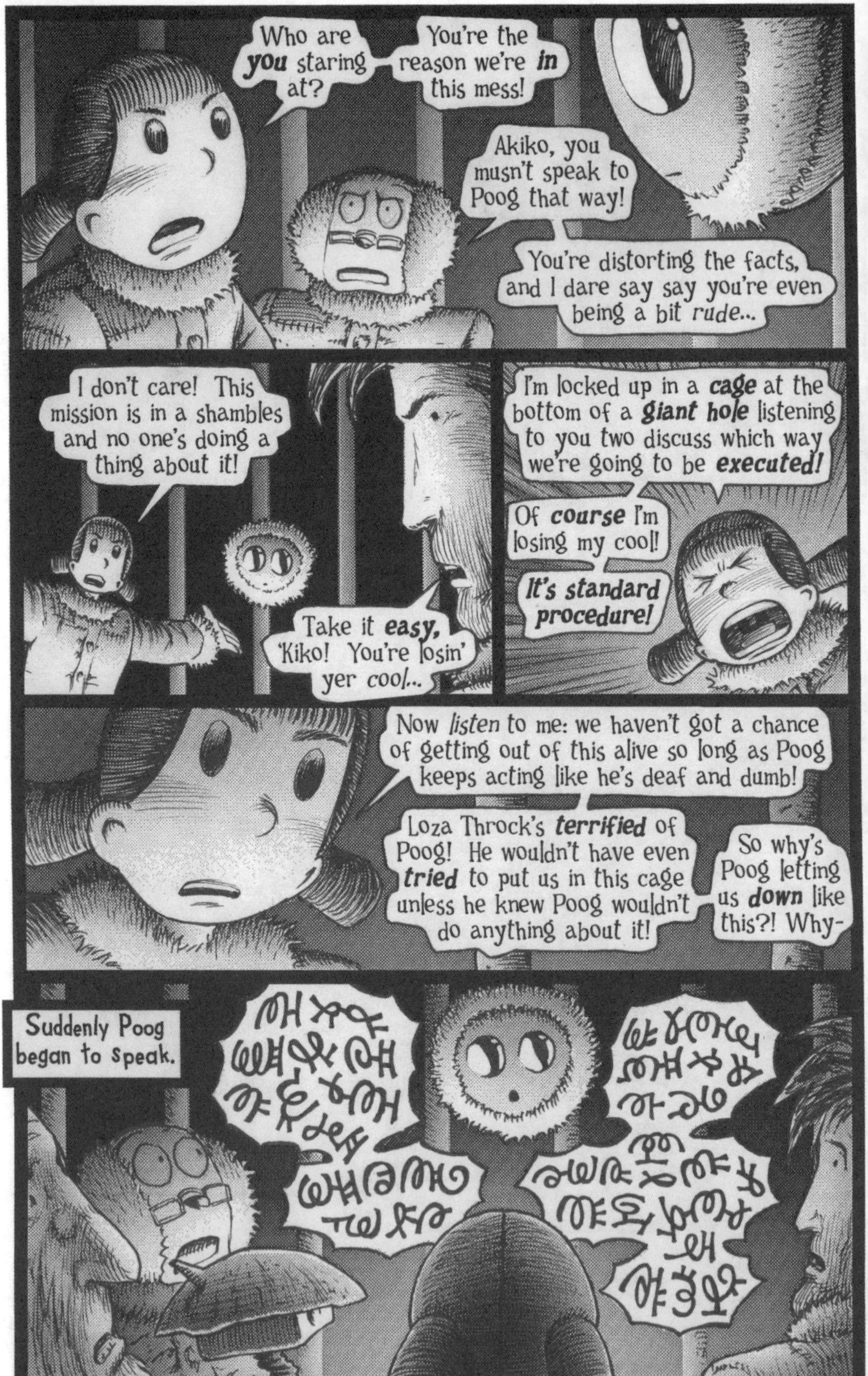
Who are you staring at?
You're the reason we're in this mess!
Akiko, you musn't speak to Poog that way!
You're distorting the facts, and I dare say say you're even being a bit rude...
I don't care! This mission is in a shambles and no one's doing a thing about it!
Take it easy, 'Kiko! You're losin' yer cool...
I'm locked up in a cage at the bottom of a giant hole listening to you two discuss which way we're going to be executed!
Of course I'm losing my cool!
It's standard procedure!
Now listen to me: we haven't got a chance of getting out of this alive so long as Poog keeps acting like he's deaf and dumb!
Loza Throck's terrified of Poog! He wouldn't have even tried to put us in this cage unless he knew Poog wouldn't do anything about it!
So why's Poog letting us down like this?! Why-
Suddenly Poog began to speak.

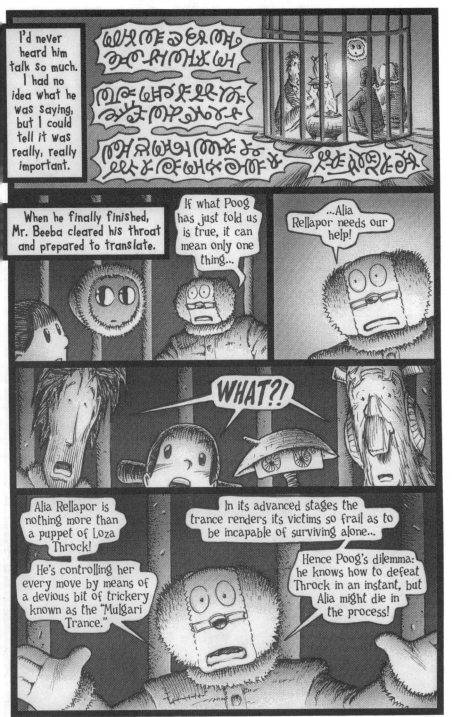

I'd never heard him talk so much. I had no idea what he was saying, but I could tell it was really, really important.

When he finally finished, Mr. Beeba cleared his throat and prepared to translate.

If what Poog has just told us is true, it can mean only one thing...

...Alia Rellapor needs our help!

WHAT?!

Alia Rellapor is nothing more than a puppet of Loza Throck!

He's controlling her every move by means of a devious bit of trickery known as the "Mulgari Trance."

In its advanced stages the trance renders its victims so frail as to be incapable of surviving alone...

Hence Poog's dilemma: he knows how to defeat Throck in an instant, but Alia might die in the process!

51

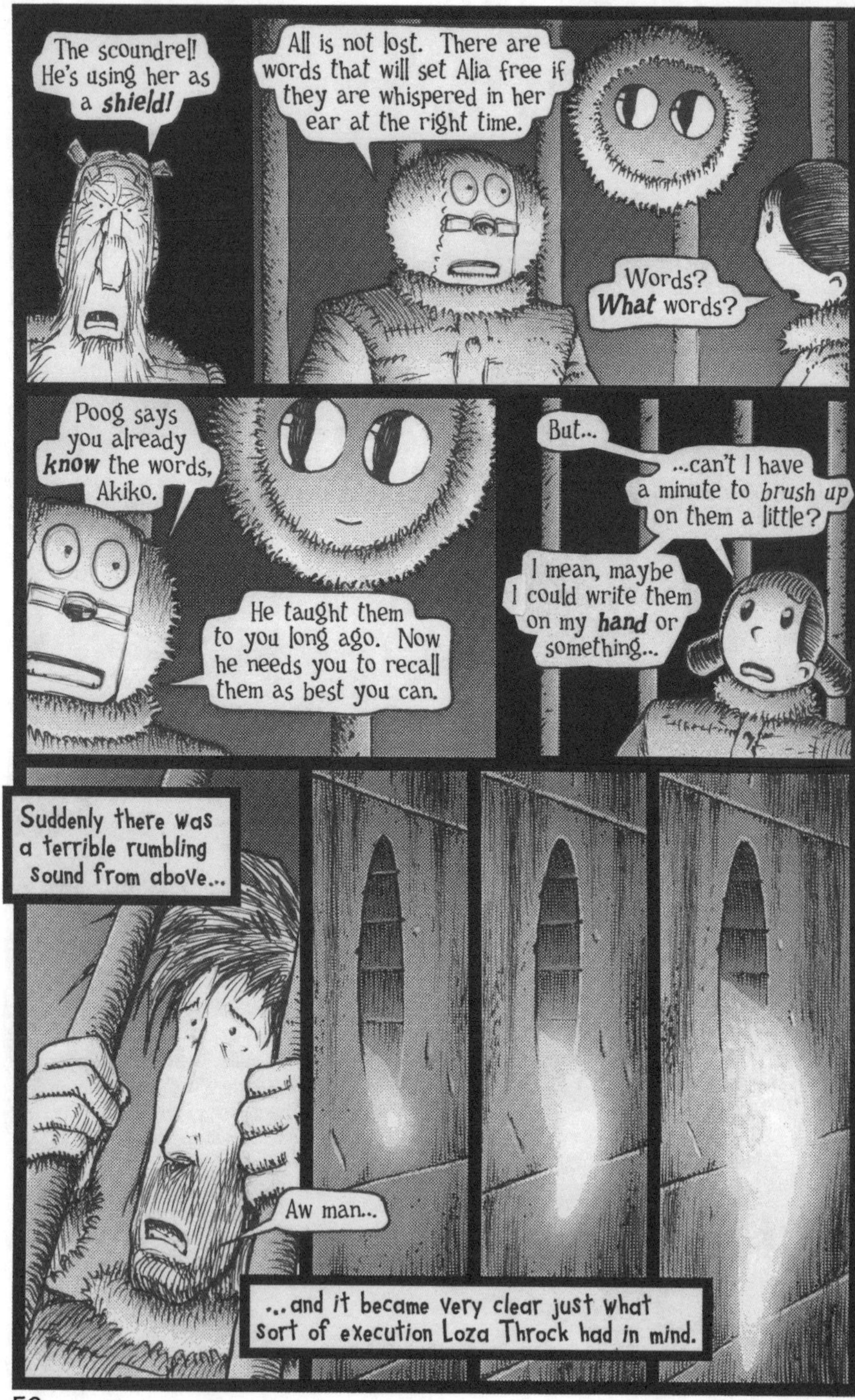
The scoundrel! He's using her as a ***shield!***
All is not lost. There are words that will set Alia free if they are whispered in her ear at the right time.
Words? ***What*** words?
Poog says you already ***know*** the words, Akiko.
He taught them to you long ago. Now he needs you to recall them as best you can.
But...
...can't I have a minute to *brush up* on them a little?
I mean, maybe I could write them on my ***hand*** or something...
Suddenly there was a terrible rumbling sound from above...
Aw man...
...and it became very clear just what sort of execution Loza Throck had in mind.

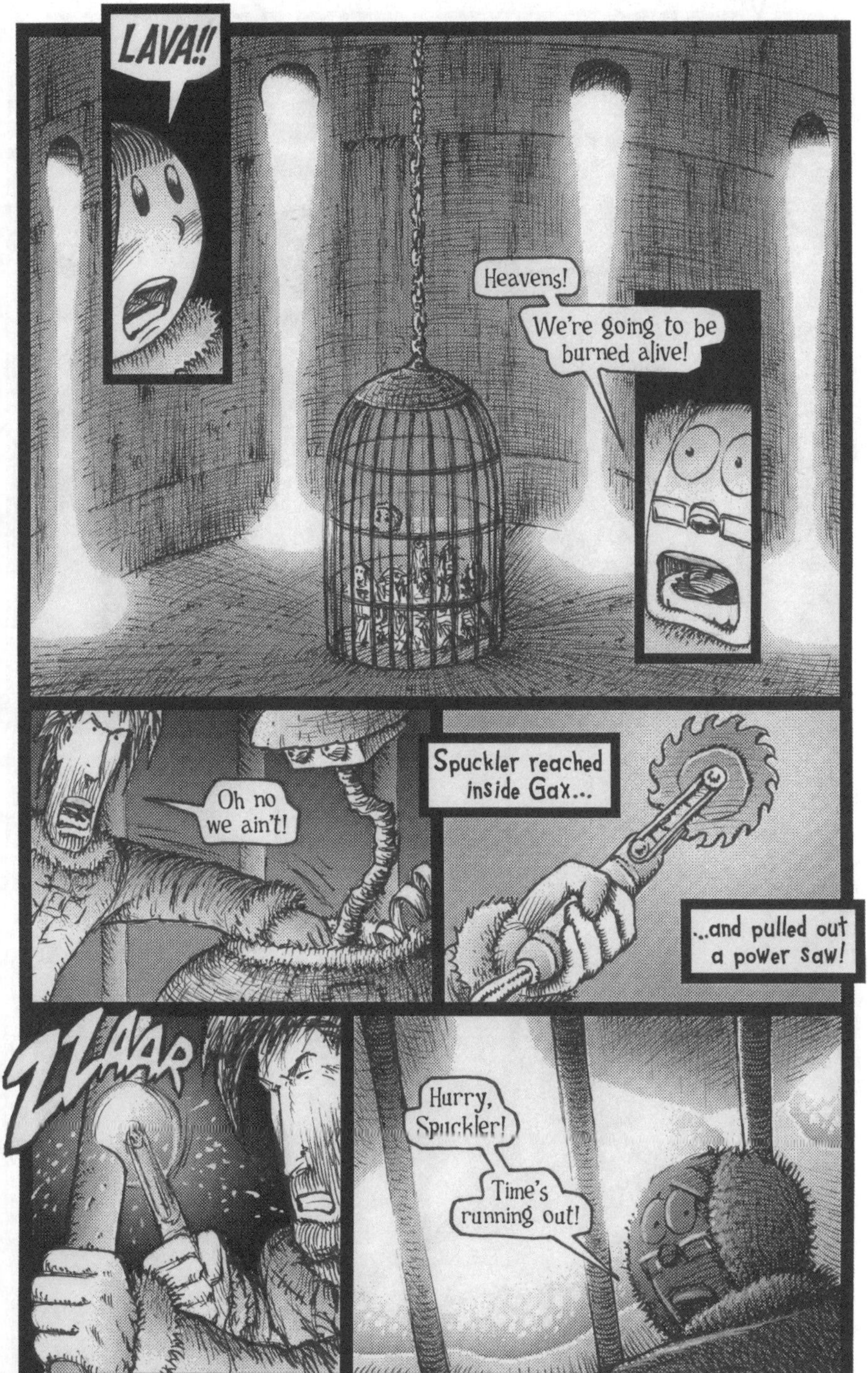
LAVA!!
Heavens!
We're going to be burned alive!
Oh no we ain't!
Spuckler reached inside Gax...
...and pulled out a power saw!
ZZWAR
Hurry, Spuckler!
Time's running out!

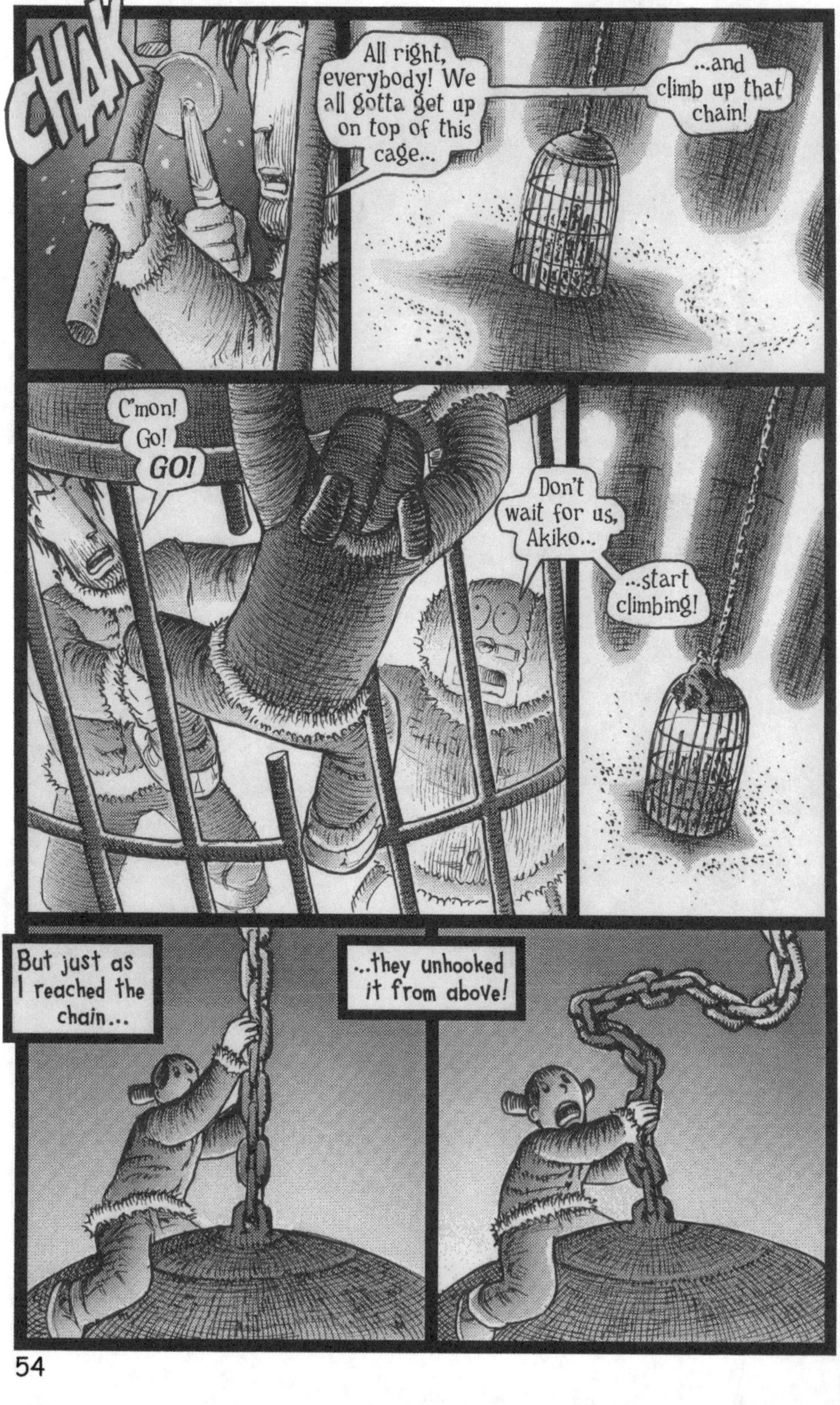
CHAK
All right, everybody! We all gotta get up on top of this cage...
...and climb up that chain!
C'mon! Go! GO!
Don't wait for us, Akiko...
...start climbing!
But just as I reached the chain...
...they unhooked it from above!

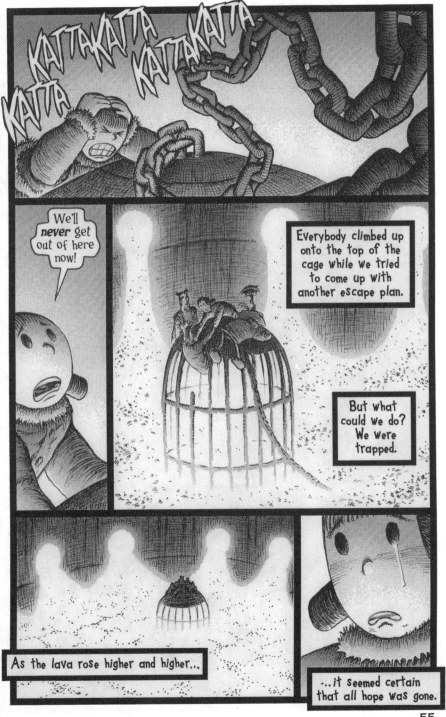

KATTAKATTA KATTAKATTA KATTAKATTA KATTA

We'll **never** get out of here now!

Everybody climbed up onto the top of the cage while we tried to come up with another escape plan.

But what could we do? We were trapped.

As the lava rose higher and higher...

...it seemed certain that all hope was gone.

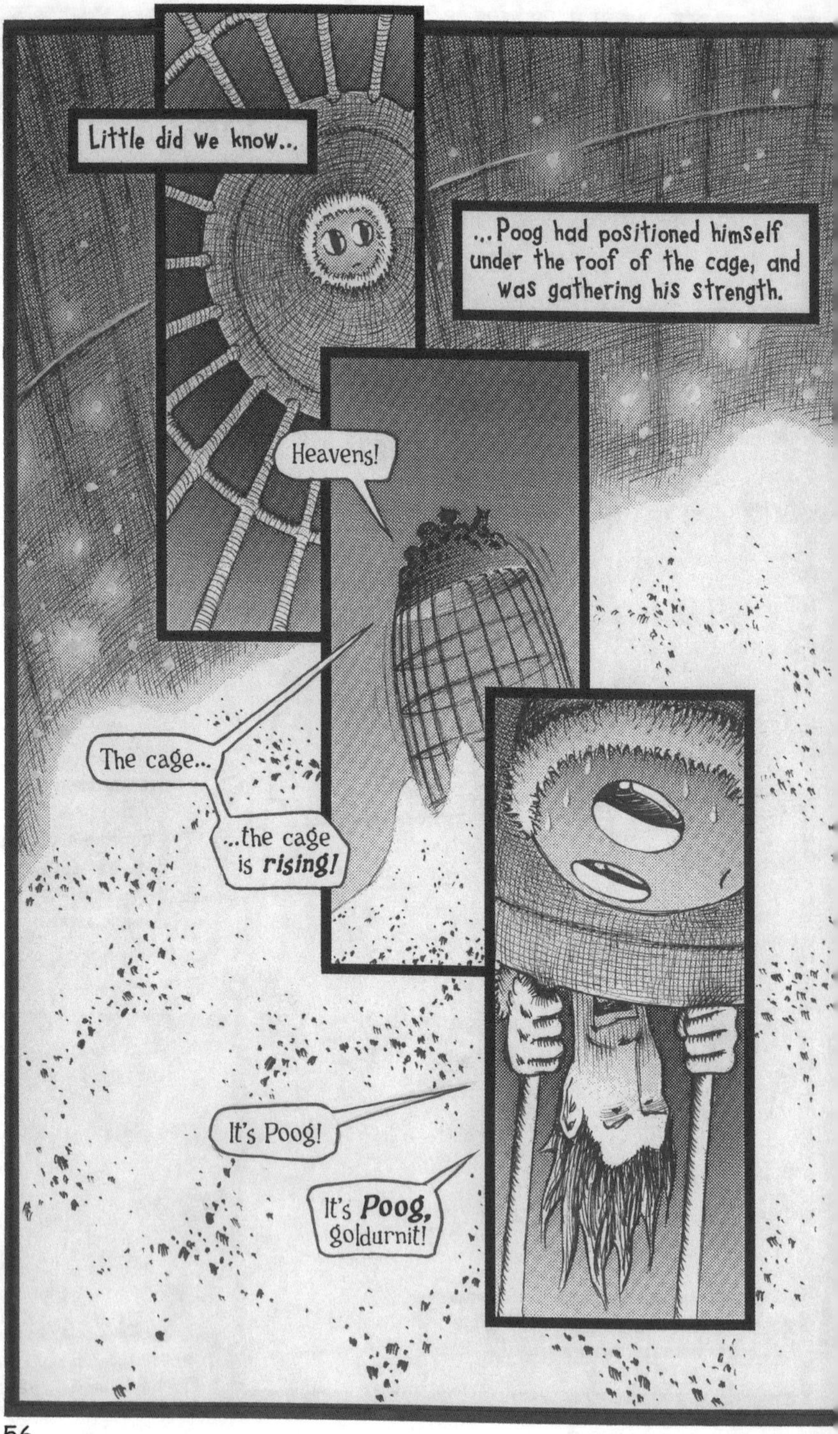
Little did we know...
...Poog had positioned himself under the roof of the cage, and was gathering his strength.
Heavens!
The cage...
...the cage is *rising!*
It's Poog!
It's ***Poog,*** goldurnit!

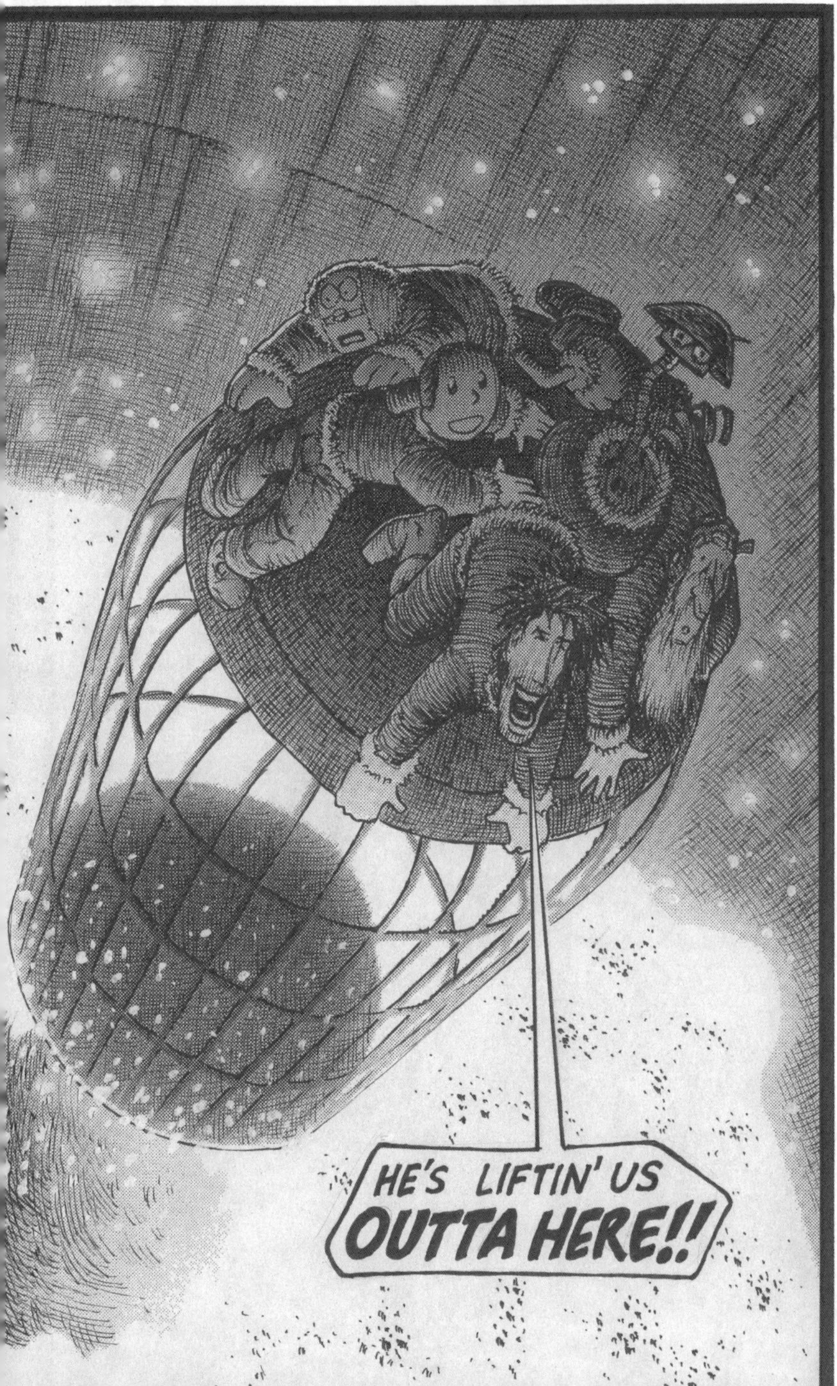
HE'S LIFTIN' US
OUTTA HERE!!

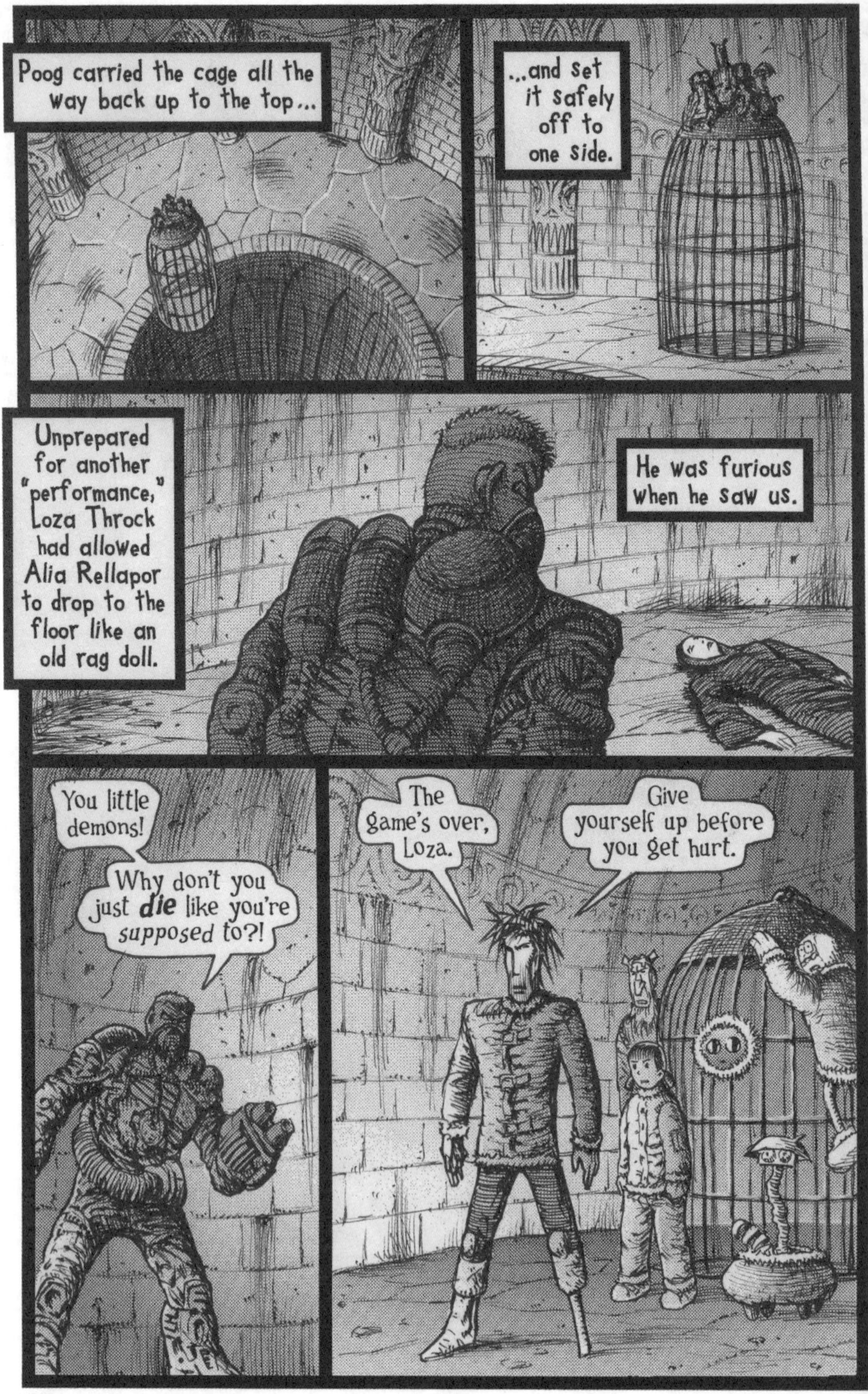
Poog carried the cage all the way back up to the top...
...and set it safely off to one side.
Unprepared for another "performance," Loza Throck had allowed Alia Rellapor to drop to the floor like an old rag doll.
He was furious when he saw us.
You little demons!
Why don't you just ***die*** like you're *supposed* to?!
The game's over, Loza.
Give yourself up before you get hurt.

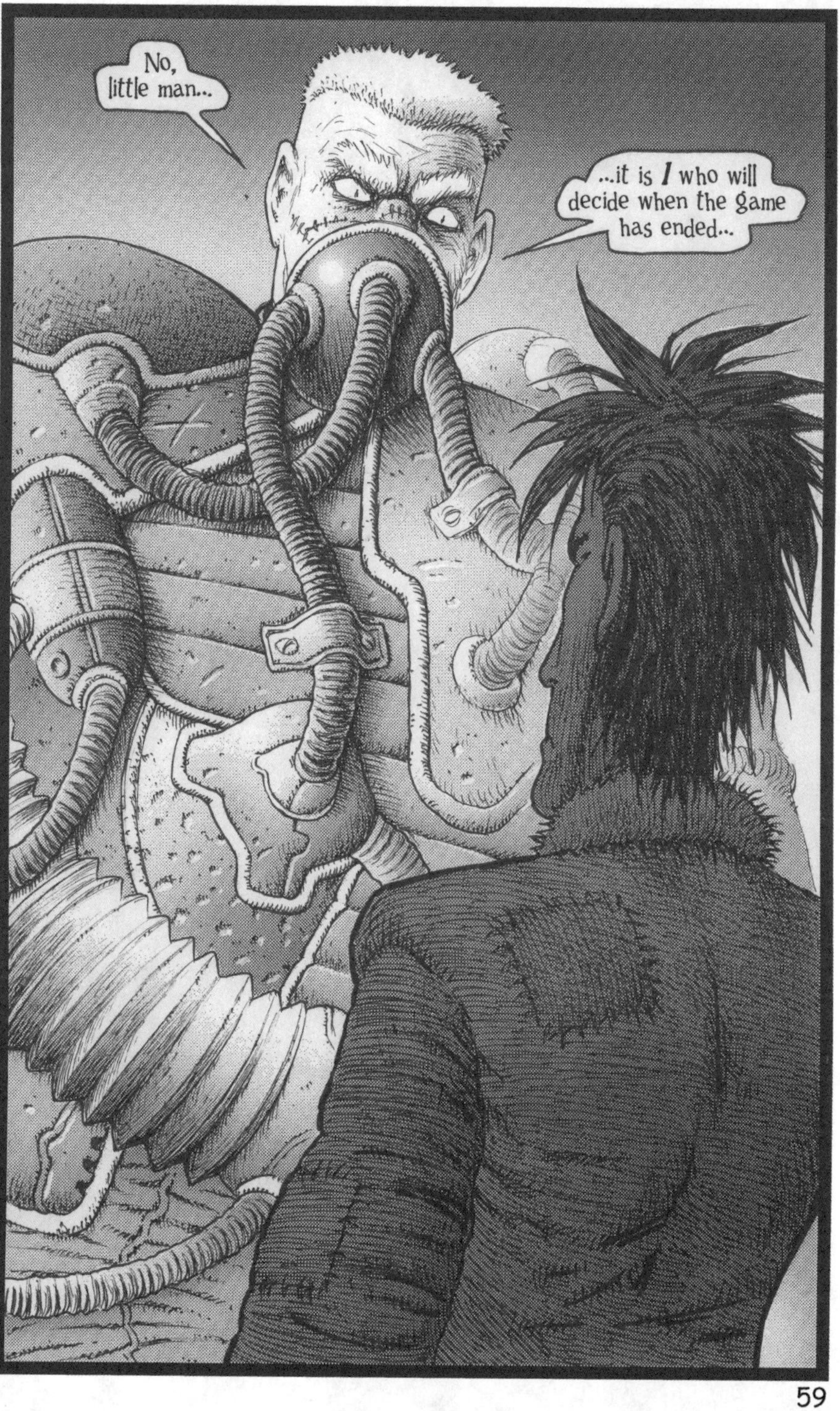
No, little man...
...it is I who will decide when the game has ended...

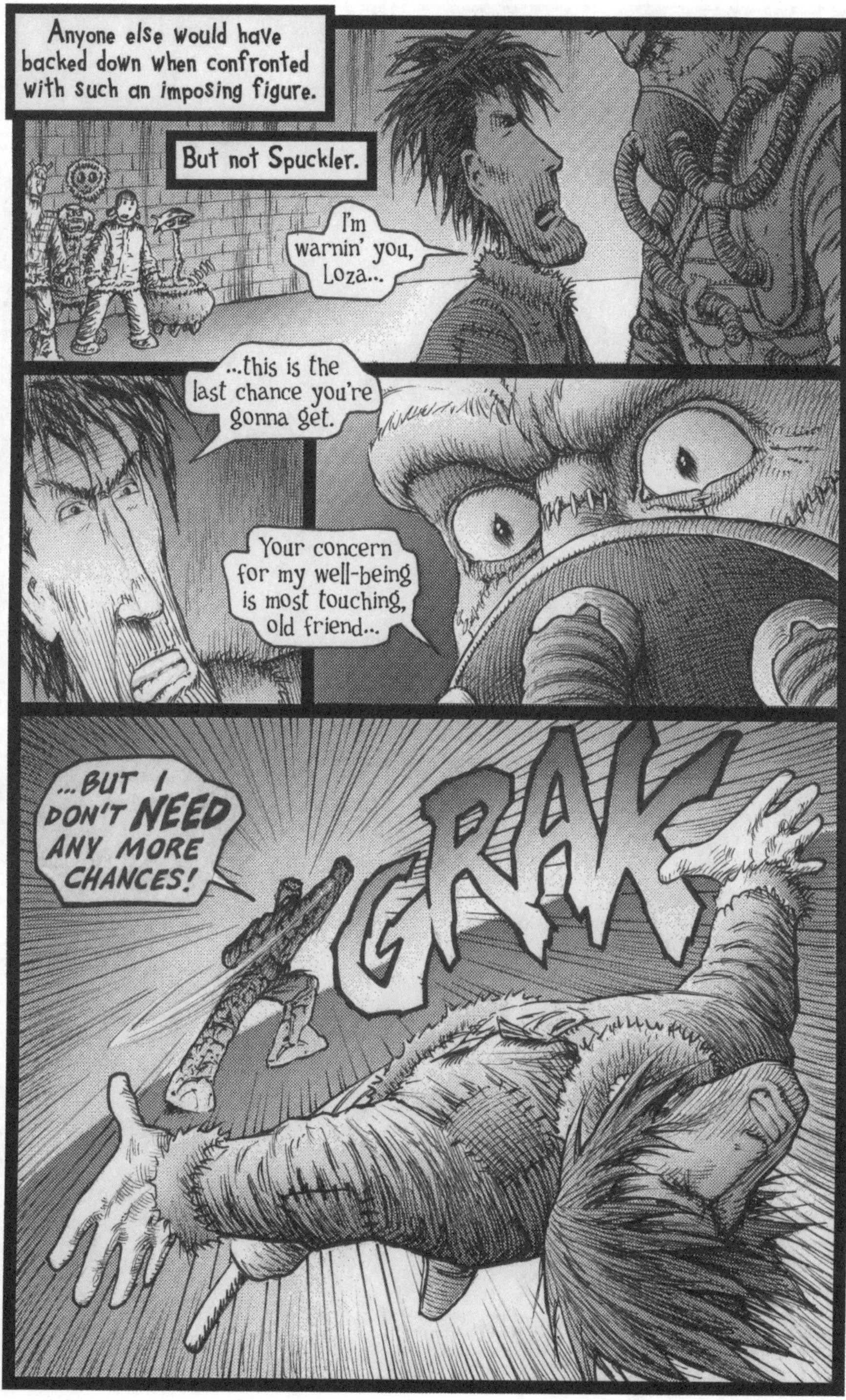

Anyone else would have backed down when confronted with such an imposing figure.
But not Spuckler.
I'm warnin' you, Loza...
...this is the last chance you're gonna get.
Your concern for my well-being is most touching, old friend...
...BUT I DON'T NEED ANY MORE CHANCES!
GRAK

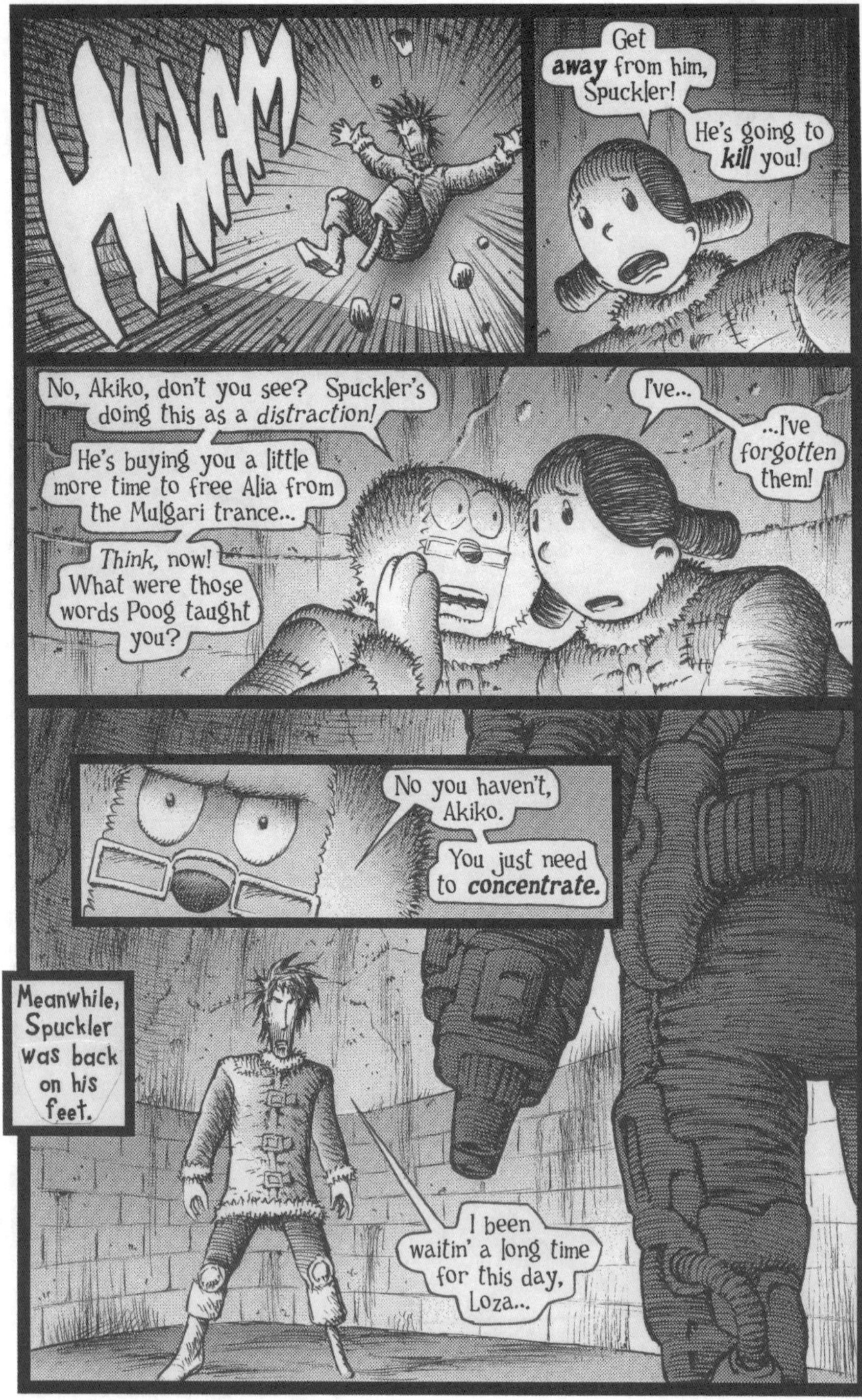
WHAM
Get **away** from him, Spuckler!
He's going to ***kill*** you!
No, Akiko, don't you see? Spuckler's doing this as a *distraction!*
He's buying you a little more time to free Alia from the Mulgari trance...
Think, now! What were those words Poog taught you?
I've...
...I've *forgotten* them!
No you haven't, Akiko.
You just need to ***concentrate.***
Meanwhile, Spuckler was back on his feet.
I been waitin' a long time for this day, Loza...

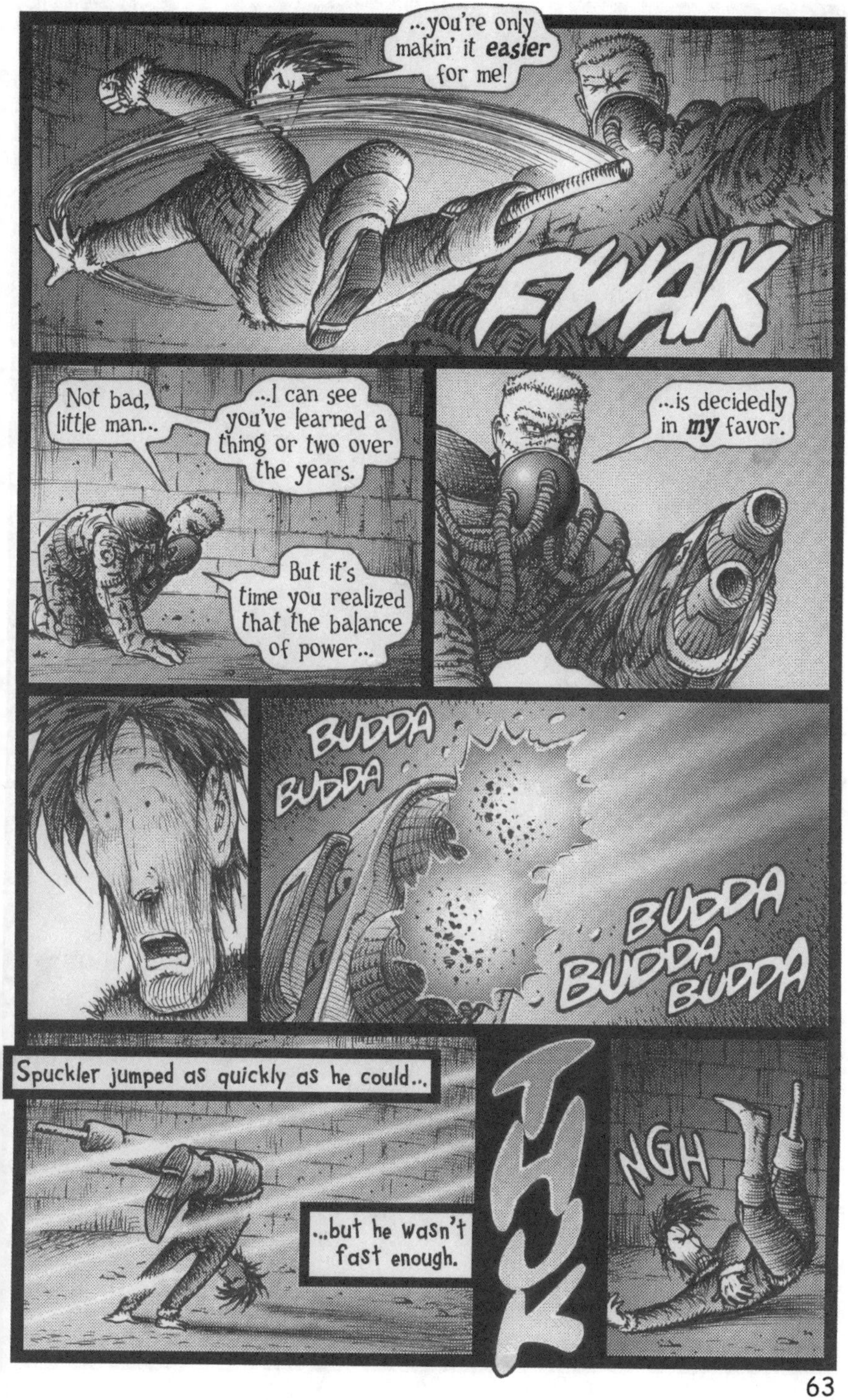

...you're only makin' it easier for me!
FWAK
Not bad, little man...
...I can see you've learned a thing or two over the years.
But it's time you realized that the balance of power...
...is decidedly in my favor.
BUDDA BUDDA
BUDDA BUDDA BUDDA
Spuckler jumped as quickly as he could...
...but he wasn't fast enough.
THUK
NGH

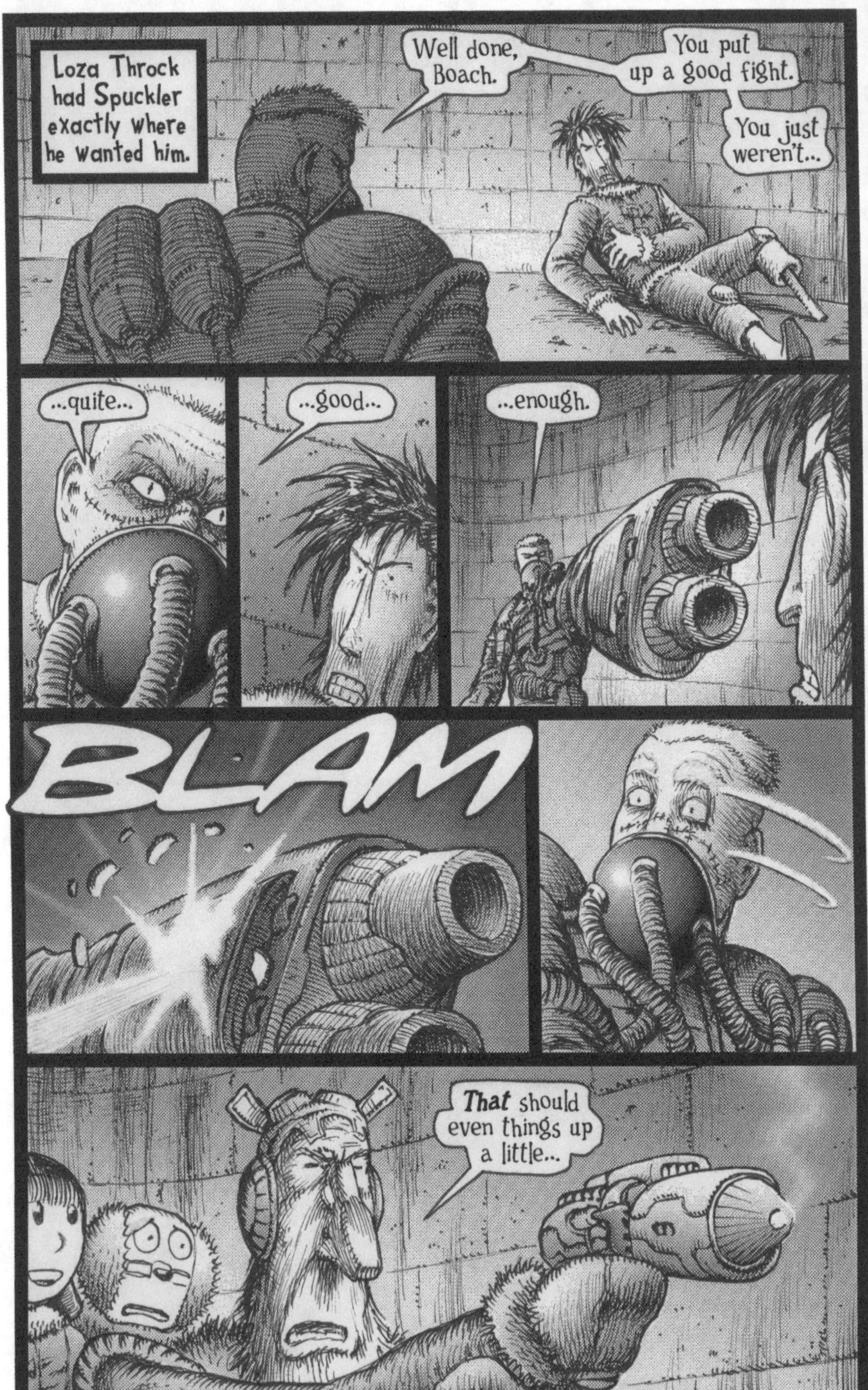

Loza Throck had Spuckler exactly where he wanted him.
Well done, Boach.
You put up a good fight.
You just weren't...
...quite...
...good...
...enough.
BLAM
That should even things up a little...

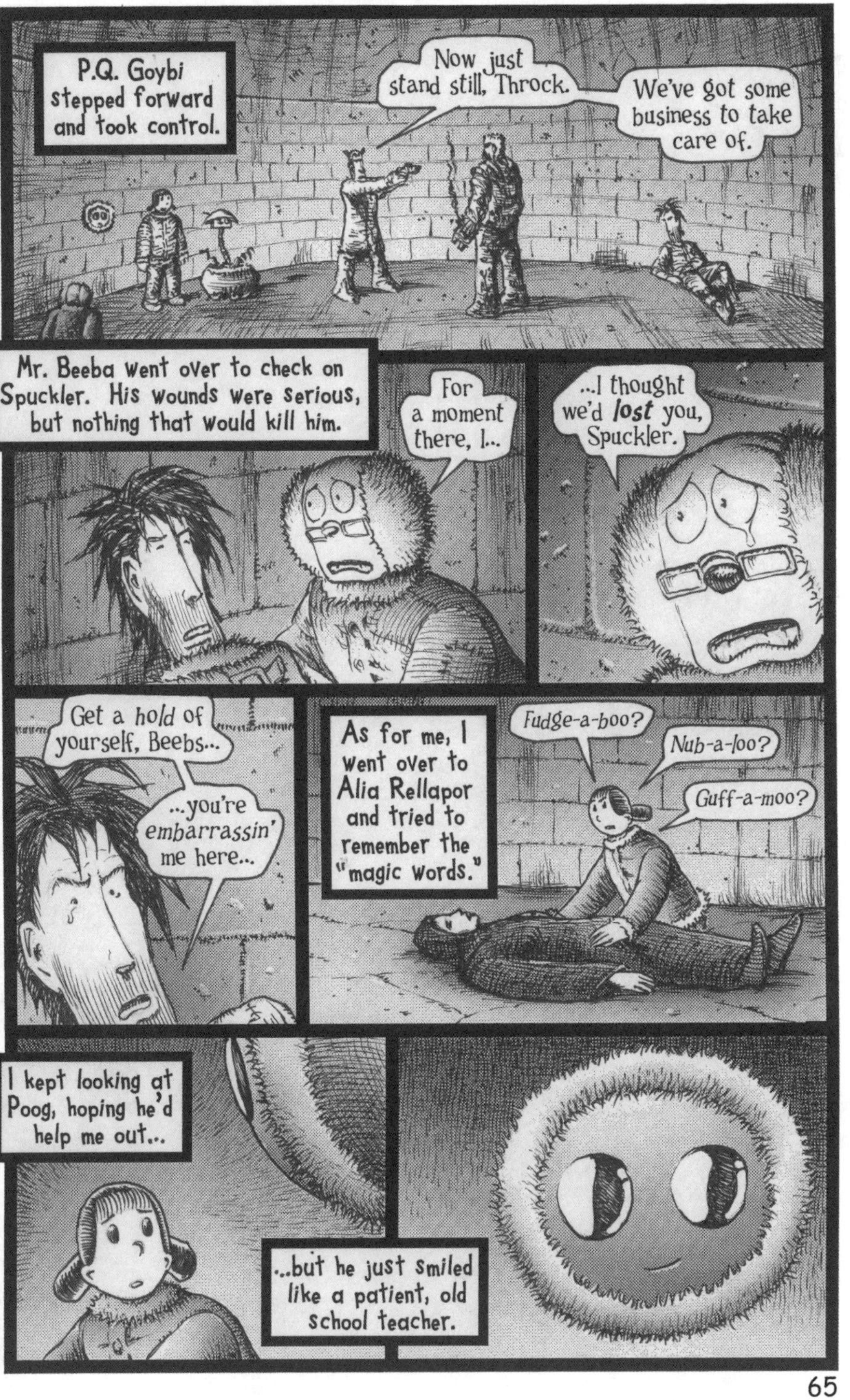
P.Q. Goybi stepped forward and took control.
Now just stand still, Throck.
We've got some business to take care of.
Mr. Beeba went over to check on Spuckler. His wounds were serious, but nothing that would kill him.
For a moment there, I...
...I thought we'd *lost* you, Spuckler.
Get a *hold* of yourself, Beebs...
...you're *embarrassin'* me here...
As for me, I went over to Alia Rellapor and tried to remember the "magic words."
Fudge-a-boo?
Nub-a-loo?
Guff-a-moo?
I kept looking at Poog, hoping he'd help me out...
...but he just smiled like a patient, old school teacher.

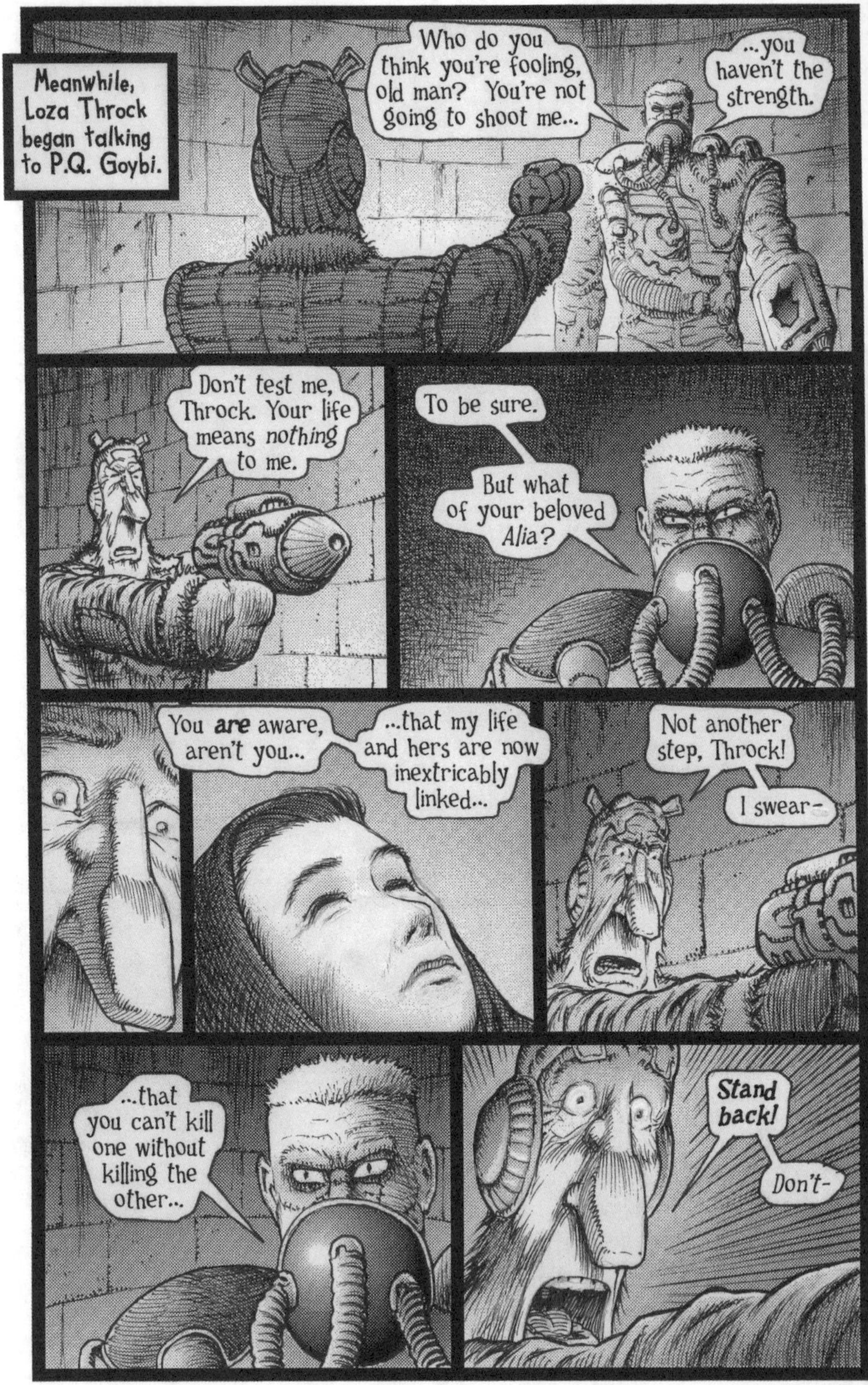
Meanwhile, Loza Throck began talking to P.Q. Goybi.
Who do you think you're fooling, old man? You're not going to shoot me...
...you haven't the strength.
Don't test me, Throck. Your life means *nothing* to me.
To be sure.
But what of your beloved *Alia*?
You **are** aware, aren't you...
...that my life and hers are now inextricably linked...
Not another step, Throck!
I swear–
...that you can't kill one without killing the other...
Stand back!
Don't–

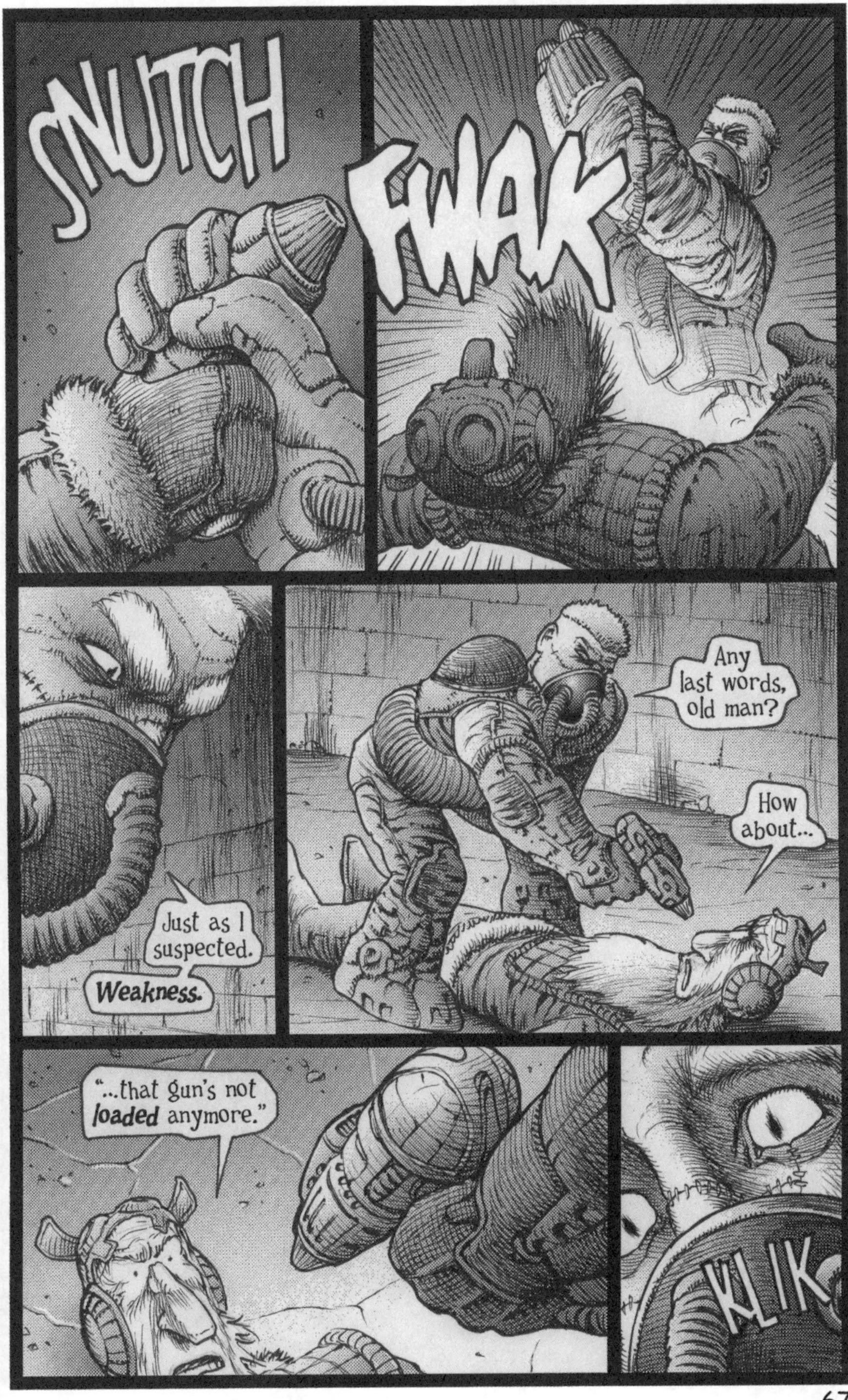
SNUTCH
FWAK
Just as I suspected.
Weakness.
Any last words, old man?
How about...
"...that gun's not loaded anymore."
KLIK

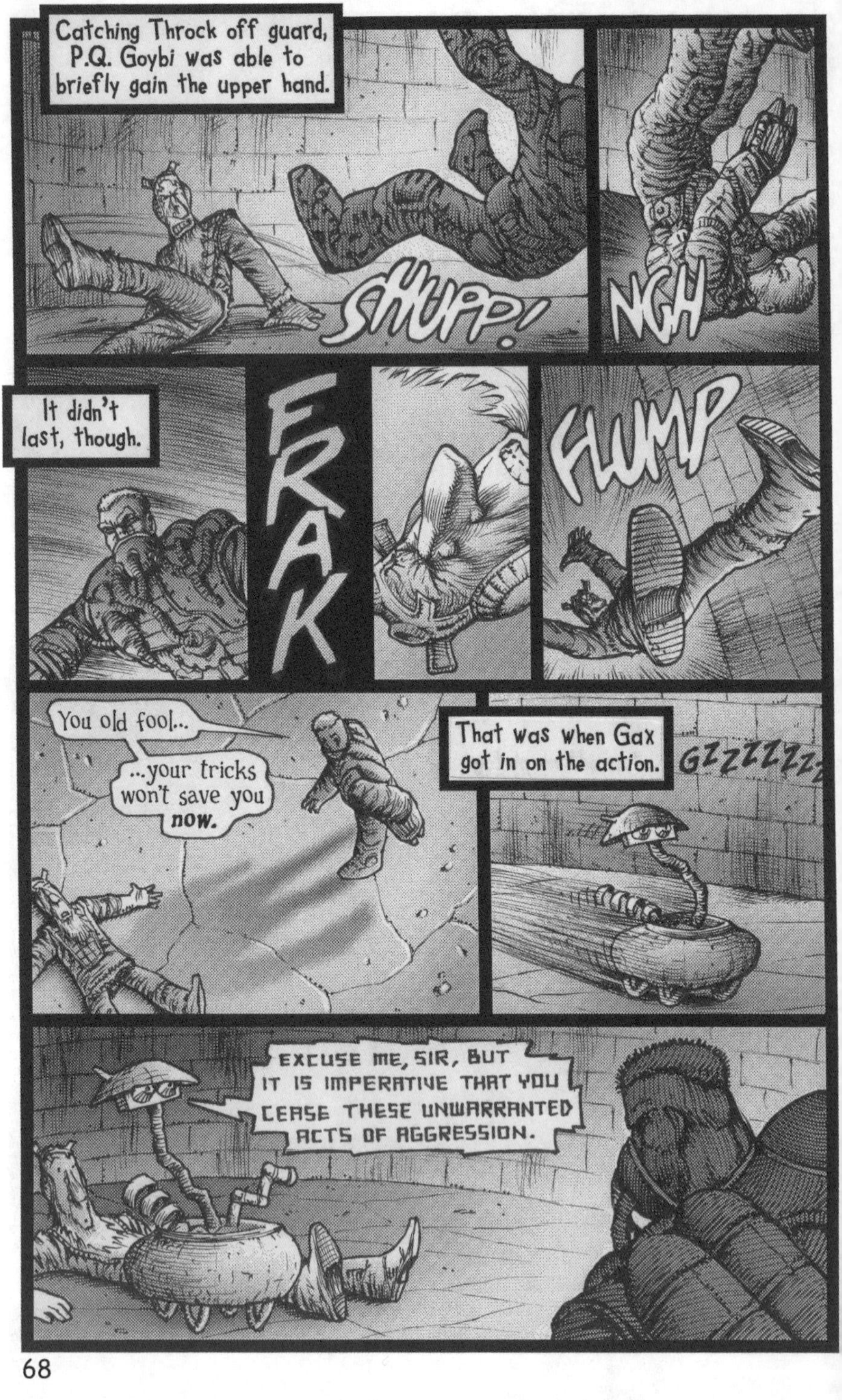

Catching Throck off guard, P.Q. Goybi was able to briefly gain the upper hand.
SHUPP!
NGH
It didn't last, though.
FRAK
FLUMP
You old fool...
...your tricks won't save you now.
That was when Gax got in on the action.
GZZZZZZ
EXCUSE ME, SIR, BUT IT IS IMPERATIVE THAT YOU CEASE THESE UNWARRANTED ACTS OF AGGRESSION.

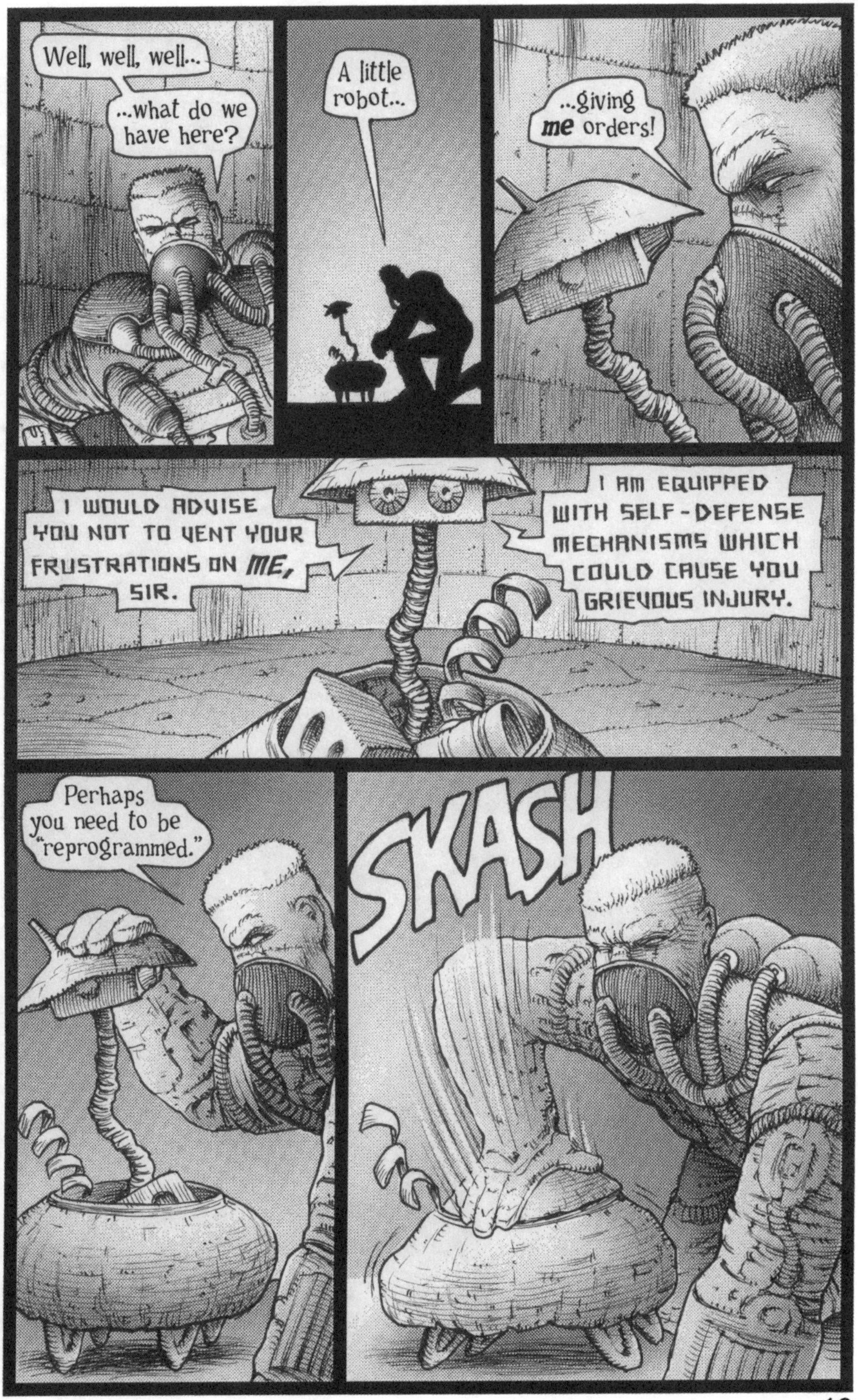
Well, well, well...
...what do we have here?
A little robot...
...giving *me* orders!
I WOULD ADVISE YOU NOT TO VENT YOUR FRUSTRATIONS ON *ME*, SIR.
I AM EQUIPPED WITH SELF-DEFENSE MECHANISMS WHICH COULD CAUSE YOU GRIEVOUS INJURY.
Perhaps you need to be "reprogrammed."
SKASH

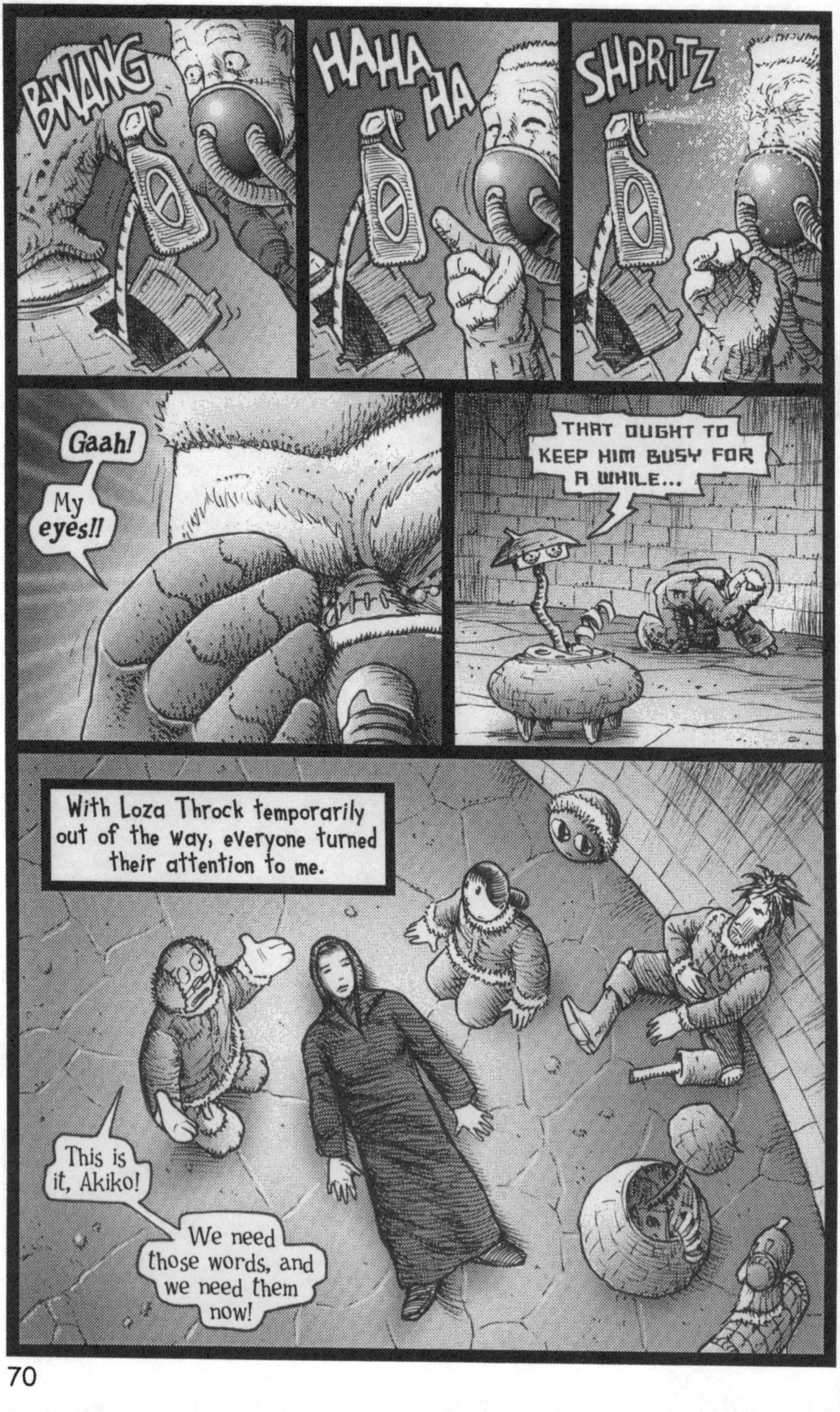
BWANG
HAHAHA HA
SHPRITZ
Gaah!
My eyes!!
THAT OUGHT TO KEEP HIM BUSY FOR A WHILE...
With Loza Throck temporarily out of the way, everyone turned their attention to me.
This is it, Akiko!
We need those words, and we need them now!

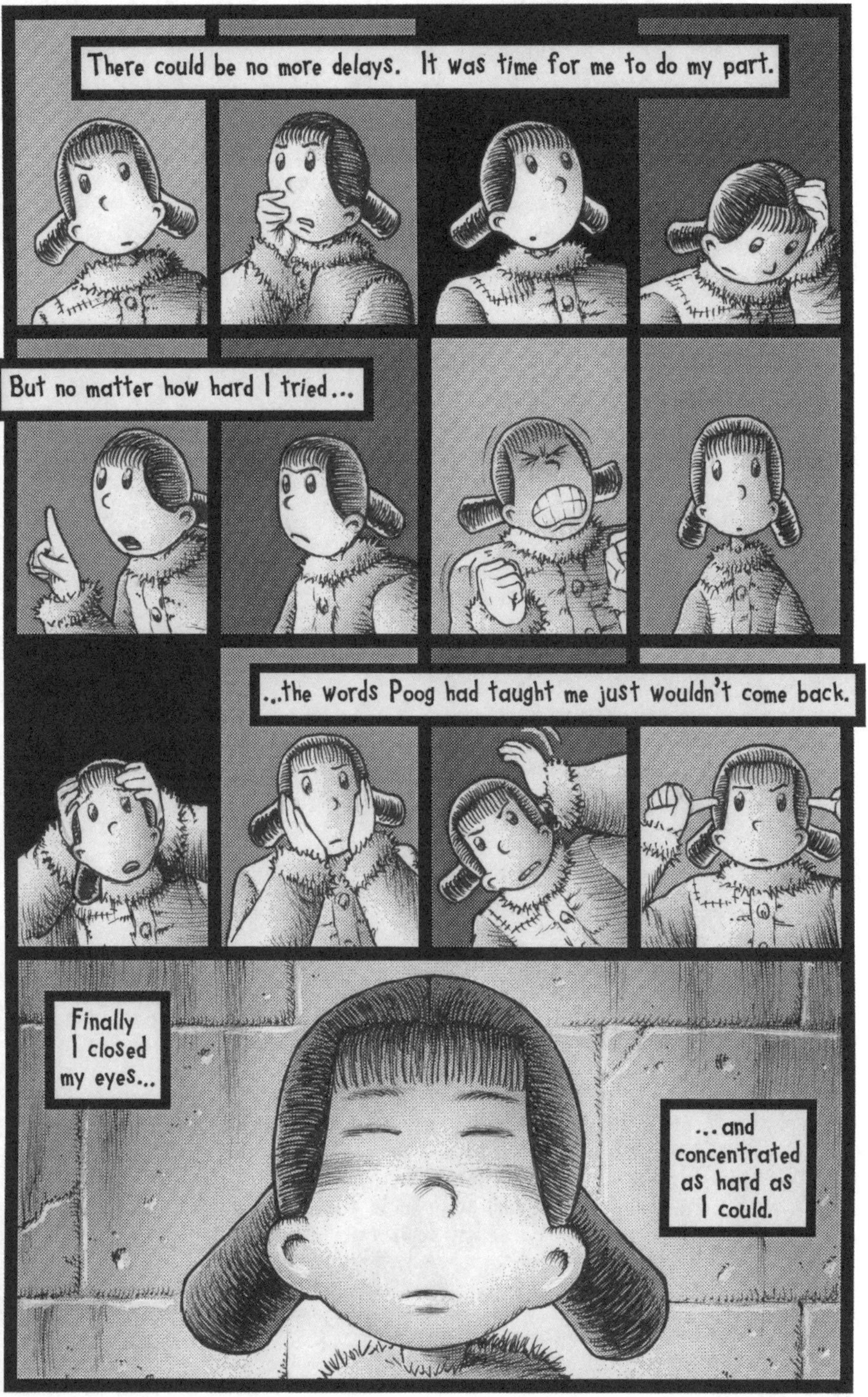
There could be no more delays. It was time for me to do my part.
But no matter how hard I tried...
...the words Poog had taught me just wouldn't come back.
Finally I closed my eyes...
...and concentrated as hard as I could.

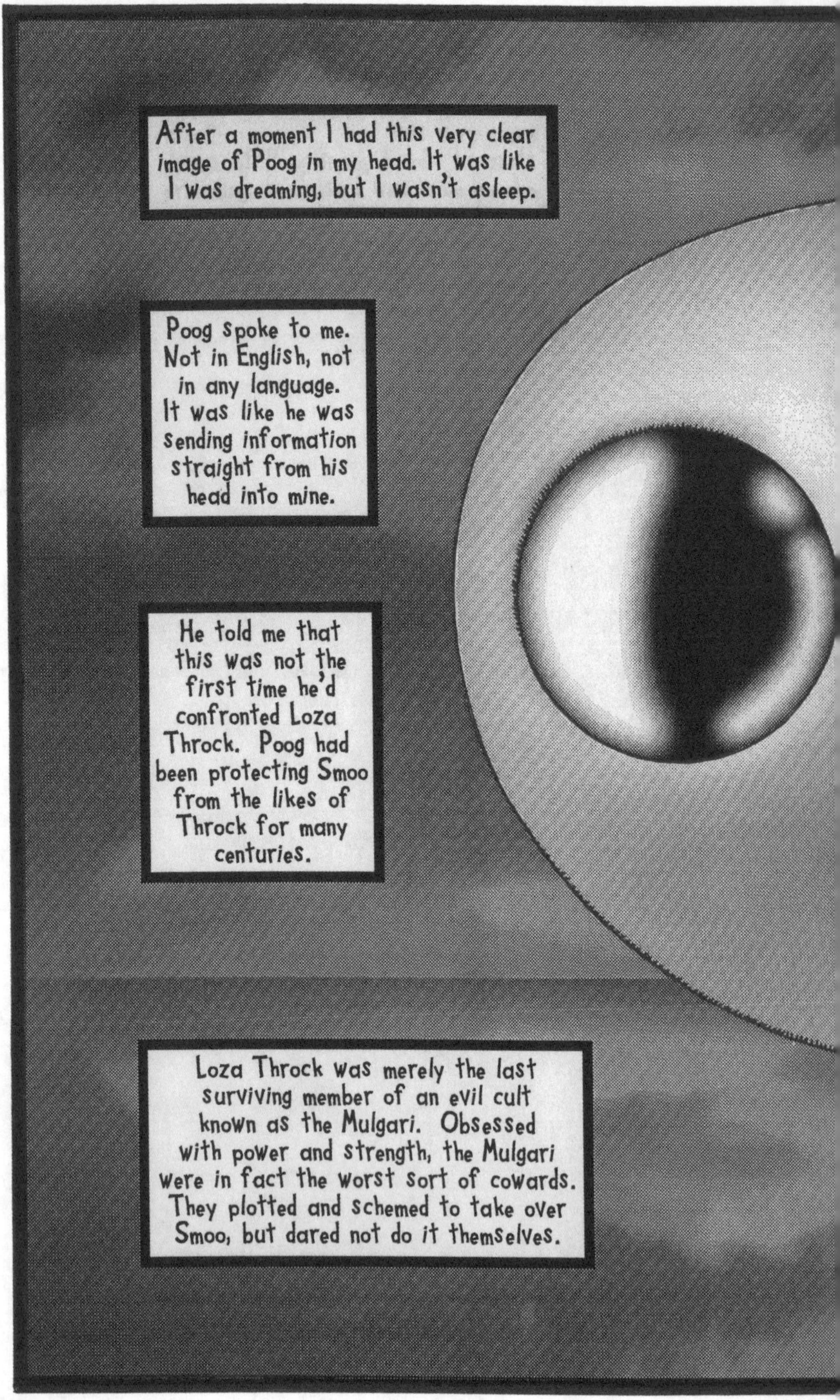
After a moment I had this very clear image of Poog in my head. It was like I was dreaming, but I wasn't asleep.
Poog spoke to me. Not in English, not in any language. It was like he was sending information straight from his head into mine.
He told me that this was not the first time he'd confronted Loza Throck. Poog had been protecting Smoo from the likes of Throck for many centuries.
Loza Throck was merely the last surviving member of an evil cult known as the Mulgari. Obsessed with power and strength, the Mulgari were in fact the worst sort of cowards. They plotted and schemed to take over Smoo, but dared not do it themselves.

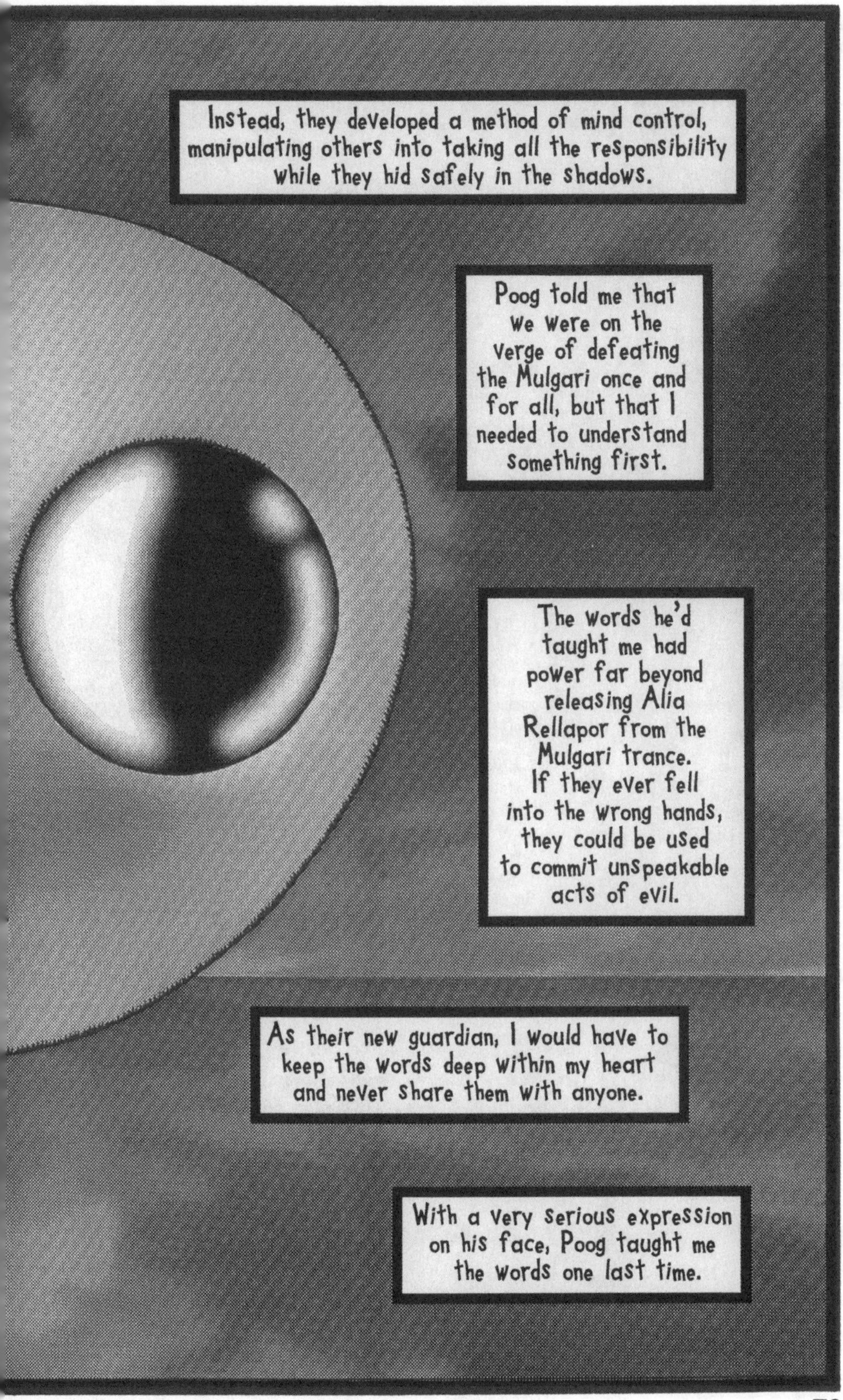
Instead, they developed a method of mind control, manipulating others into taking all the responsibility while they hid safely in the shadows.
Poog told me that we were on the verge of defeating the Mulgari once and for all, but that I needed to understand something first.
The words he'd taught me had power far beyond releasing Alia Rellapor from the Mulgari trance. If they ever fell into the wrong hands, they could be used to commit unspeakable acts of evil.
As their new guardian, I would have to keep the words deep within my heart and never share them with anyone.
With a very serious expression on his face, Poog taught me the words one last time.

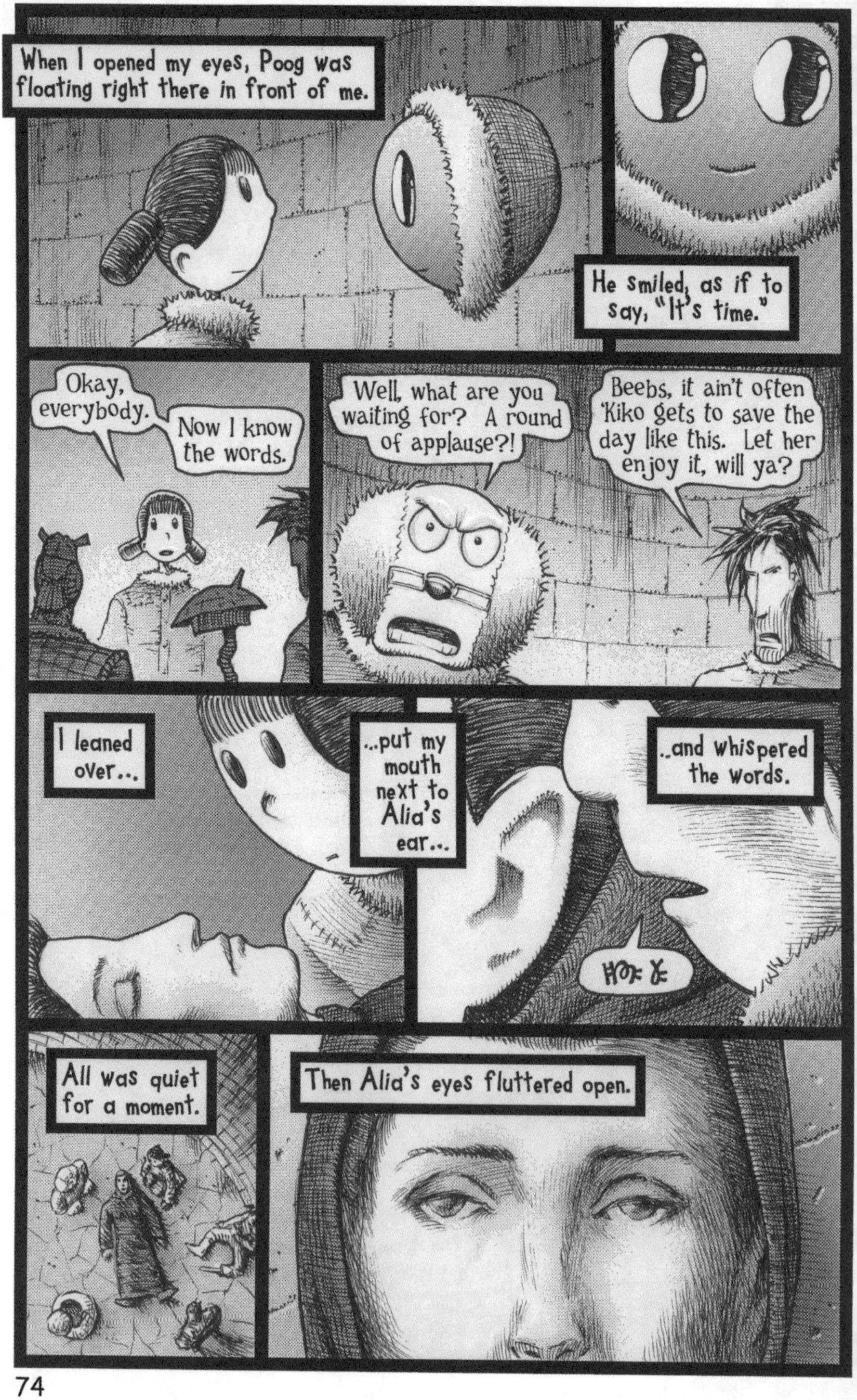
When I opened my eyes, Poog was floating right there in front of me.
He smiled, as if to say, "It's time."
Okay, everybody.
Now I know the words.
Well, what are you waiting for? A round of applause?!
Beebs, it ain't often 'Kiko gets to save the day like this. Let her enjoy it, will ya?
I leaned over...
...put my mouth next to Alia's ear...
..and whispered the words.
All was quiet for a moment.
Then Alia's eyes fluttered open.

Alia!

Are you okay?

Goybi?

You...

...you *remember* me!

We mustn't cause her to strain herself...

Coming out of the Mulgari Trance throws one into an extreme state of exhaustion!

Sure enough, Alia closed her eyes and went right back to sleep.

That was when Poog made a terrifying announcement.

ᑐᕐᗩᑌᕐ ᔭᖴᕑᗯᒪᗴ ᕼᖴᕑ ᕑᗰ ᖷ ᒪᗯ ᕼᖴᗘᕼ!

Poog says that Loza is preparing to leave Smoo at this very moment!

An escape ship is docked and waiting for him at the other end of the castle. And that's not all...

...he's taking the Prince with him!

NO!! We've got to stop him!!

75

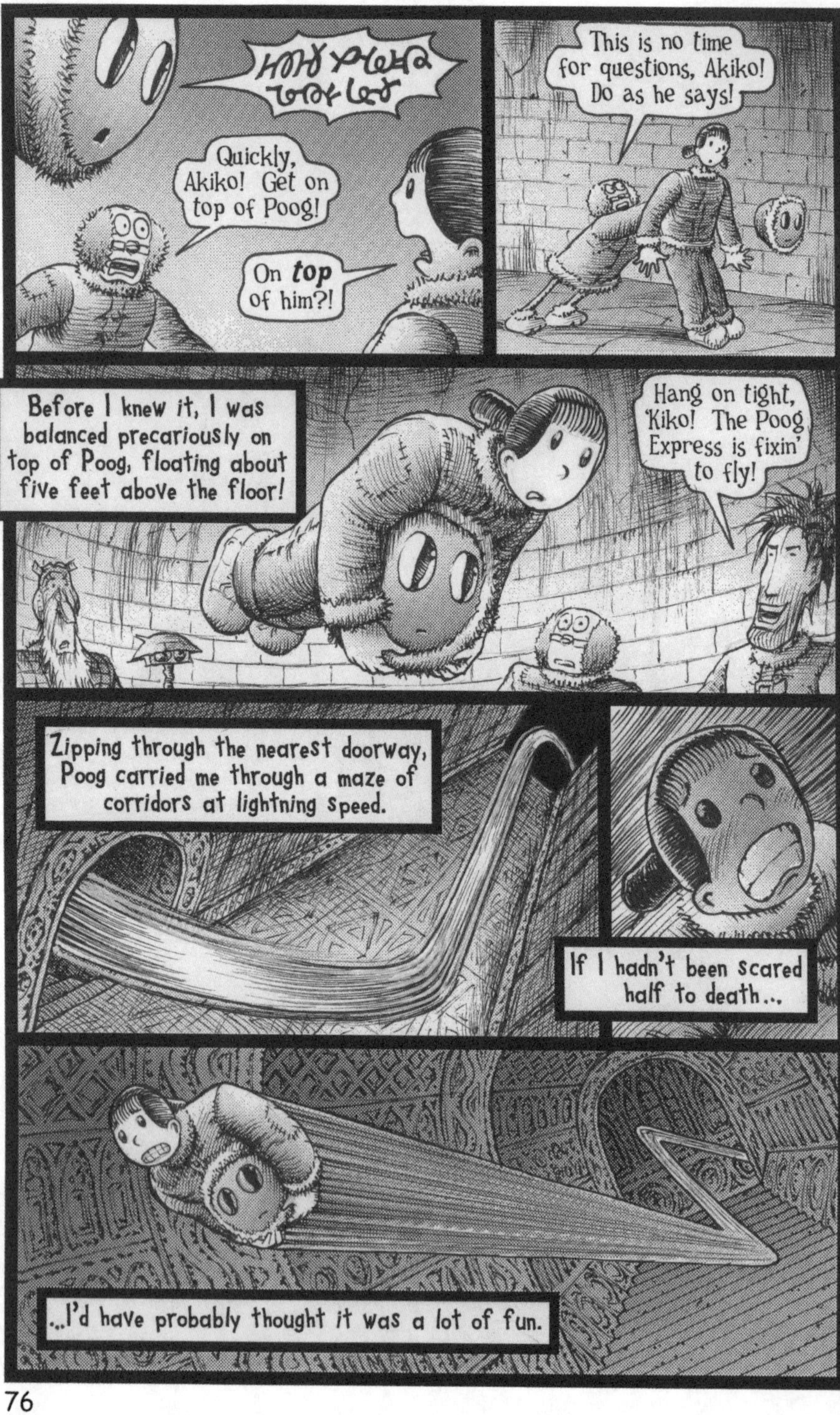
Quickly, Akiko! Get on top of Poog!
On *top* of him?!
This is no time for questions, Akiko! Do as he says!
Before I knew it, I was balanced precariously on top of Poog, floating about five feet above the floor!
Hang on tight, 'Kiko! The Poog Express is fixin' to fly!
Zipping through the nearest doorway, Poog carried me through a maze of corridors at lightning speed.
If I hadn't been scared half to death...
...I'd have probably thought it was a lot of fun.

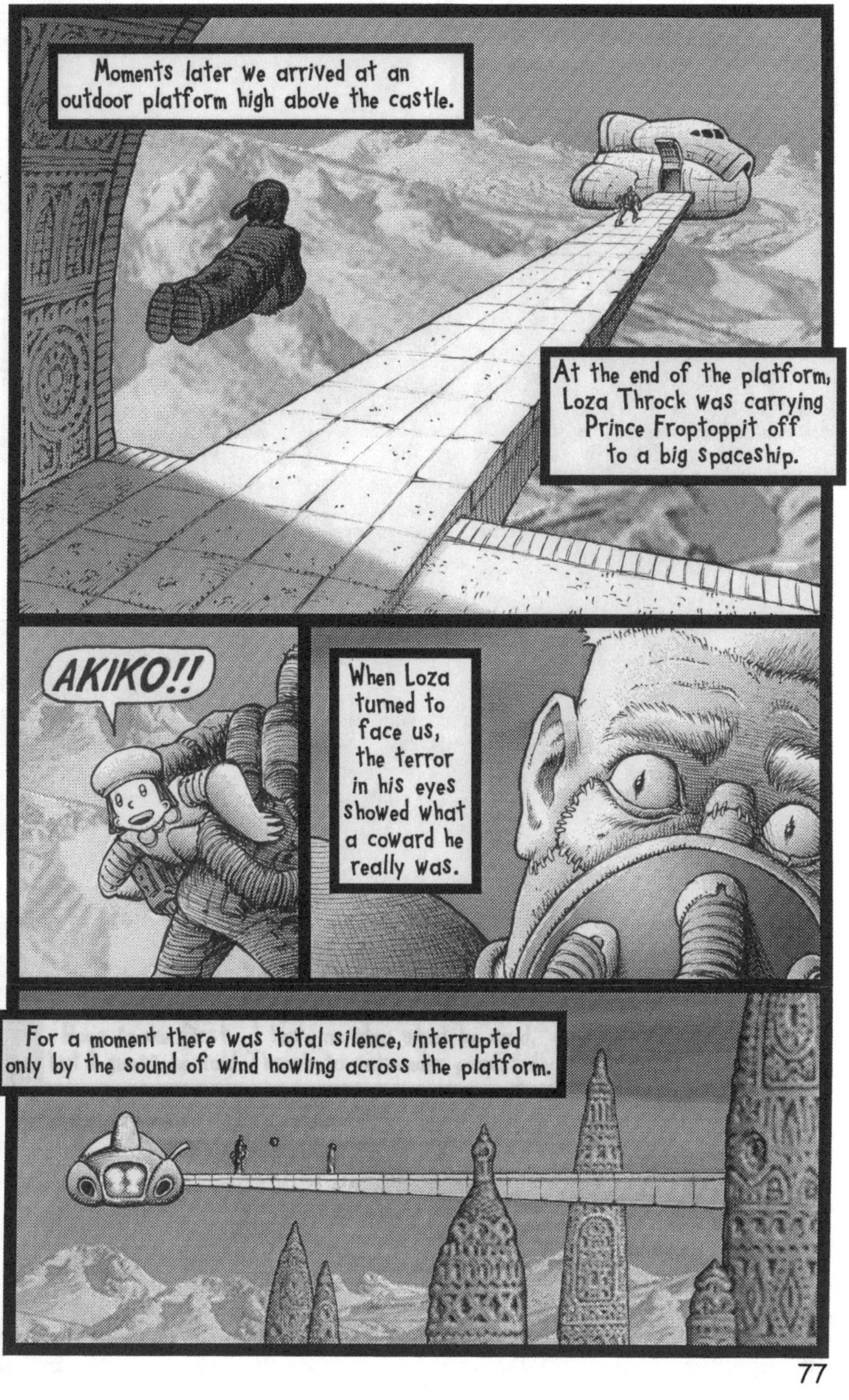
Moments later we arrived at an outdoor platform high above the castle.
At the end of the platform, Loza Throck was carrying Prince Froptoppit off to a big spaceship.
AKIKO!!
When Loza turned to face us, the terror in his eyes showed what a coward he really was.
For a moment there was total silence, interrupted only by the sound of wind howling across the platform.

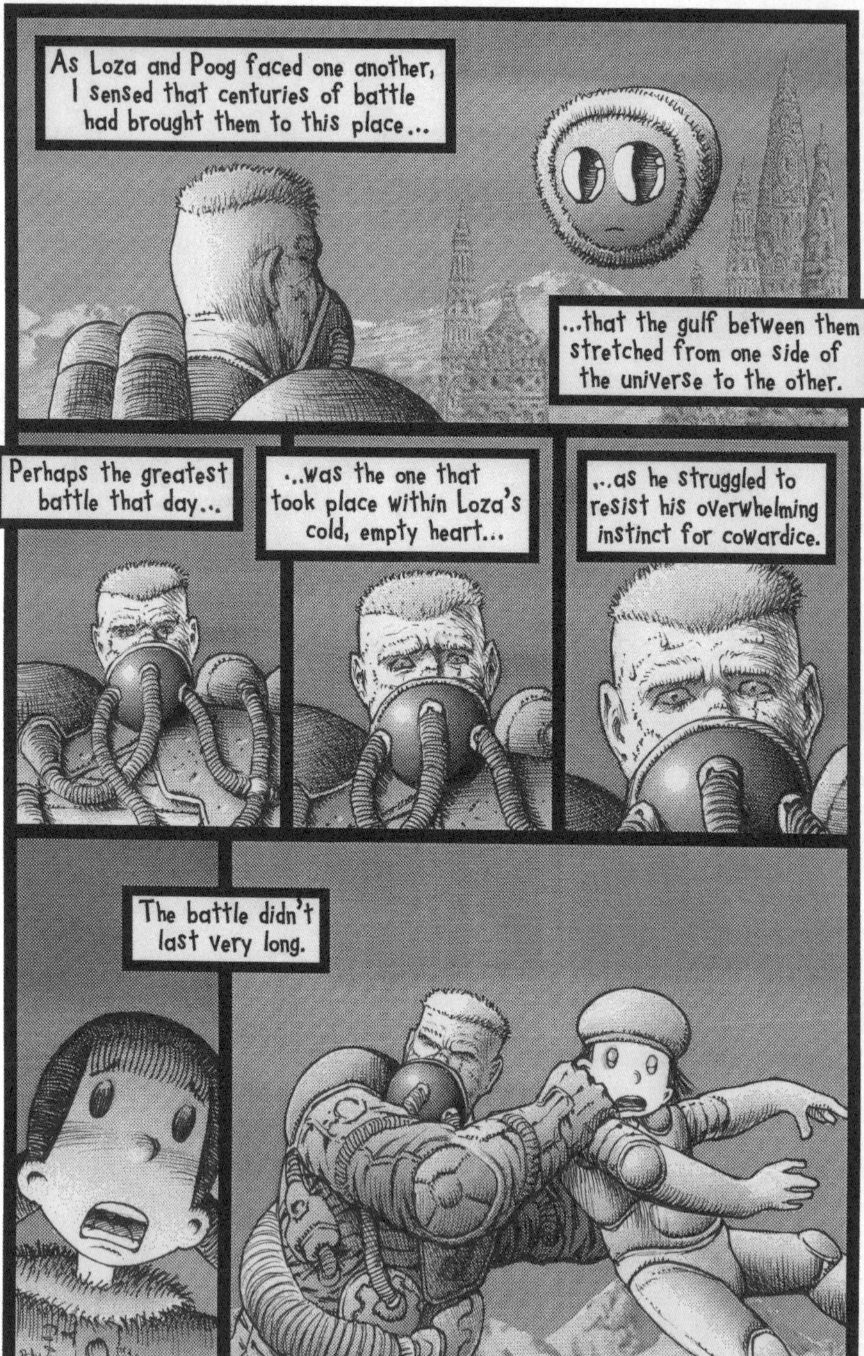
As Loza and Poog faced one another, I sensed that centuries of battle had brought them to this place...
...that the gulf between them stretched from one side of the universe to the other.
Perhaps the greatest battle that day...
...was the one that took place within Loza's cold, empty heart...
...as he struggled to resist his overwhelming instinct for cowardice.
The battle didn't last very long.

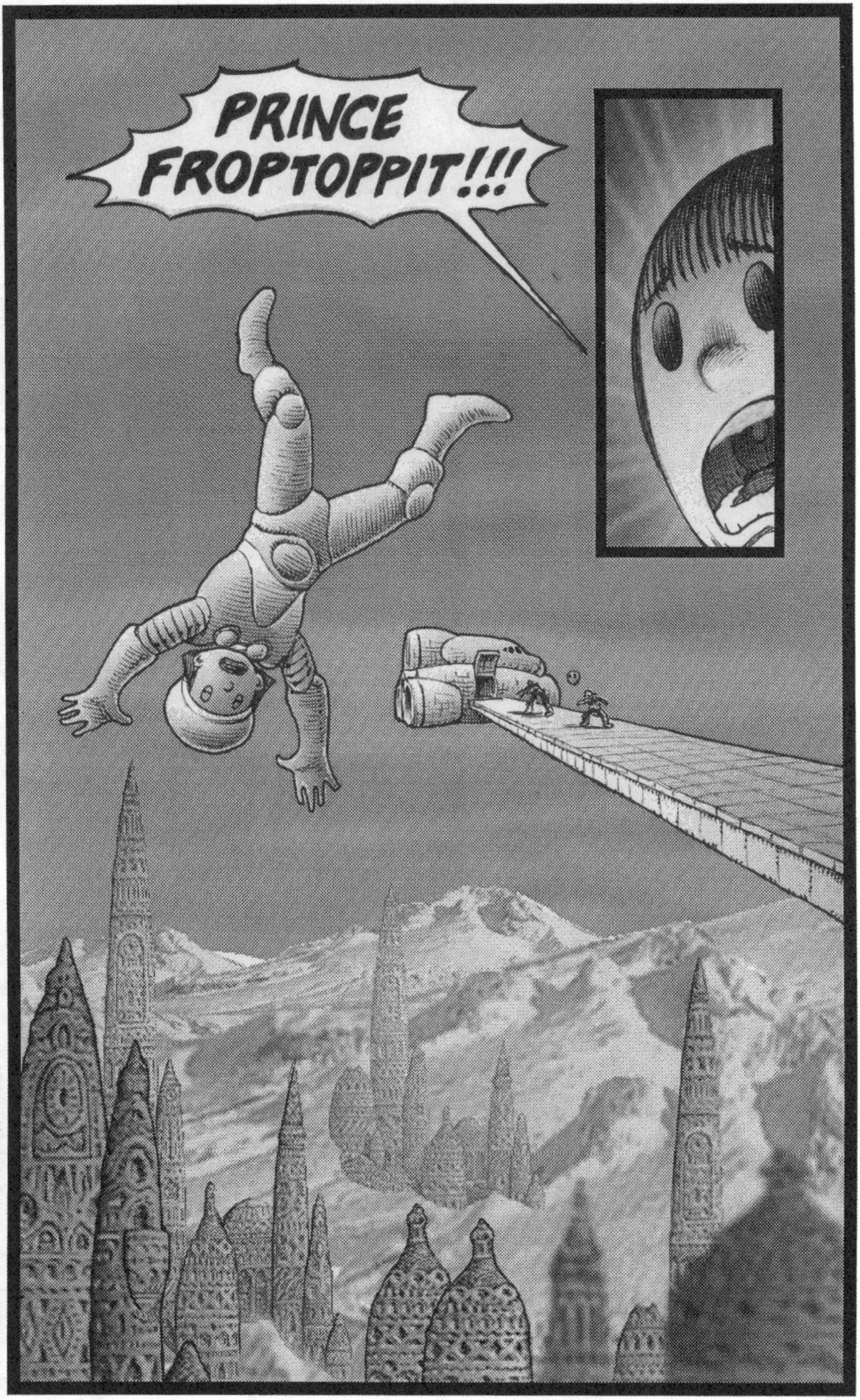
PRINCE FROPTOPPIT!!!

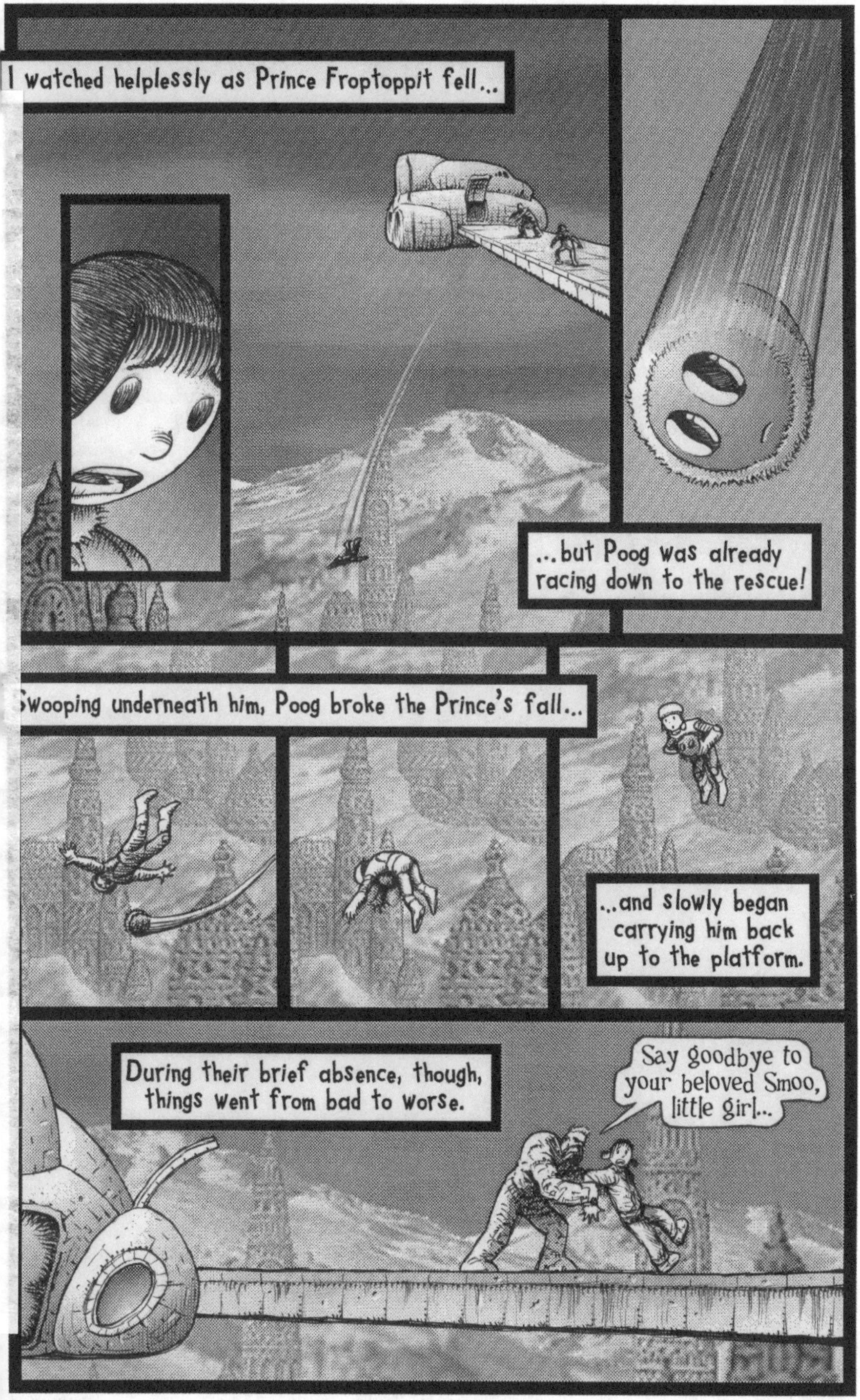
I watched helplessly as Prince Froptoppit fell...
...but Poog was already racing down to the rescue!
Swooping underneath him, Poog broke the Prince's fall...
...and slowly began carrying him back up to the platform.
During their brief absence, though, things went from bad to worse.
Say goodbye to your beloved Smoo, little girl...

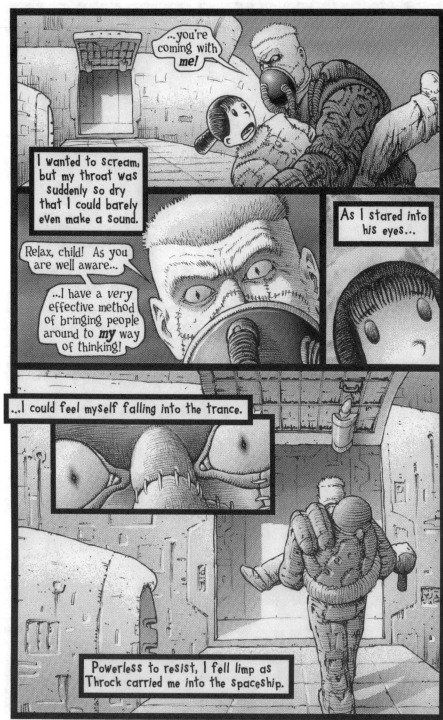

...you're coming with *me!*

I wanted to scream, but my throat was suddenly so dry that I could barely even make a sound.

Relax, child! As you are well aware...

...I have a *very* effective method of bringing people around to *my* way of thinking!

As I stared into his eyes...

...I could feel myself falling into the trance.

Powerless to resist, I fell limp as Throck carried me into the spaceship.

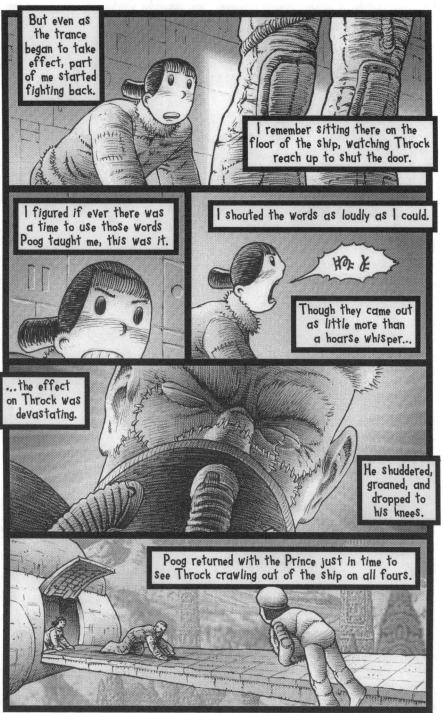

But even as the trance began to take effect, part of me started fighting back.

I remember sitting there on the floor of the ship, watching Throck reach up to shut the door.

I figured if ever there was a time to use those words Poog taught me, this was it.

I shouted the words as loudly as I could.

Though they came out as little more than a hoarse whisper...

...the effect on Throck was devastating.

He shuddered, groaned, and dropped to his knees.

Poog returned with the Prince just in time to see Throck crawling out of the ship on all fours.

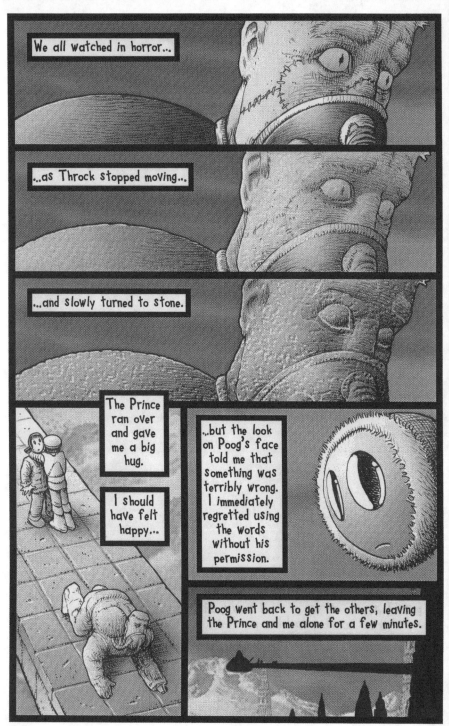

We all watched in horror...

..as Throck stopped moving...

...and slowly turned to stone.

The Prince ran over and gave me a big hug.

I should have felt happy...

..but the look on Poog's face told me that something was terribly wrong. I immediately regretted using the words without his permission.

Poog went back to get the others, leaving the Prince and me alone for a few minutes.

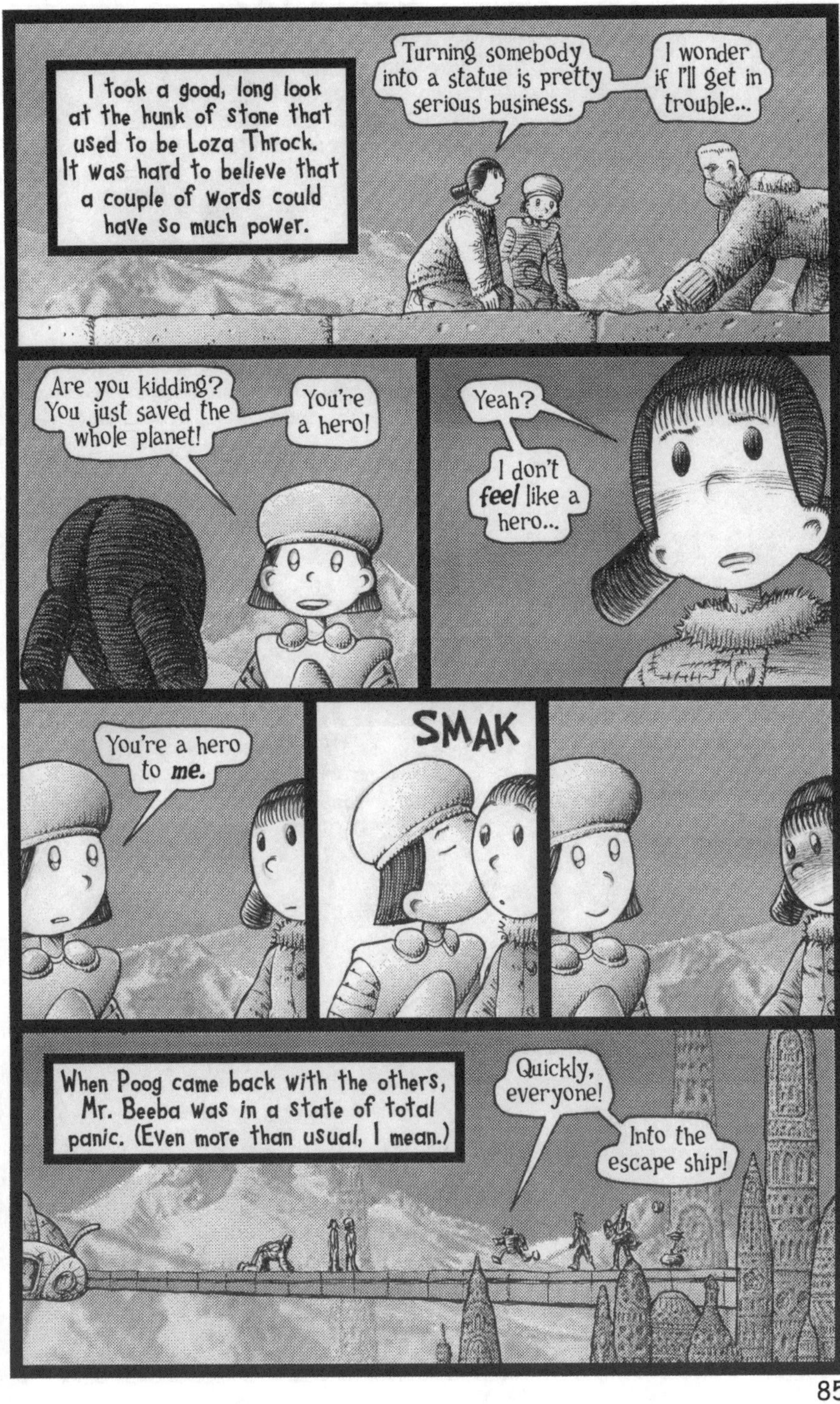
I took a good, long look at the hunk of stone that used to be Loza Throck. It was hard to believe that a couple of words could have so much power.
Turning somebody into a statue is pretty serious business.
I wonder if I'll get in trouble...
Are you kidding? You just saved the whole planet!
You're a hero!
Yeah?
I don't *feel* like a hero...
You're a hero to *me.*
SMAK
When Poog came back with the others, Mr. Beeba was in a state of total panic. (Even more than usual, I mean.)
Quickly, everyone!
Into the escape ship!

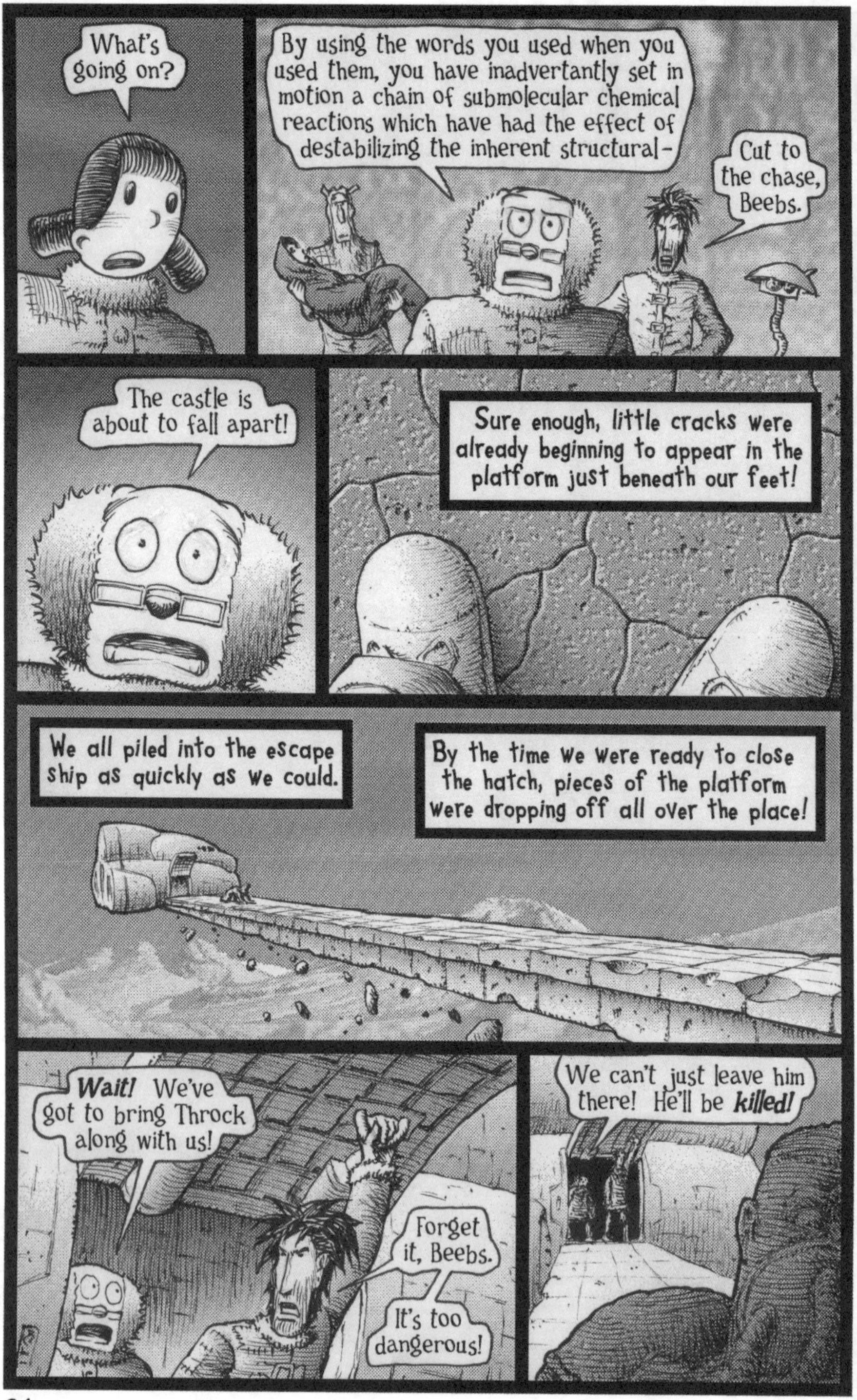
What's going on?
By using the words you used when you used them, you have inadvertantly set in motion a chain of submolecular chemical reactions which have had the effect of destabilizing the inherent structural-
Cut to the chase, Beebs.
The castle is about to fall apart!
Sure enough, little cracks were already beginning to appear in the platform just beneath our feet!
We all piled into the escape ship as quickly as we could.
By the time we were ready to close the hatch, pieces of the platform were dropping off all over the place!
Wait! We've got to bring Throck along with us!
Forget it, Beebs.
It's too dangerous!
We can't just leave him there! He'll be ***killed!***

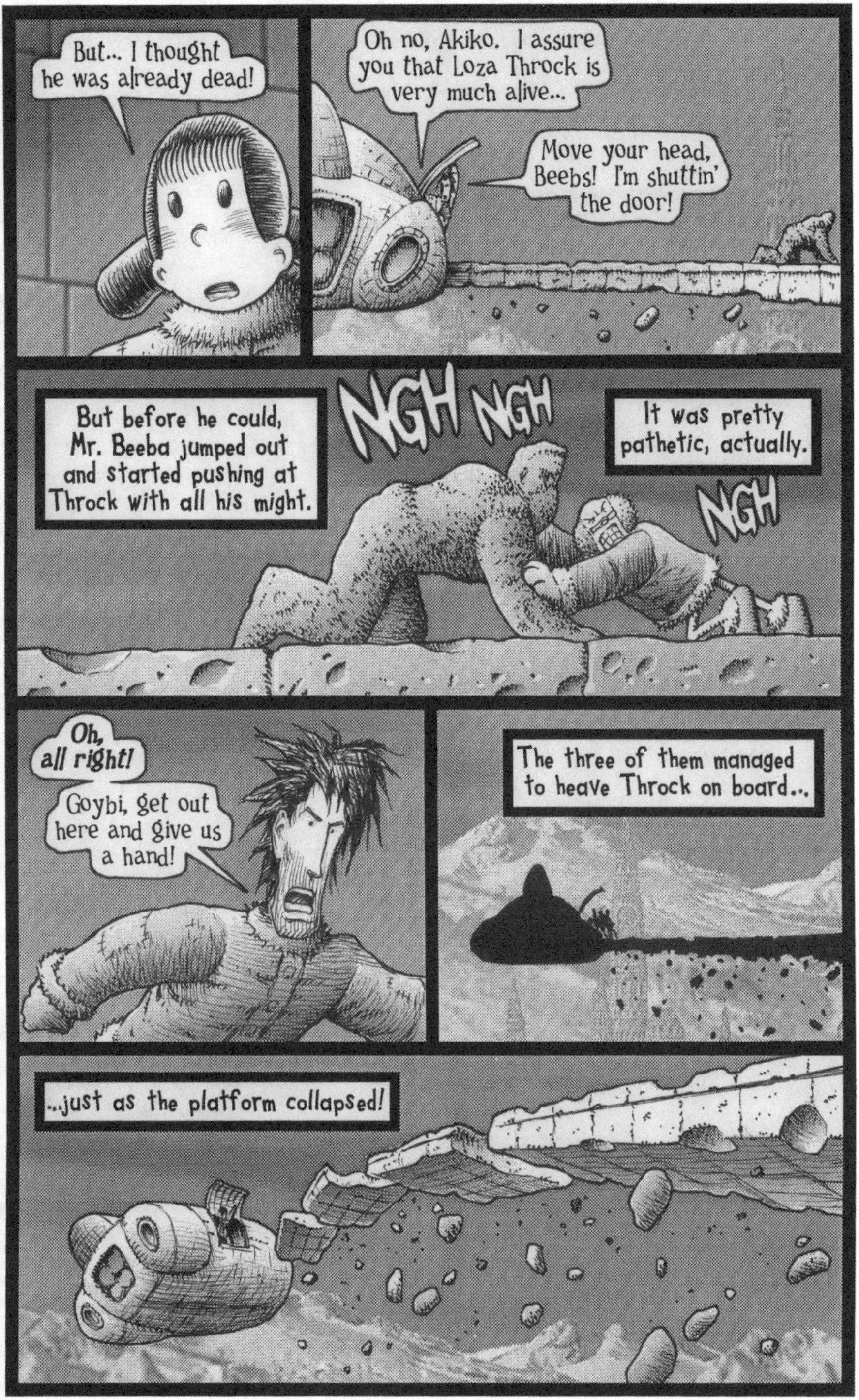

But... I thought he was already dead!
Oh no, Akiko. I assure you that Loza Throck is very much alive...
Move your head, Beebs! I'm shuttin' the door!
But before he could, Mr. Beeba jumped out and started pushing at Throck with all his might.
NGH NGH
It was pretty pathetic, actually.
NGH
Oh, all right!
Goybi, get out here and give us a hand!
The three of them managed to heave Throck on board...
...just as the platform collapsed!

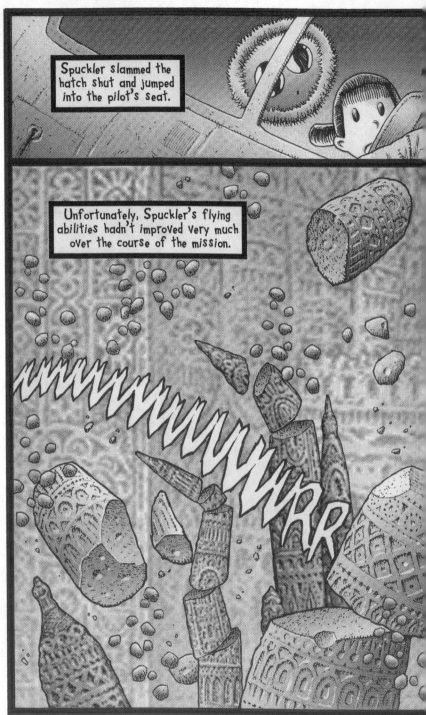

Spuckler slammed the hatch shut and jumped into the pilot's seat.

Unfortunately, Spuckler's flying abilities hadn't improved very much over the course of the mission.

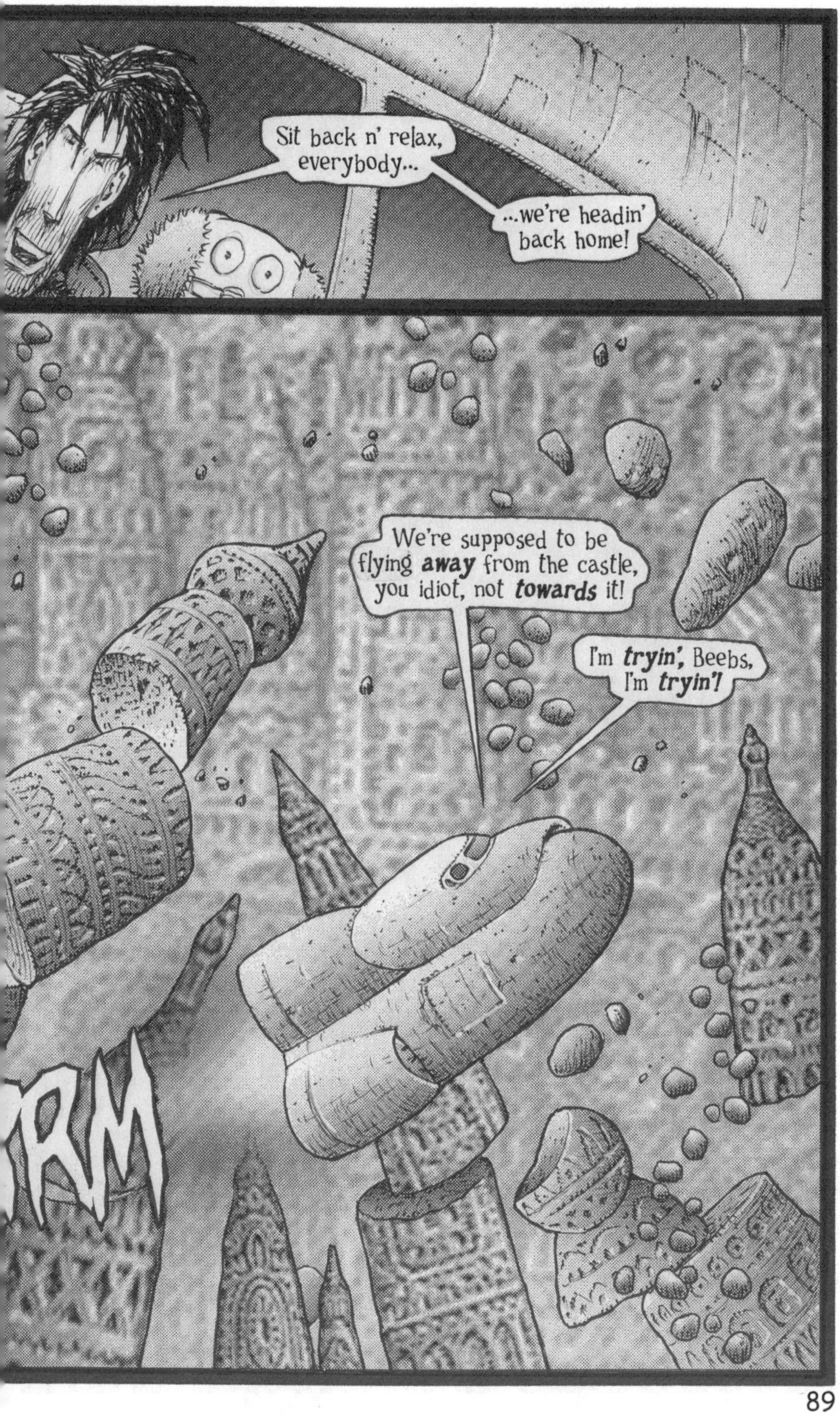
Sit back n' relax, everybody...
...we're headin' back home!
We're supposed to be flying **away** from the castle, you idiot, not ***towards*** it!
I'm ***tryin',*** Beebs, I'm ***tryin'!***
RM

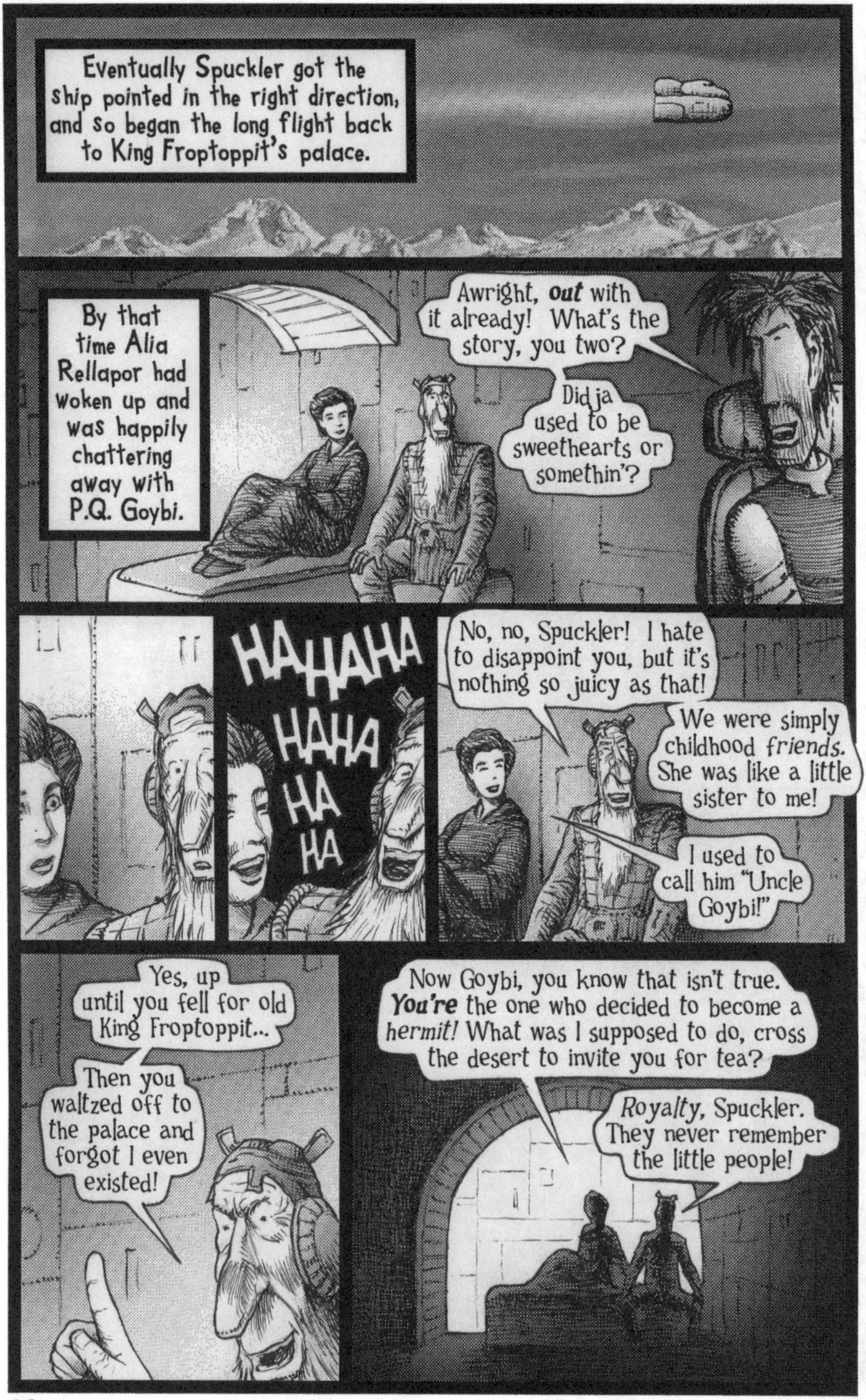
Eventually Spuckler got the ship pointed in the right direction, and so began the long flight back to King Froptoppit's palace.
By that time Alia Rellapor had woken up and was happily chattering away with P.Q. Goybi.
Awright, **out** with it already! What's the story, you two?
Didja used to be sweethearts or somethin'?
HAHAHA HAHA HA HA
No, no, Spuckler! I hate to disappoint you, but it's nothing so juicy as that!
We were simply childhood *friends.* She was like a little sister to me!
I used to call him "Uncle Goybi!"
Yes, up until you fell for old King Froptoppit...
Then you waltzed off to the palace and forgot I even existed!
Now Goybi, you know that isn't true. ***You're*** the one who decided to become a *hermit!* What was I supposed to do, cross the desert to invite you for tea?
Royalty, Spuckler. They never remember the little people!

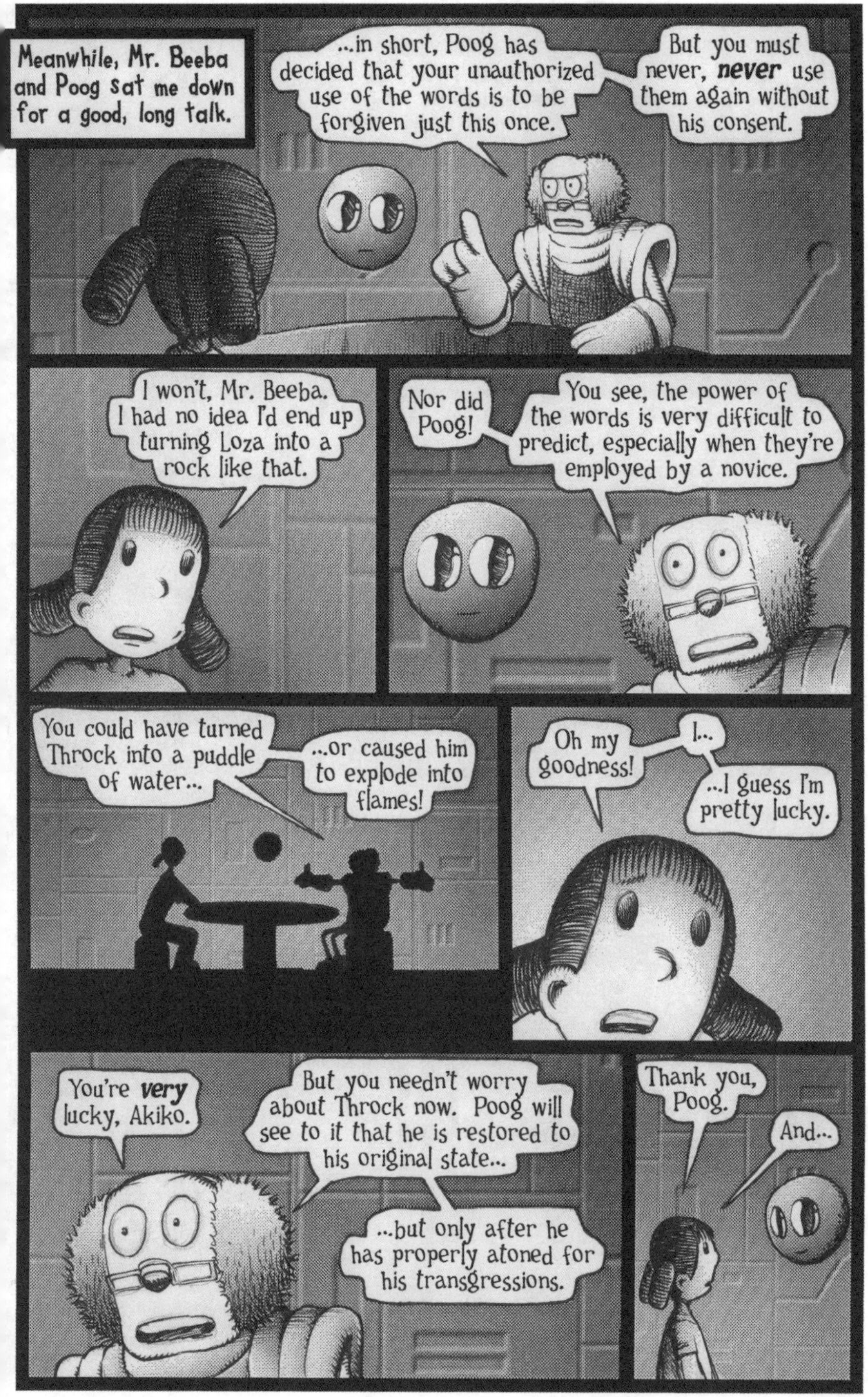

Meanwhile, Mr. Beeba and Poog sat me down for a good, long talk.
...in short, Poog has decided that your unauthorized use of the words is to be forgiven just this once.
But you must never, ***never*** use them again without his consent.
I won't, Mr. Beeba. I had no idea I'd end up turning Loza into a rock like that.
Nor did Poog!
You see, the power of the words is very difficult to predict, especially when they're employed by a novice.
You could have turned Throck into a puddle of water...
...or caused him to explode into flames!
Oh my goodness!
I...
...I guess I'm pretty lucky.
You're ***very*** lucky, Akiko.
But you needn't worry about Throck now. Poog will see to it that he is restored to his original state...
...but only after he has properly atoned for his transgressions.
Thank you, Poog.
And...

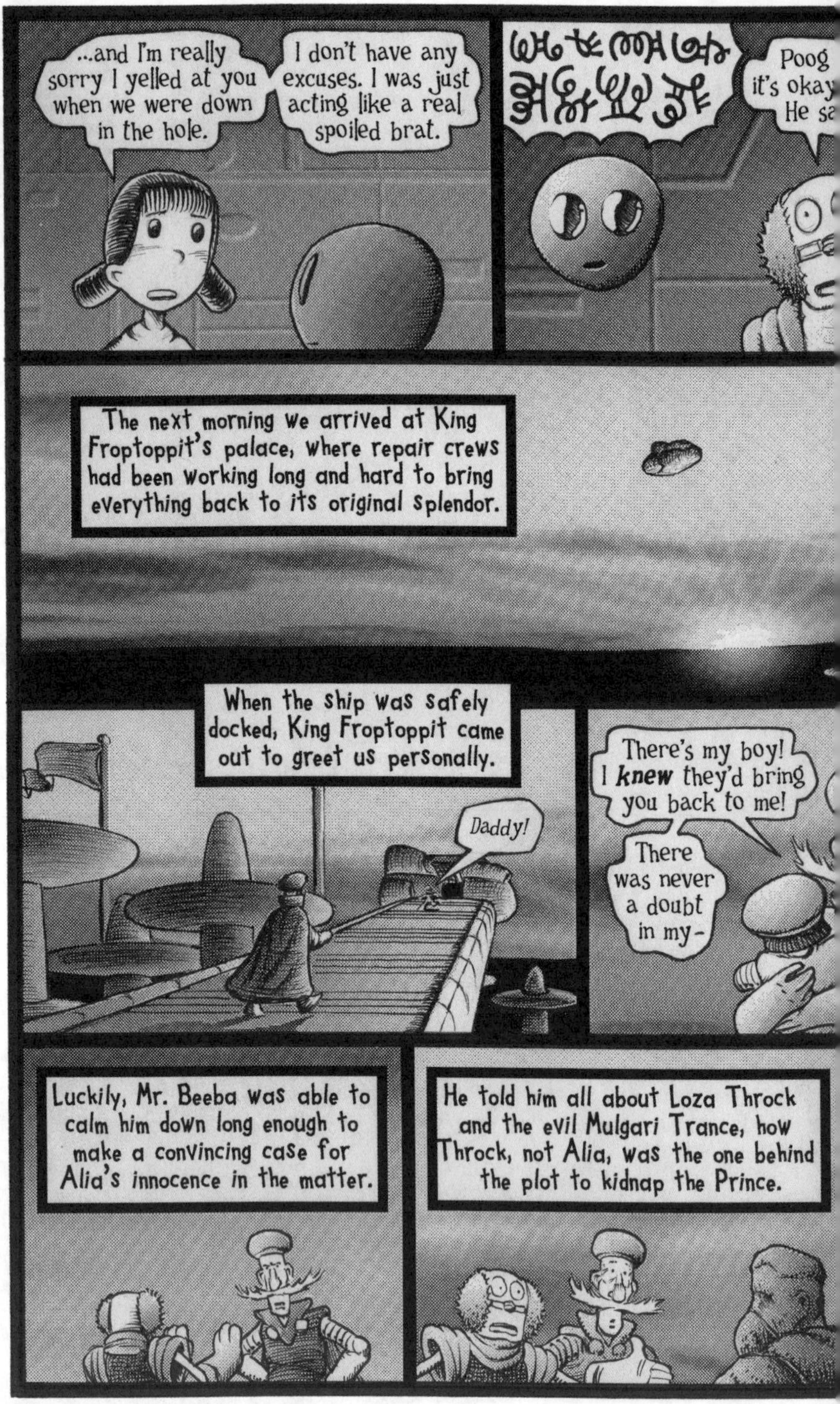
...and I'm really sorry I yelled at you when we were down in the hole.
I don't have any excuses. I was just acting like a real spoiled brat.
Poog it's okay
The next morning we arrived at King Froptoppit's palace, where repair crews had been working long and hard to bring everything back to its original splendor.
When the ship was safely docked, King Froptoppit came out to greet us personally.
Daddy!
There's my boy! I **knew** they'd bring you back to me!
There was never a doubt in my-
Luckily, Mr. Beeba was able to calm him down long enough to make a convincing case for Alia's innocence in the matter.
He told him all about Loza Throck and the evil Mulgari Trance, how Throck, not Alia, was the one behind the plot to kidnap the Prince.

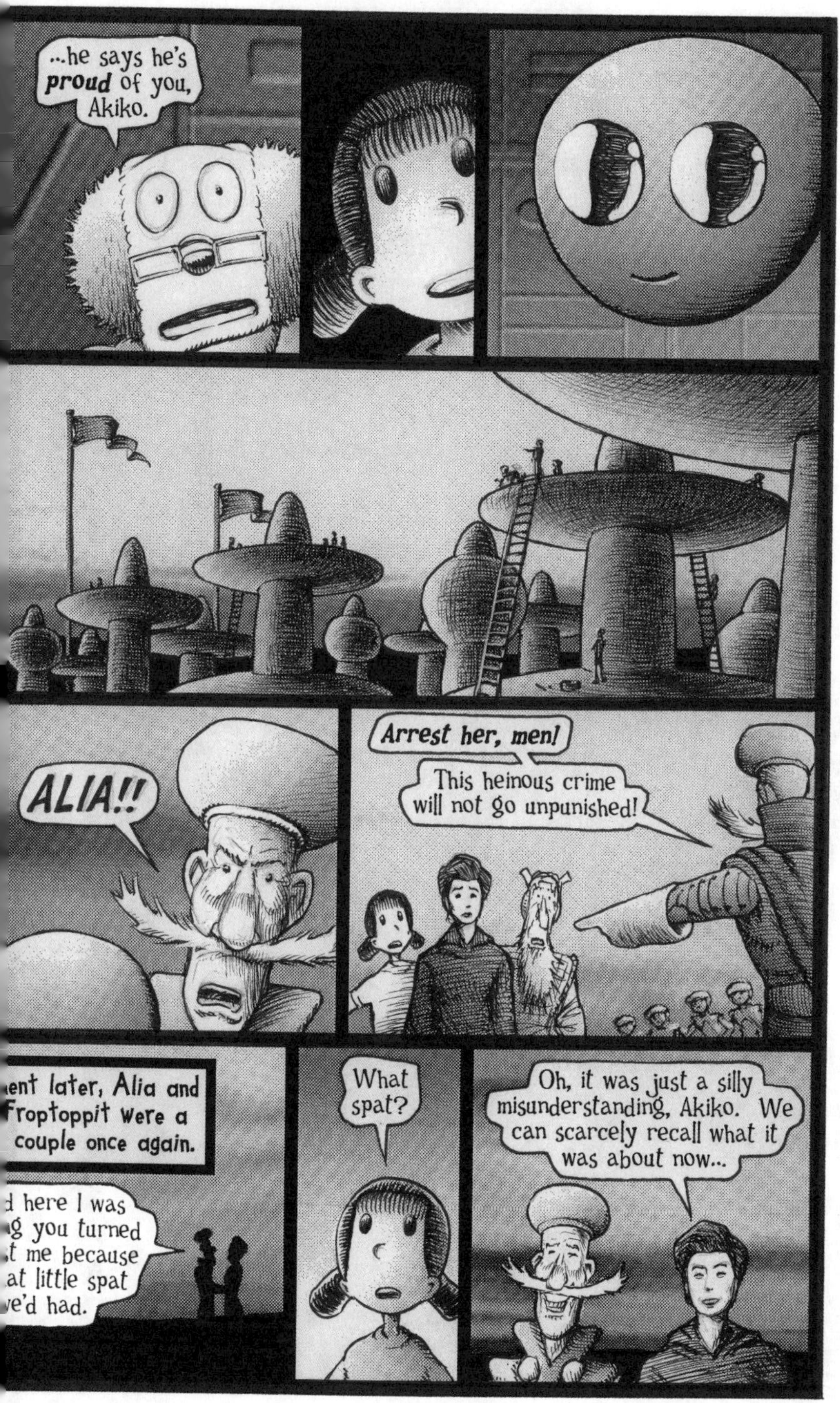
...he says he's **proud** of you, Akiko.
ALIA!!
Arrest her, men!
This heinous crime will not go unpunished!
ent later, Alia and Froptoppit were a couple once again.
d here I was g you turned t me because at little spat e'd had.
What spat?
Oh, it was just a silly misunderstanding, Akiko. We can scarcely recall what it was about now...

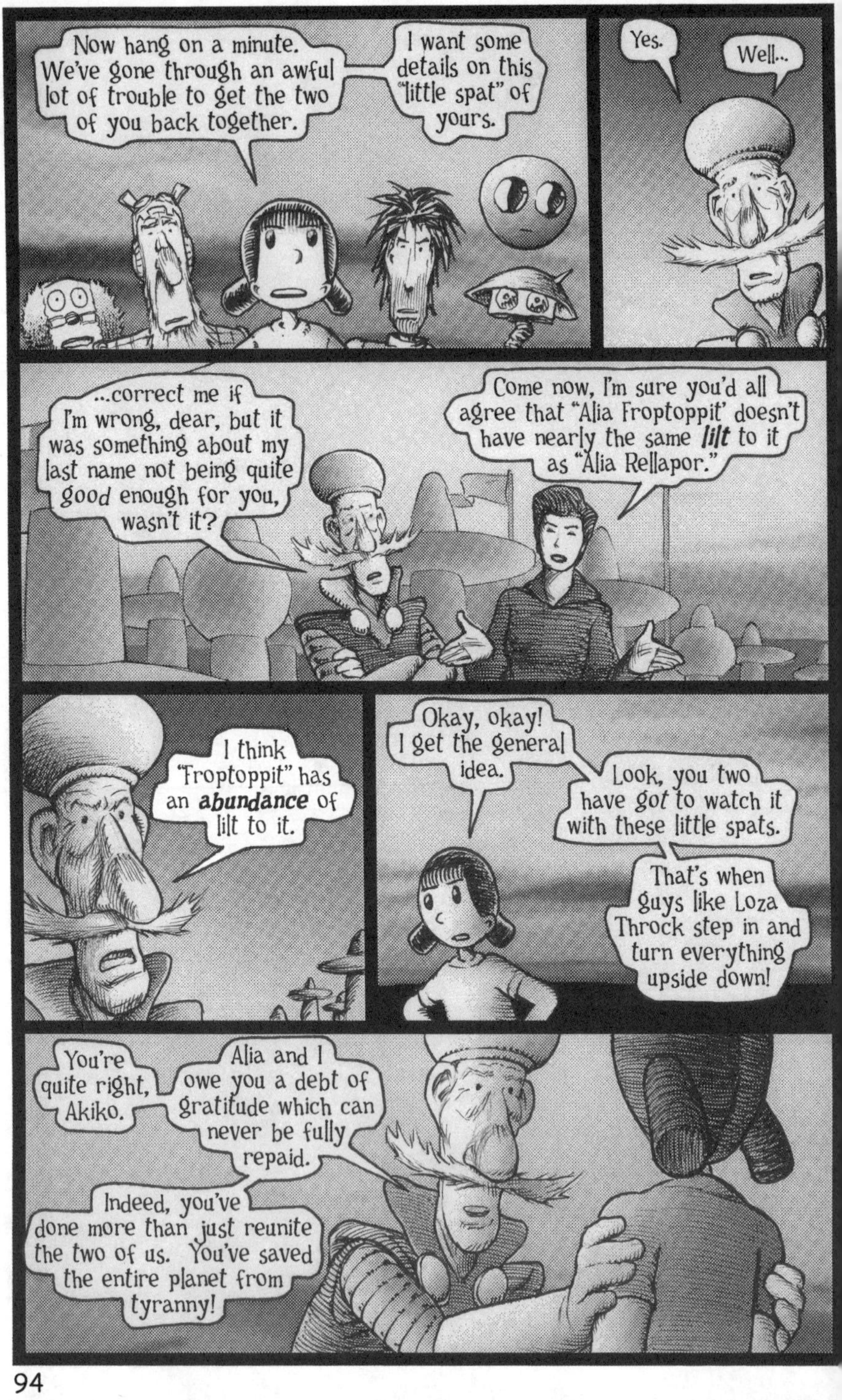
Now hang on a minute. We've gone through an awful lot of trouble to get the two of you back together.
I want some details on this "little spat" of yours.
Yes.
Well...
...correct me if I'm wrong, dear, but it was something about my last name not being quite good enough for you, wasn't it?
Come now, I'm sure you'd all agree that "Alia Froptoppit' doesn't have nearly the same lilt to it as "Alia Rellapor."
I think "Froptoppit" has an abundance of lilt to it.
Okay, okay! I get the general idea.
Look, you two have got to watch it with these little spats.
That's when guys like Loza Throck step in and turn everything upside down!
You're quite right, Akiko.
Alia and I owe you a debt of gratitude which can never be fully repaid.
Indeed, you've done more than just reunite the two of us. You've saved the entire planet from tyranny!

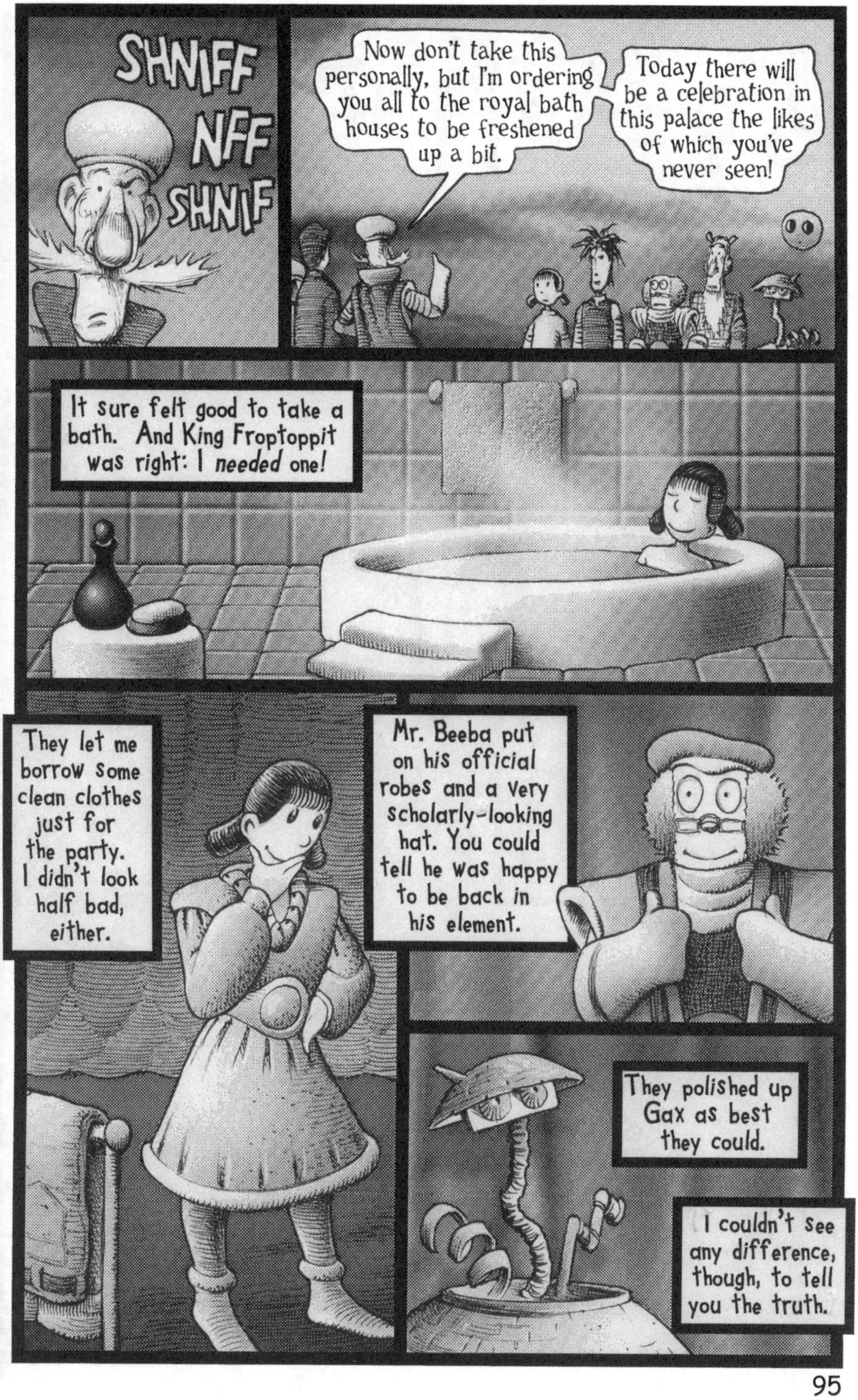
SHNIFF
NFF
SHNIF
Now don't take this personally, but I'm ordering you all to the royal bath houses to be freshened up a bit.
Today there will be a celebration in this palace the likes of which you've never seen!
It sure felt good to take a bath. And King Froptoppit was right: I *needed* one!
They let me borrow some clean clothes just for the party. I didn't look half bad, either.
Mr. Beeba put on his official robes and a very scholarly-looking hat. You could tell he was happy to be back in his element.
They polished up Gax as best they could.
I couldn't see any difference, though, to tell you the truth.

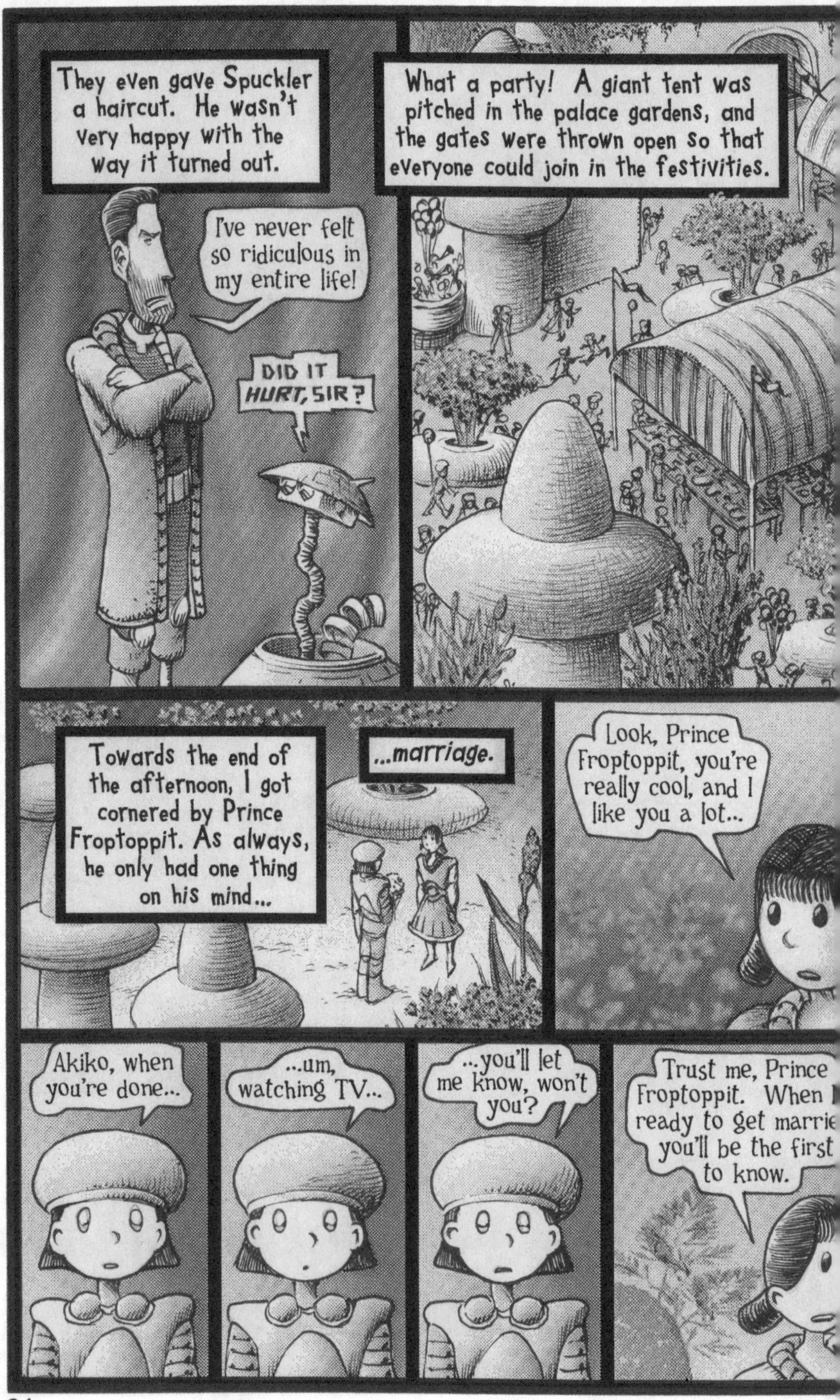
They even gave Spuckler a haircut. He wasn't very happy with the way it turned out.
I've never felt so ridiculous in my entire life!
DID IT HURT, SIR?
What a party! A giant tent was pitched in the palace gardens, and the gates were thrown open so that everyone could join in the festivities.
Towards the end of the afternoon, I got cornered by Prince Froptoppit. As always, he only had one thing on his mind...
...marriage.
Look, Prince Froptoppit, you're really cool, and I like you a lot...
Akiko, when you're done...
...um, watching TV...
...you'll let me know, won't you?
Trust me, Prince Froptoppit. When
ready to get marrie
you'll be the first
to know.

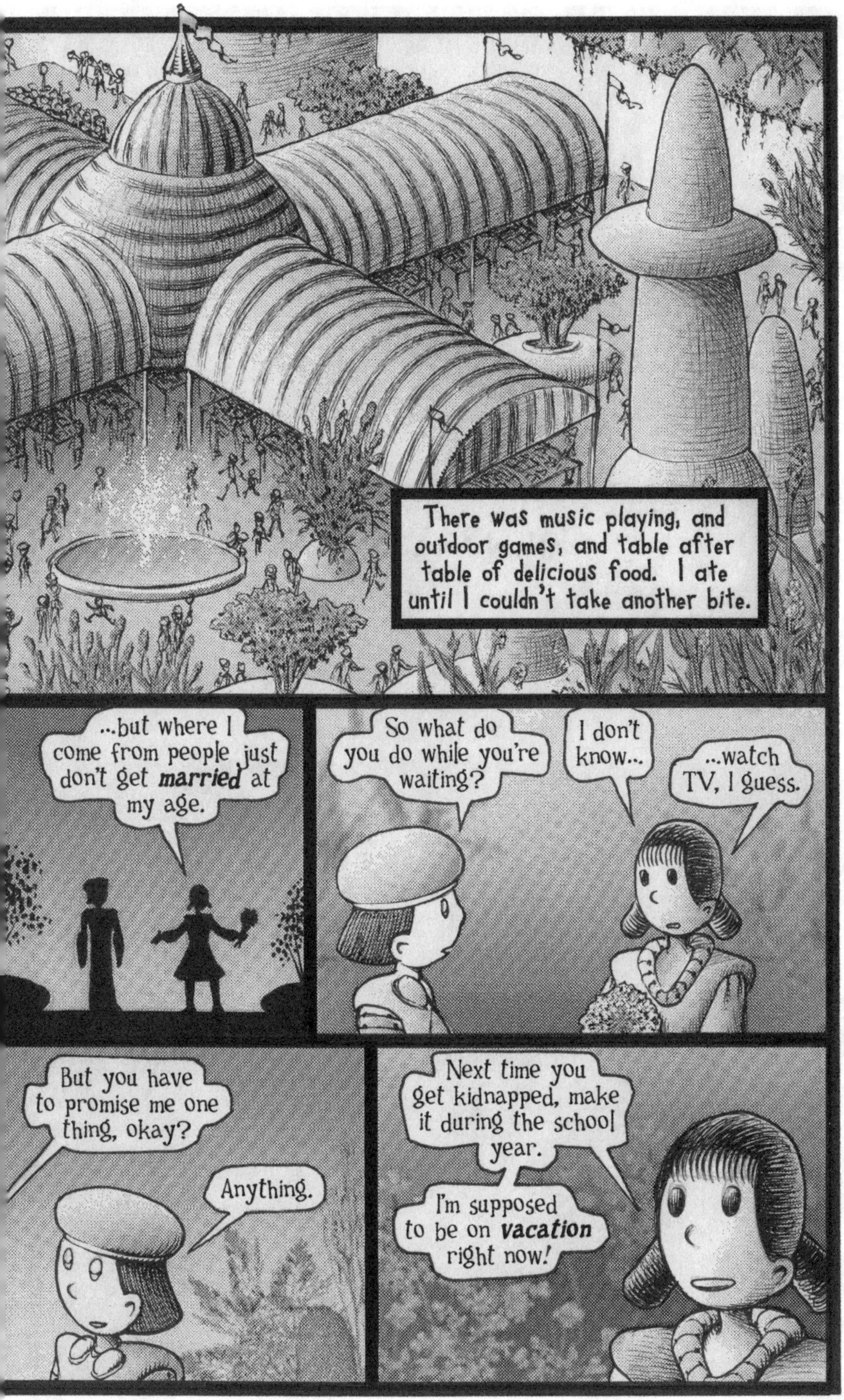
There was music playing, and outdoor games, and table after table of delicious food. I ate until I couldn't take another bite.
...but where I come from people just don't get married at my age.
So what do you do while you're waiting?
I don't know...
...watch TV, I guess.
But you have to promise me one thing, okay?
Anything.
Next time you get kidnapped, make it during the school year.
I'm supposed to be on vacation right now!

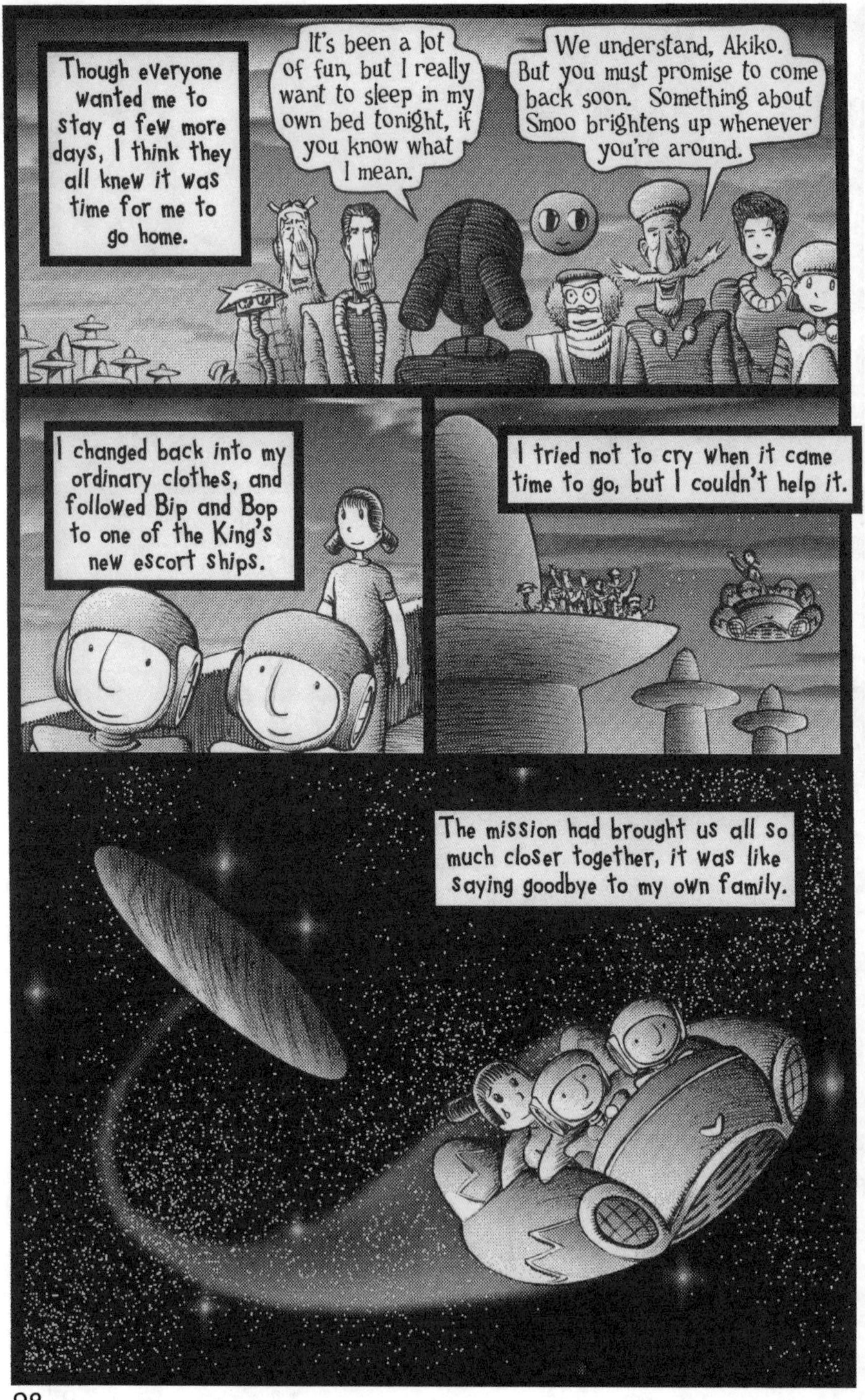

Though everyone wanted me to stay a few more days, I think they all knew it was time for me to go home.
It's been a lot of fun, but I really want to sleep in my own bed tonight, if you know what I mean.
We understand, Akiko. But you must promise to come back soon. Something about Smoo brightens up whenever you're around.
I changed back into my ordinary clothes, and followed Bip and Bop to one of the King's new escort ships.
I tried not to cry when it came time to go, but I couldn't help it.
The mission had brought us all so much closer together, it was like saying goodbye to my own family.

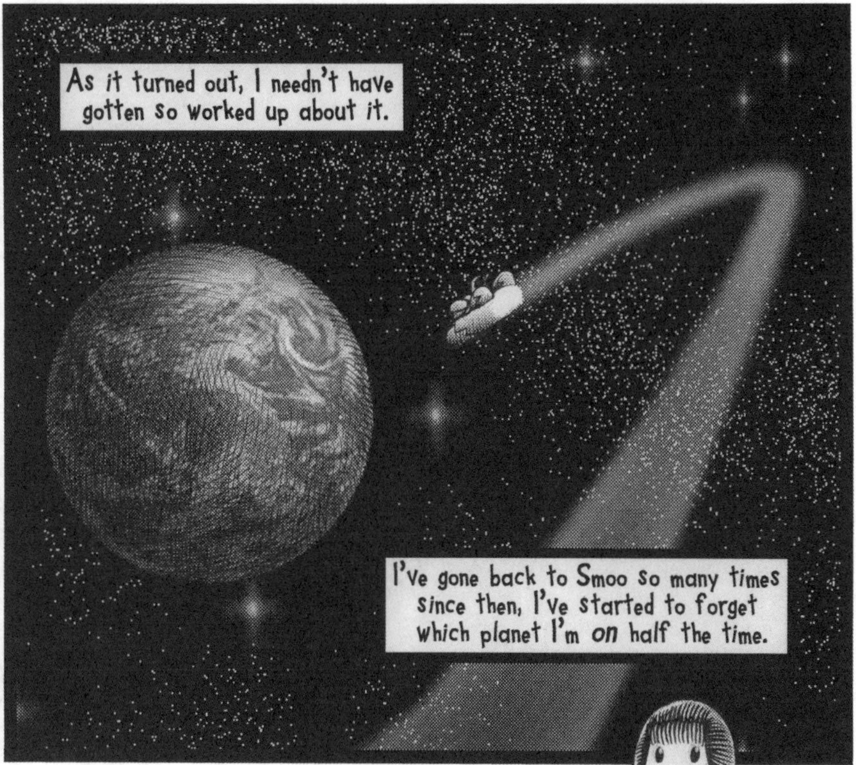
As it turned out, I needn't have gotten so worked up about it.
I've gone back to Smoo so many times since then, I've started to forget which planet I'm *on* half the time.

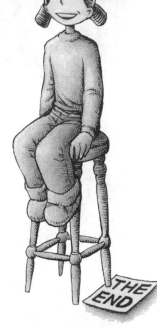

Now don't get me wrong.
I still like it here on earth.

I mean, what's not to like?
There's plenty of trees almost
everywhere you go, and people talking to
one another, and animals all over the place...
Take it from me: as planets go,
this *is* one of the best.

Still...

...I have to admit that
every time I see an ice cream truck
coming down the road, I wonder if it's
King Froptoppit, back to take me
off to Smoo again.

Mostly it's not.
But when it *is*, my heart always
beats a little bit faster.

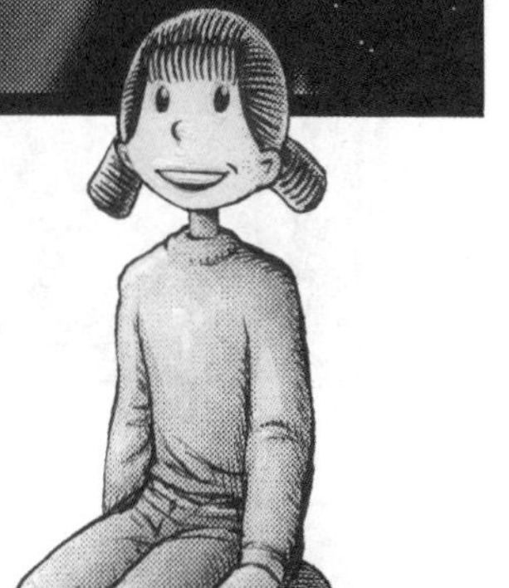
THE END

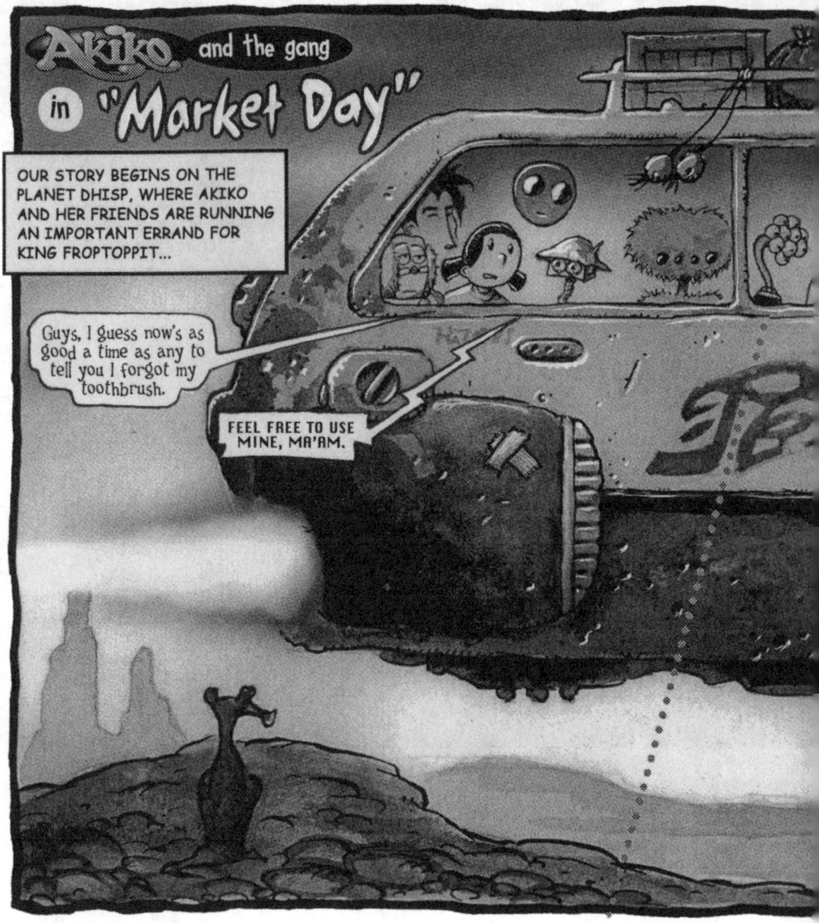
Akiko and the gang
in "Market Day"
OUR STORY BEGINS ON THE PLANET DHISP, WHERE AKIKO AND HER FRIENDS ARE RUNNING AN IMPORTANT ERRAND FOR KING FROPTOPPIT...
Guys, I guess now's as good a time as any to tell you I forgot my toothbrush.
FEEL FREE TO USE MINE, MA'AM.

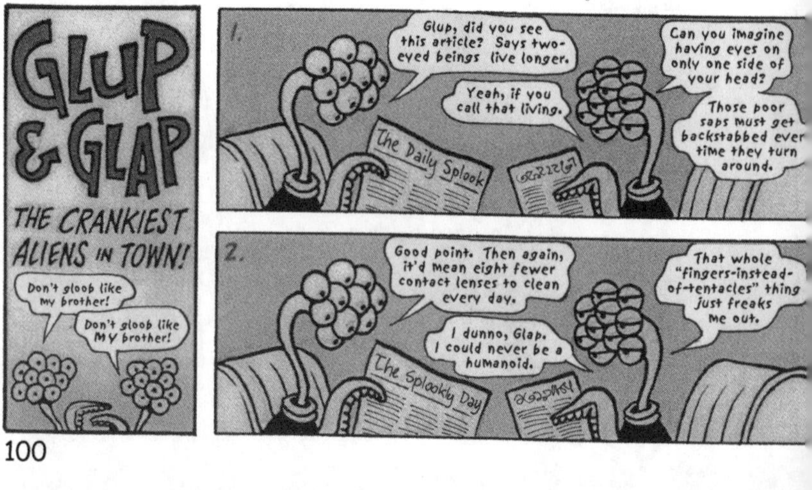
GLUP & GLAP
THE CRANKIEST ALIENS IN TOWN!
Don't gloob like my brother!
Don't gloob like MY brother!
1.
Glup, did you see this article? Says two-eyed beings live longer.
Yeah, if you call that living.
Can you imagine having eyes on only one side of your head?
Those poor saps must get backstabbed ever time they turn around.
The Daily Splook
2.
Good point. Then again, it'd mean eight fewer contact lenses to clean every day.
I dunno, Glap. I could never be a humanoid.
That whole "fingers-instead-of-tentacles" thing just freaks me out.
The Splookly Day

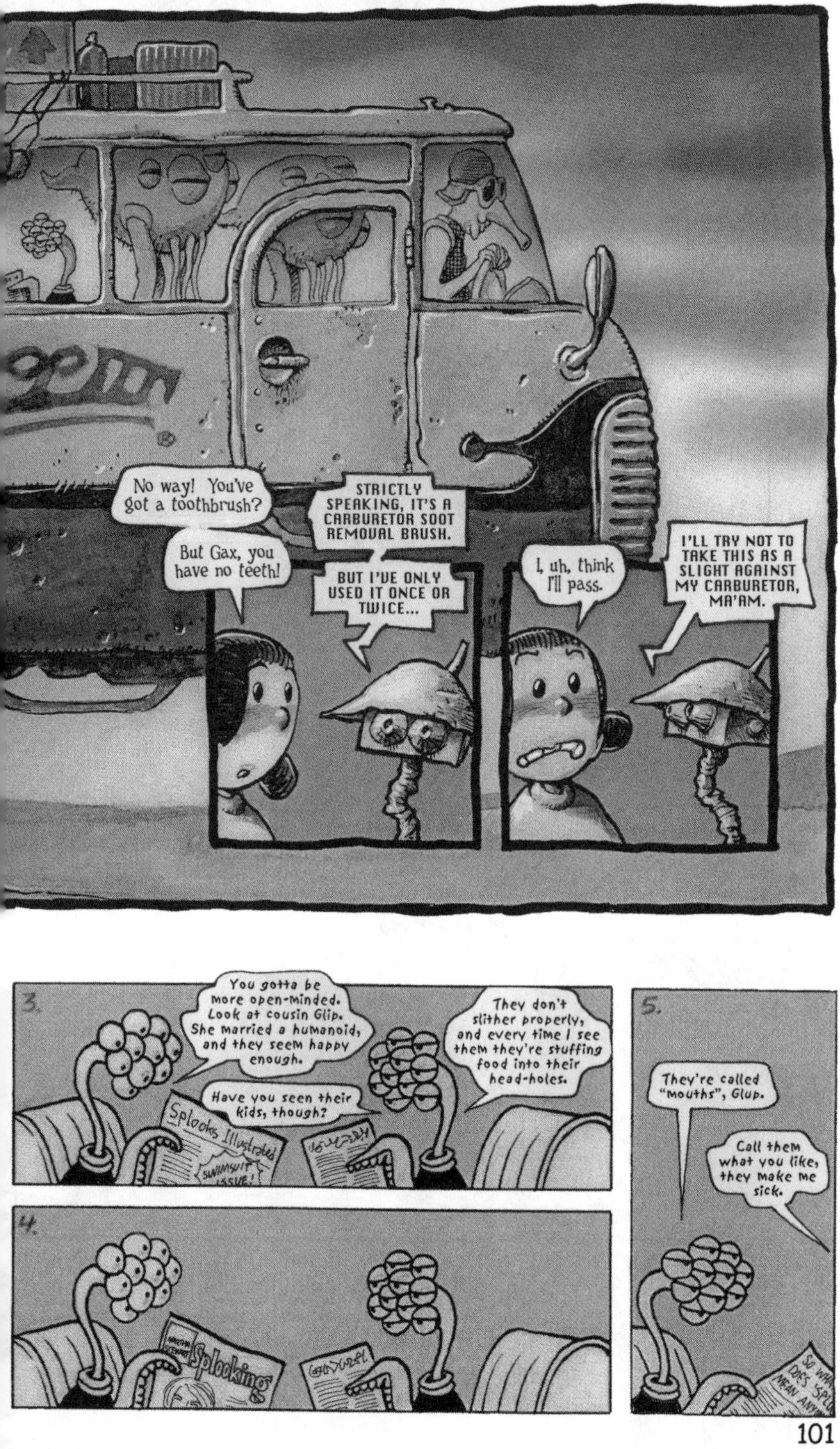
No way! You've got a toothbrush?
STRICTLY SPEAKING, IT'S A CARBURETOR SOOT REMOVAL BRUSH.
But Gax, you have no teeth!
BUT I'VE ONLY USED IT ONCE OR TWICE...
I, uh, think I'll pass.
I'LL TRY NOT TO TAKE THIS AS A SLIGHT AGAINST MY CARBURETOR, MA'AM.
3.
You gotta be more open-minded. Look at cousin Glip. She married a humanoid, and they seem happy enough.
They don't slither properly, and every time I see them they're stuffing food into their head-holes.
Have you seen their kids, though?
Splooks Illustrated
SWIMSUIT ISSUE!
4.
Splooking
5.
They're called "mouths", Glup.
Call them what you like, they make me sick.

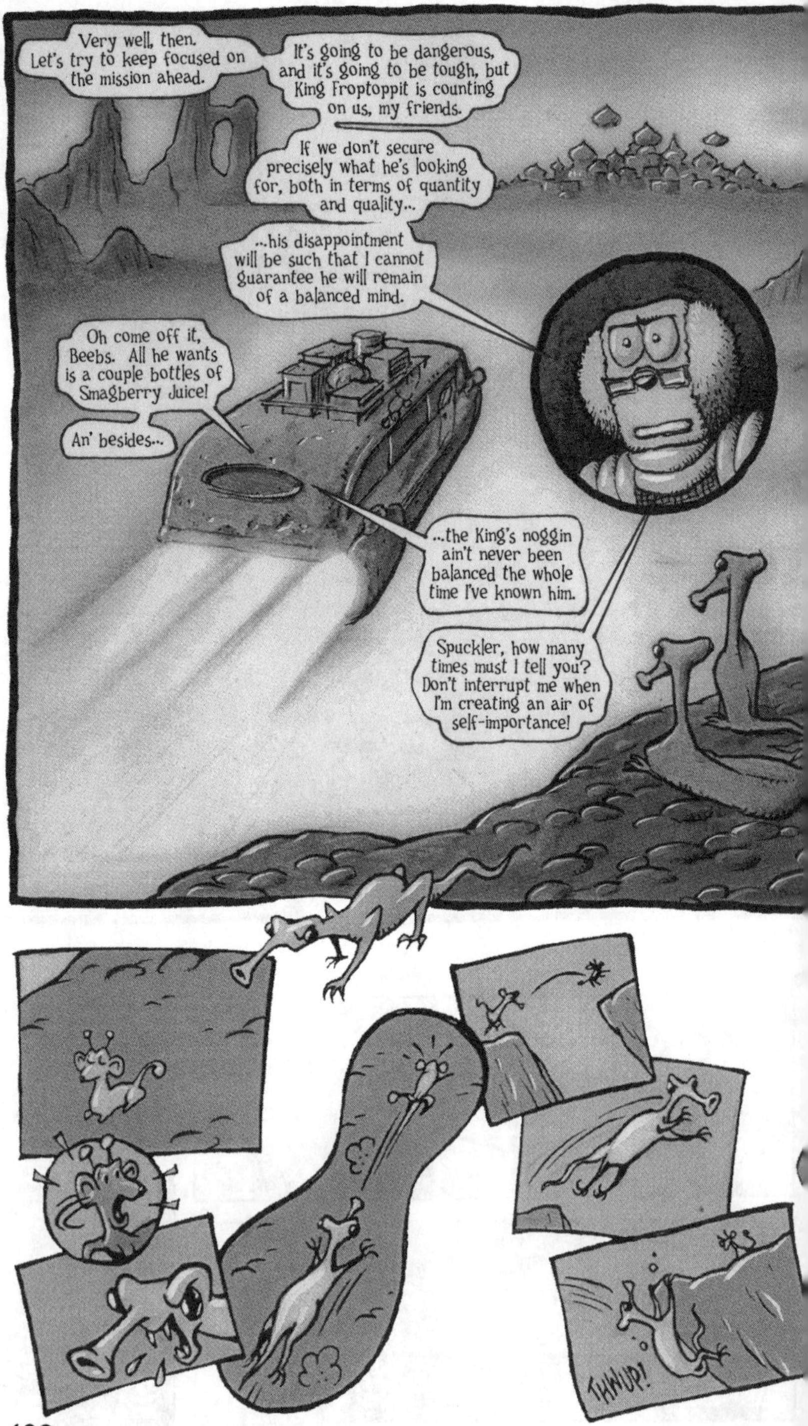
Very well, then. Let's try to keep focused on the mission ahead.
It's going to be dangerous, and it's going to be tough, but King Froptoppit is counting on us, my friends.
If we don't secure precisely what he's looking for, both in terms of quantity and quality...
...his disappointment will be such that I cannot guarantee he will remain of a balanced mind.
Oh come off it, Beebs. All he wants is a couple bottles of Smagberry Juice!
An' besides...
...the King's noggin ain't never been balanced the whole time I've known him.
Spuckler, how many times must I tell you? Don't interrupt me when I'm creating an air of self-importance!
THWUP!

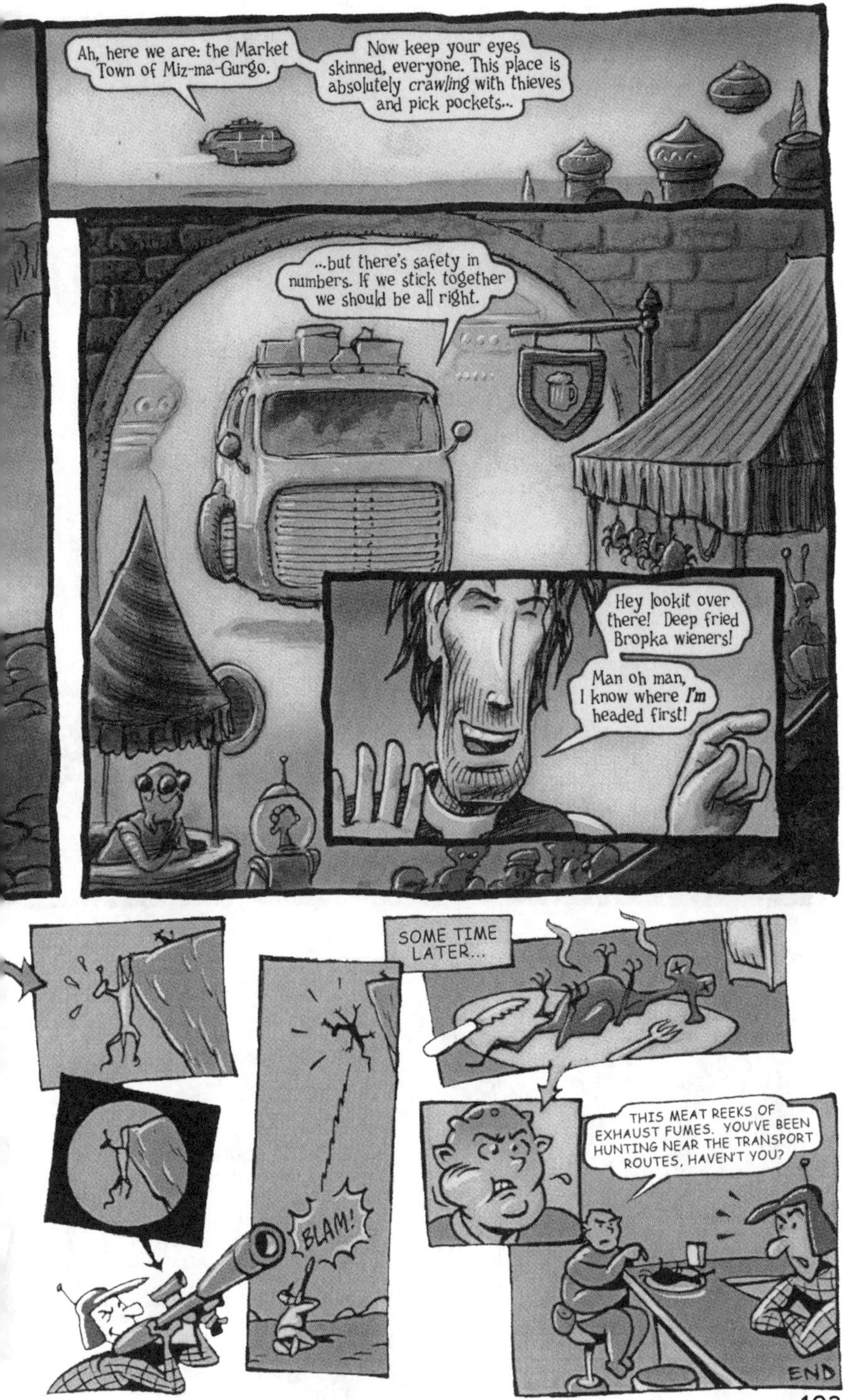
Ah, here we are: the Market Town of Miz-ma-Gurgo.
Now keep your eyes skinned, everyone. This place is absolutely *crawling* with thieves and pick pockets...
...but there's safety in numbers. If we stick together we should be all right.
Hey lookit over there! Deep fried Bropka wieners!
Man oh man, I know where *I'm* headed first!
BLAM!
SOME TIME LATER...
THIS MEAT REEKS OF EXHAUST FUMES. YOU'VE BEEN HUNTING NEAR THE TRANSPORT ROUTES, HAVEN'T YOU?
END

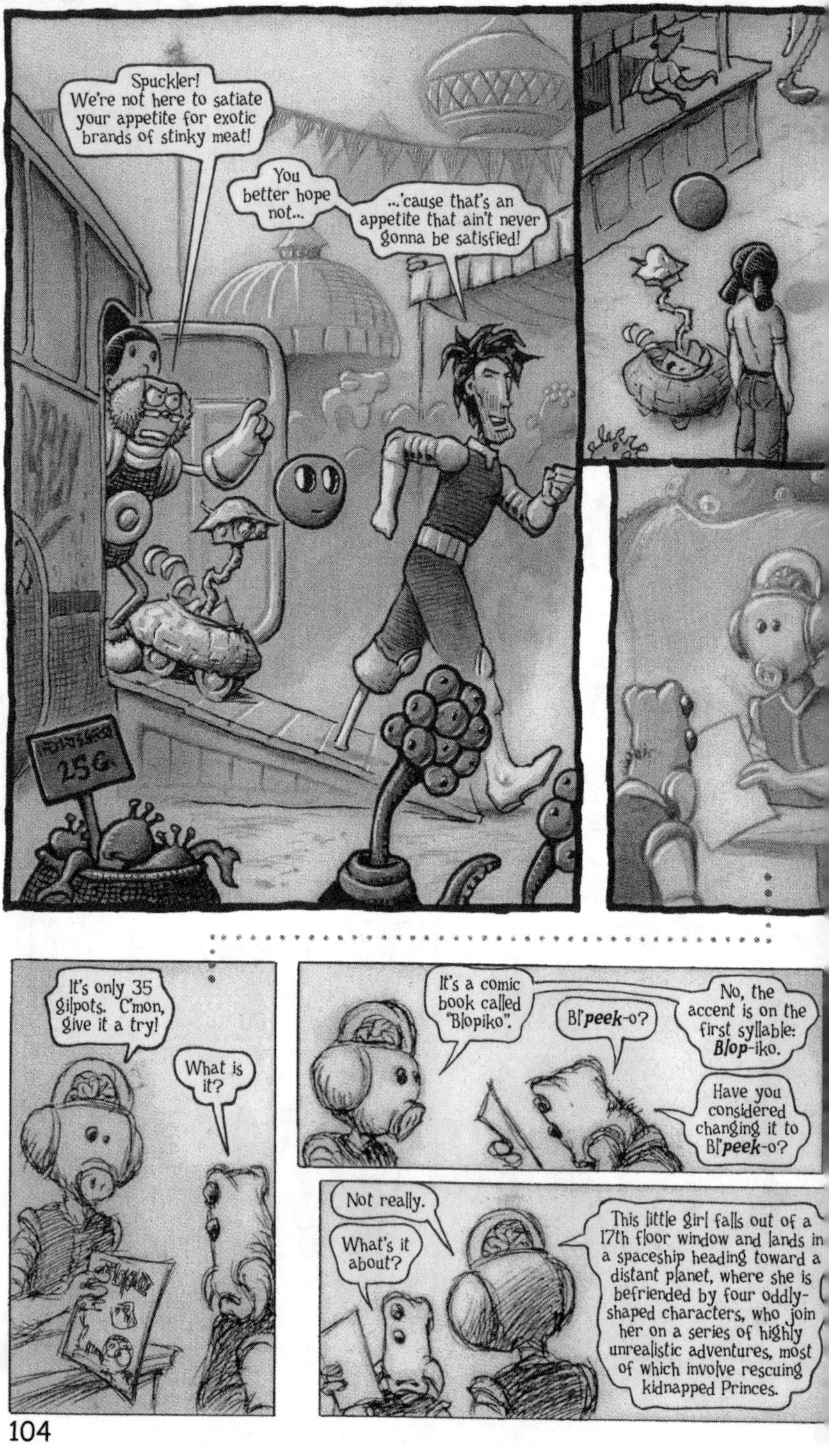
Spuckler! We're not here to satiate your appetite for exotic brands of stinky meat!
You better hope not...
...'cause that's an appetite that ain't never gonna be satisfied!
It's only 35 gilpots. C'mon, give it a try!
What is it?
It's a comic book called "Blopiko".
Bl'peek-o?
No, the accent is on the first syllable: Blop-iko.
Have you considered changing it to Bl'peek-o?
Not really.
What's it about?
This little girl falls out of a 17th floor window and lands in a spaceship heading toward a distant planet, where she is befriended by four oddly-shaped characters, who join her on a series of highly unrealistic adventures, most of which involve rescuing kidnapped Princes.

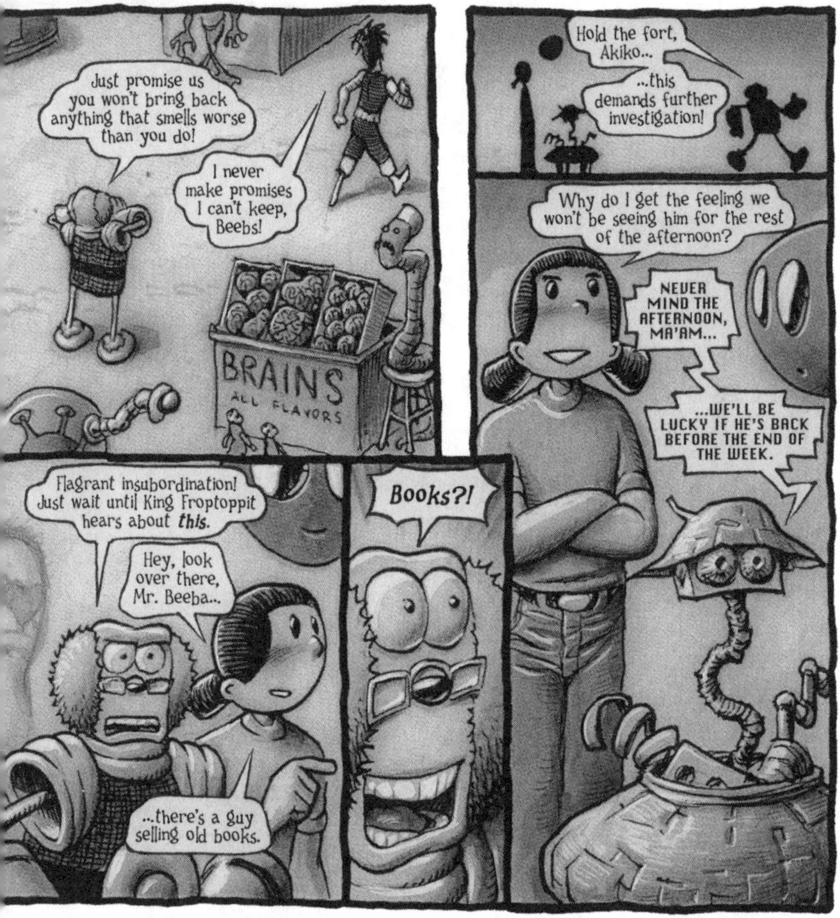
Just promise us you won't bring back anything that smells worse than you do!
I never make promises I can't keep, Beebs!
BRAINS
ALL FLAVORS
Hold the fort, Akiko...
...this demands further investigation!
Why do I get the feeling we won't be seeing him for the rest of the afternoon?
NEVER MIND THE AFTERNOON, MA'AM...
...WE'LL BE LUCKY IF HE'S BACK BEFORE THE END OF THE WEEK.
Flagrant insubordination! Just wait until King Froptoppit hears about *this*.
Hey, look over there, Mr. Beeba...
...there's a guy selling old books.
Books?!

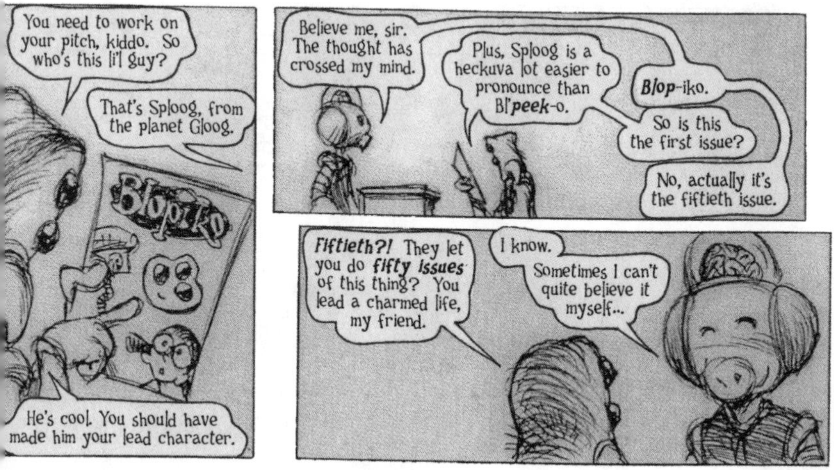
You need to work on your pitch, kiddo. So who's this li'l guy?
That's Sploog, from the planet Gloog.
He's cool. You should have made him your lead character.
Believe me, sir. The thought has crossed my mind.
Plus, Sploog is a heckuva lot easier to pronounce than Bl'*peek*-o.
Blop-iko.
So is this the first issue?
No, actually it's the fiftieth issue.
Fiftieth?! They let you do *fifty issues* of this thing? You lead a charmed life, my friend.
I know.
Sometimes I can't quite believe it myself...

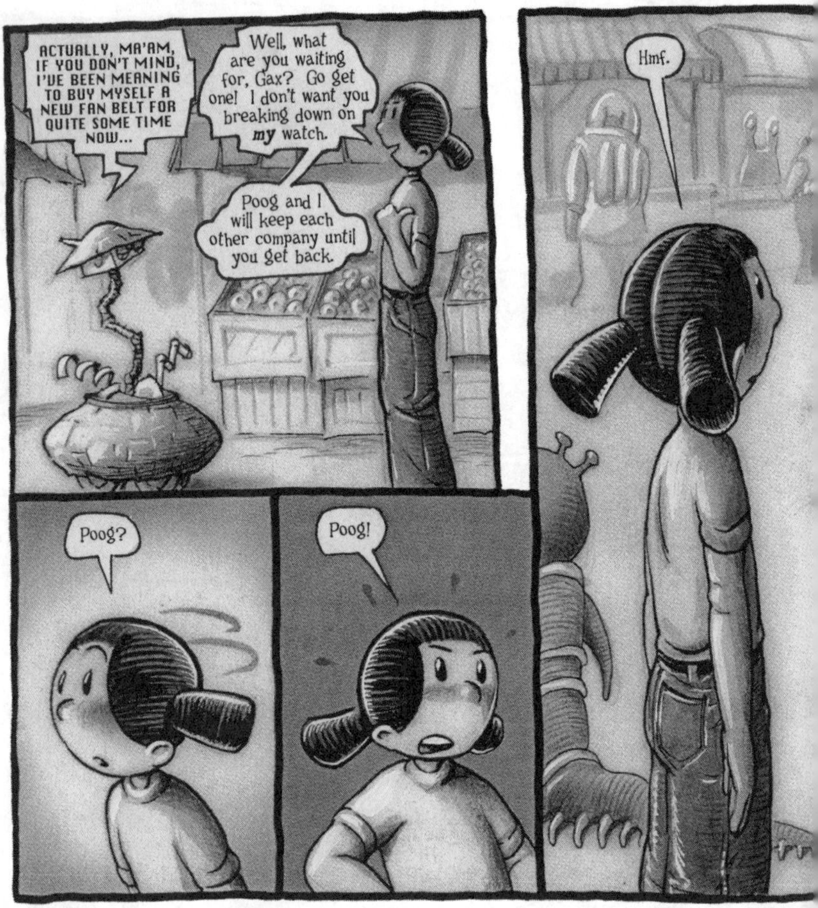
ACTUALLY, MA'AM, IF YOU DON'T MIND, I'VE BEEN MEANING TO BUY MYSELF A NEW FAN BELT FOR QUITE SOME TIME NOW...
Well, what are you waiting for, Gax? Go get one! I don't want you breaking down on **my** watch.
Poog and I will keep each other company until you get back.
Hmf.
Poog?
Poog!

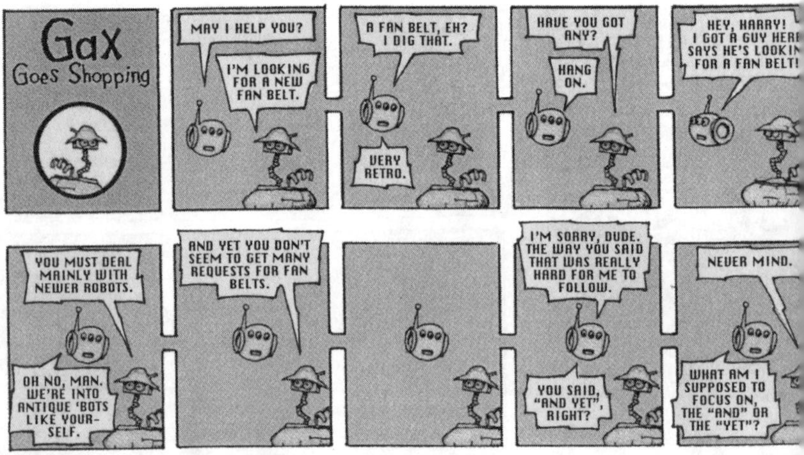
Gax
Goes Shopping
MAY I HELP YOU?
I'M LOOKING FOR A NEW FAN BELT.
A FAN BELT, EH? I DIG THAT.
VERY RETRO.
HAVE YOU GOT ANY?
HANG ON.
HEY, HARRY! I GOT A GUY HER SAYS HE'S LOOKIN FOR A FAN BELT!
YOU MUST DEAL MAINLY WITH NEWER ROBOTS.
OH NO, MAN. WE'RE INTO ANTIQUE 'BOTS LIKE YOURSELF.
AND YET YOU DON'T SEEM TO GET MANY REQUESTS FOR FAN BELTS.
I'M SORRY, DUDE. THE WAY YOU SAID THAT WAS REALLY HARD FOR ME TO FOLLOW.
YOU SAID, "AND YET", RIGHT?
NEVER MIND.
WHAT AM I SUPPOSED TO FOCUS ON, THE "AND" OR THE "YET"?

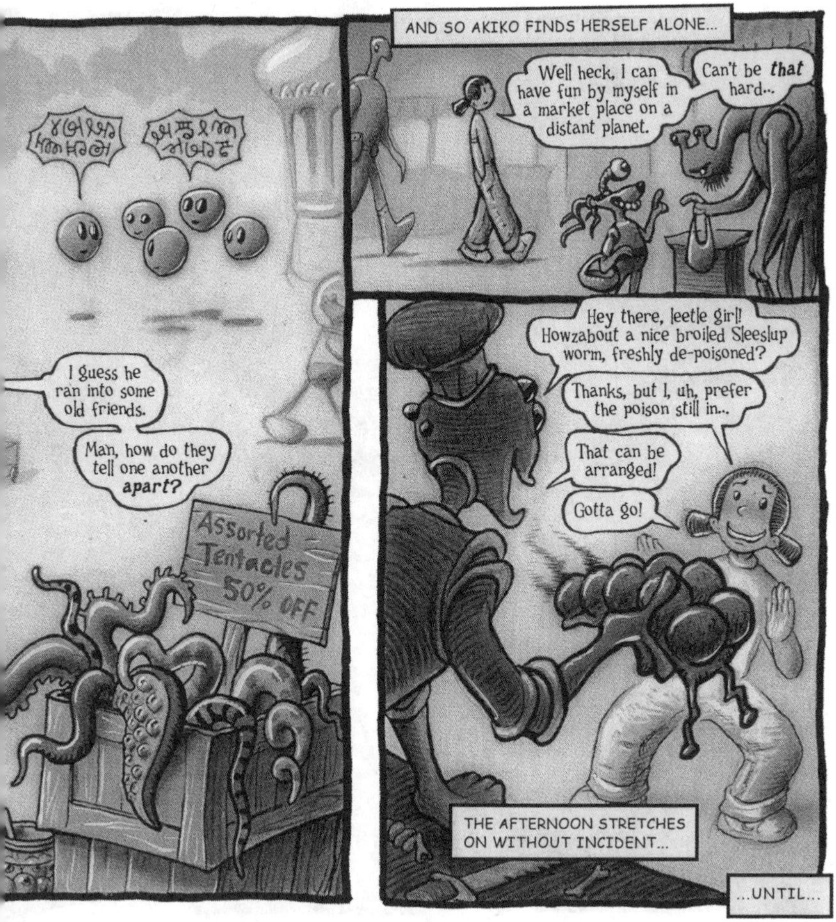
I guess he ran into some old friends.
Man, how do they tell one another *apart?*
Assorted Tentacles 50% OFF
AND SO AKIKO FINDS HERSELF ALONE...
Well heck, I can have fun by myself in a market place on a distant planet.
Can't be *that* hard...
Hey there, leetle girl! Howzabout a nice broiled Sleeslup worm, freshly de-poisoned?
Thanks, but I, uh, prefer the poison still in...
That can be arranged!
Gotta go!
THE AFTERNOON STRETCHES ON WITHOUT INCIDENT...
...UNTIL...

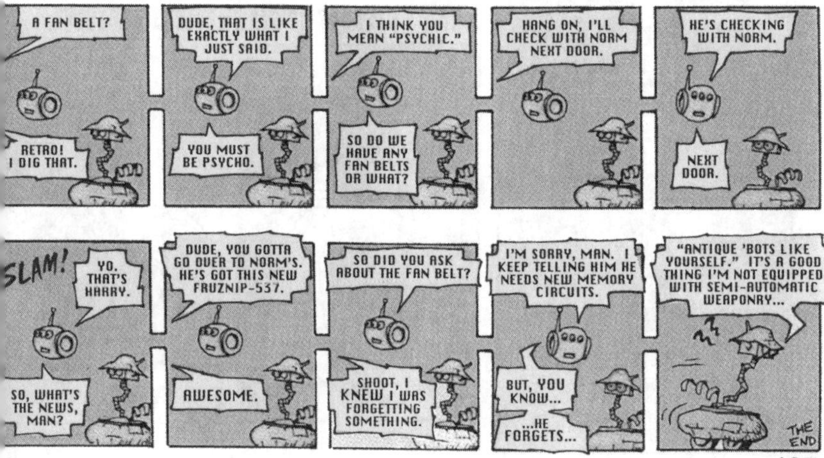
A FAN BELT?
RETRO! I DIG THAT.
DUDE, THAT IS LIKE EXACTLY WHAT I JUST SAID.
YOU MUST BE PSYCHO.
I THINK YOU MEAN "PSYCHIC."
SO DO WE HAVE ANY FAN BELTS OR WHAT?
HANG ON, I'LL CHECK WITH NORM NEXT DOOR.
HE'S CHECKING WITH NORM.
NEXT DOOR.
SLAM!
YO. THAT'S HARRY.
SO, WHAT'S THE NEWS, MAN?
DUDE, YOU GOTTA GO OVER TO NORM'S. HE'S GOT THIS NEW FRUZNIP-537.
AWESOME.
SO DID YOU ASK ABOUT THE FAN BELT?
SHOOT, I KNEW I WAS FORGETTING SOMETHING.
I'M SORRY, MAN. I KEEP TELLING HIM HE NEEDS NEW MEMORY CIRCUITS.
BUT, YOU KNOW...
...HE FORGETS...
"ANTIQUE 'BOTS LIKE YOURSELF." IT'S A GOOD THING I'M NOT EQUIPPED WITH SEMI-AUTOMATIC WEAPONRY...
THE END

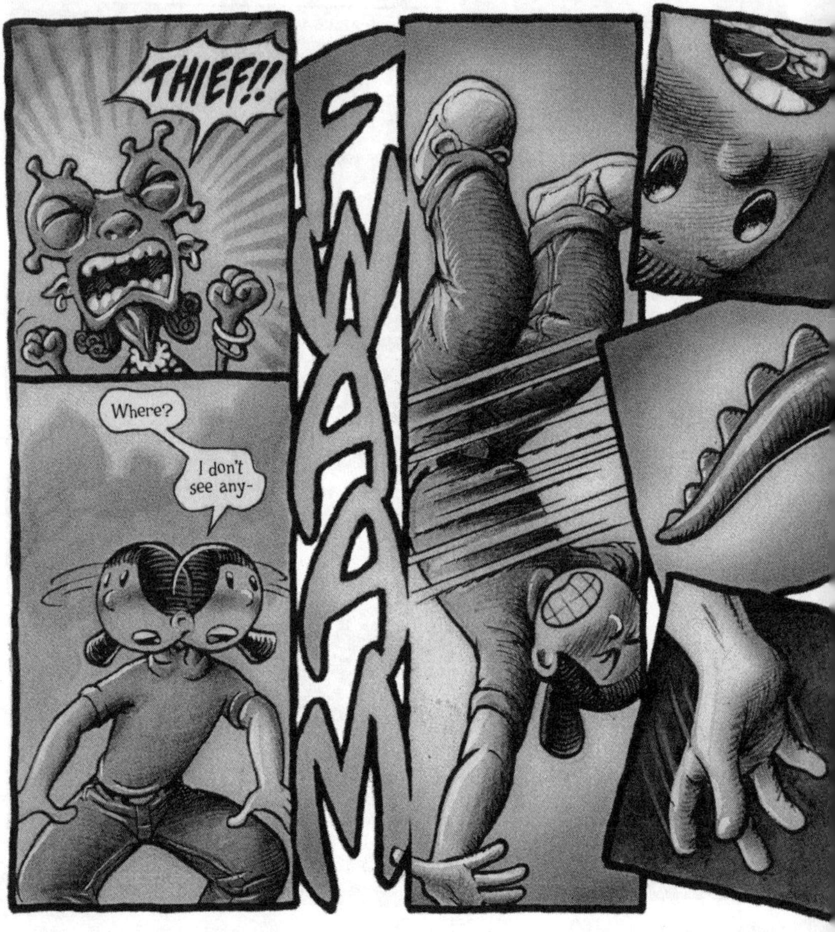
THIEF!!
Where?
I don't see any-
WHAM!

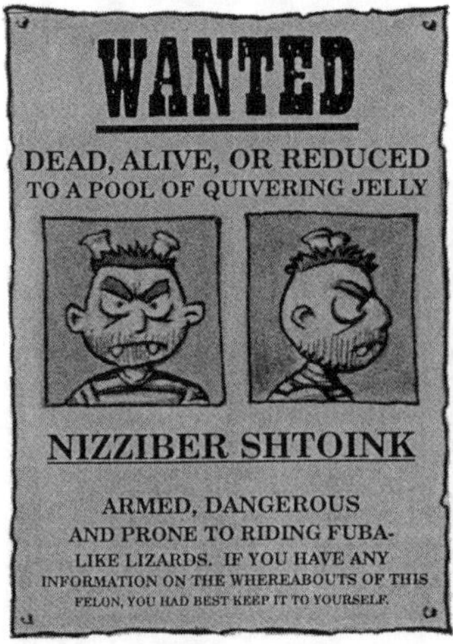
WANTED
DEAD, ALIVE, OR REDUCED TO A POOL OF QUIVERING JELLY
NIZZIBER SHTOINK
ARMED, DANGEROUS AND PRONE TO RIDING FUBA-LIKE LIZARDS. IF YOU HAVE ANY INFORMATION ON THE WHEREABOUTS OF THIS FELON, YOU HAD BEST KEEP IT TO YOURSELF.

A BRIEF HISTORY OF HIS PREVIOUS EXPLOITS:

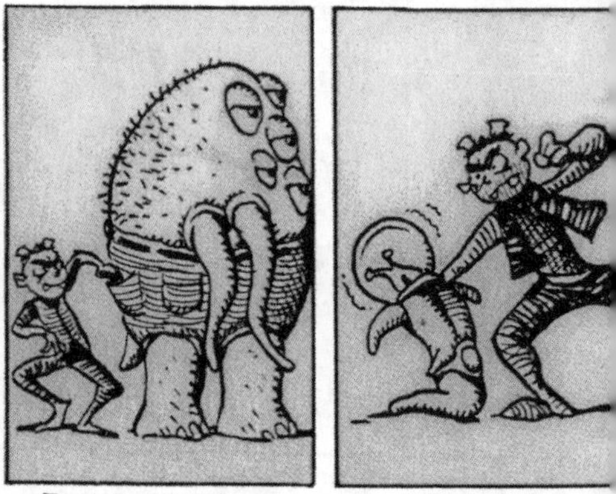

PICKPOCKETING ASSAULT

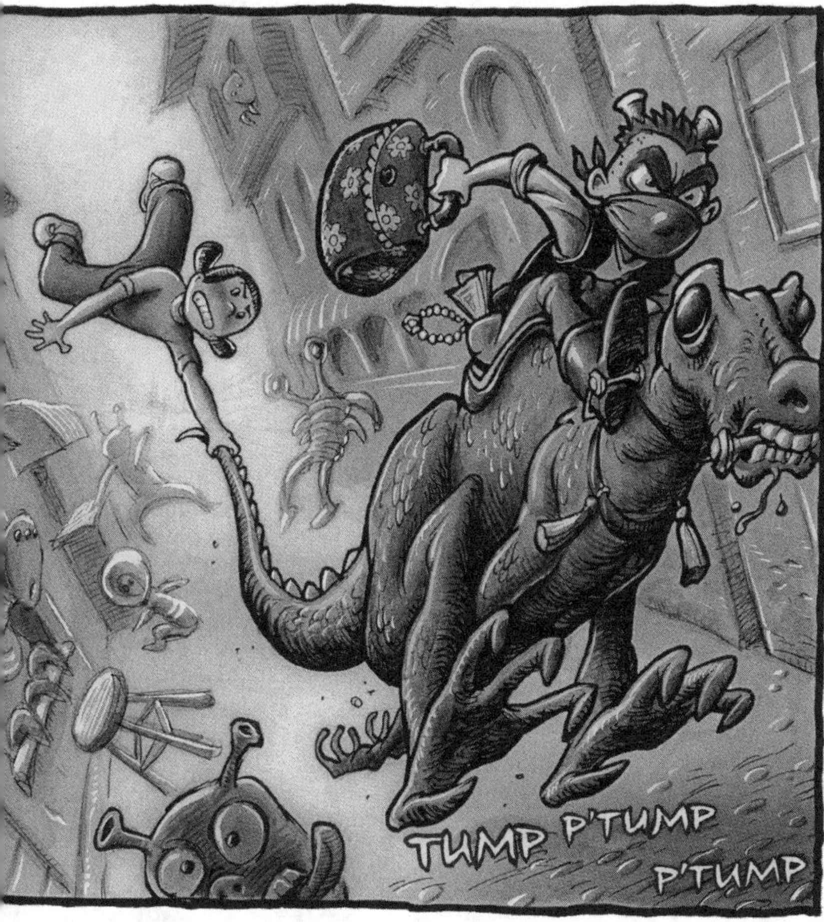
TUMP P'TUMP
P'TUMP

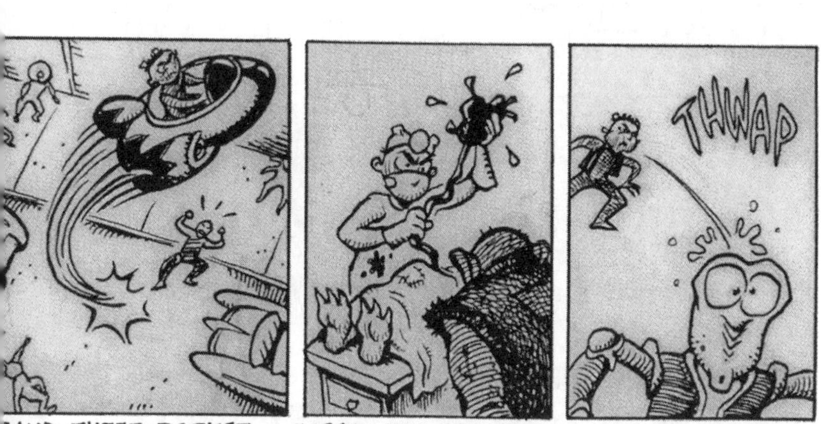
THWAP

RAND THEFT ROCKET ILLEGAL ORGAN TRANSPLANTS EXCESSIVE SPITTING

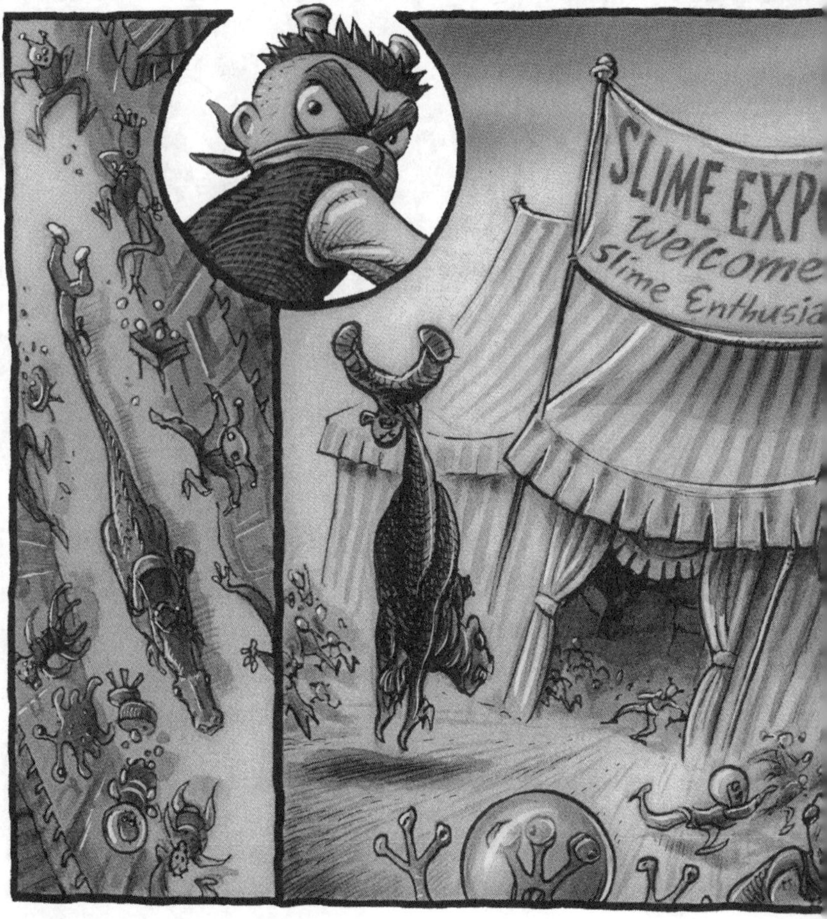
SLIME EXPO
Welcome
slime Enthusia

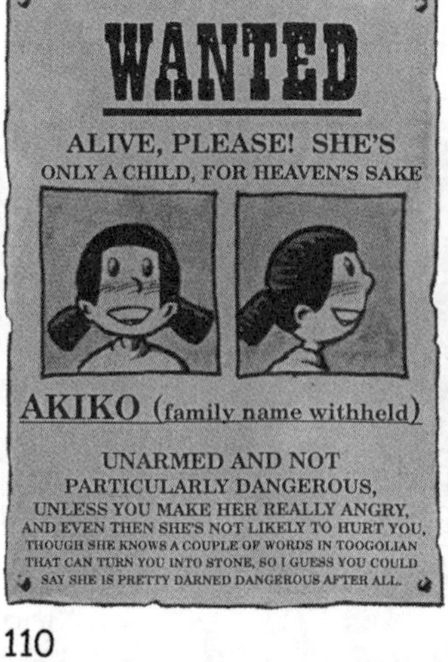
WANTED
ALIVE, PLEASE! SHE'S ONLY A CHILD, FOR HEAVEN'S SAKE
AKIKO (family name withheld)
UNARMED AND NOT PARTICULARLY DANGEROUS, UNLESS YOU MAKE HER REALLY ANGRY, AND EVEN THEN SHE'S NOT LIKELY TO HURT YOU, THOUGH SHE KNOWS A COUPLE OF WORDS IN TOOGOLIAN THAT CAN TURN YOU INTO STONE, SO I GUESS YOU COULD SAY SHE IS PRETTY DARNED DANGEROUS AFTER ALL.

A BRIEF HISTORY OF HER PREVIOUS EXPLOITS:

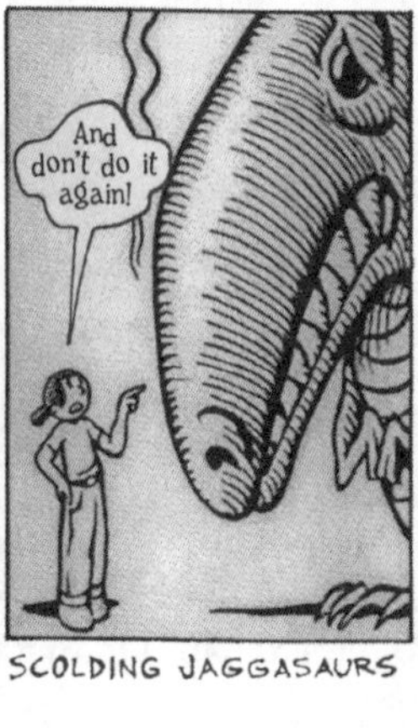
And don't do it again!

SCOLDING JAGGASAURS

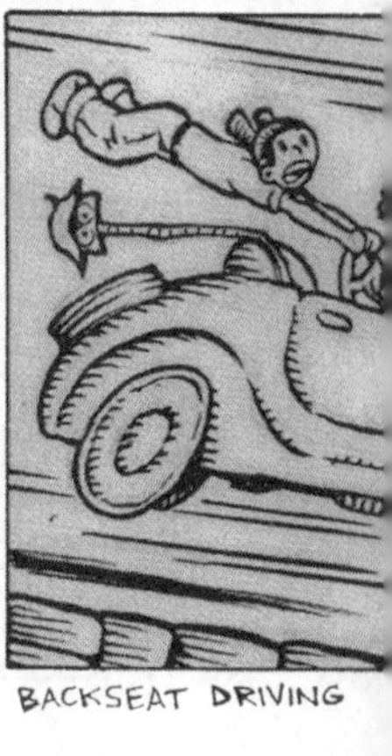

BACKSEAT DRIVING

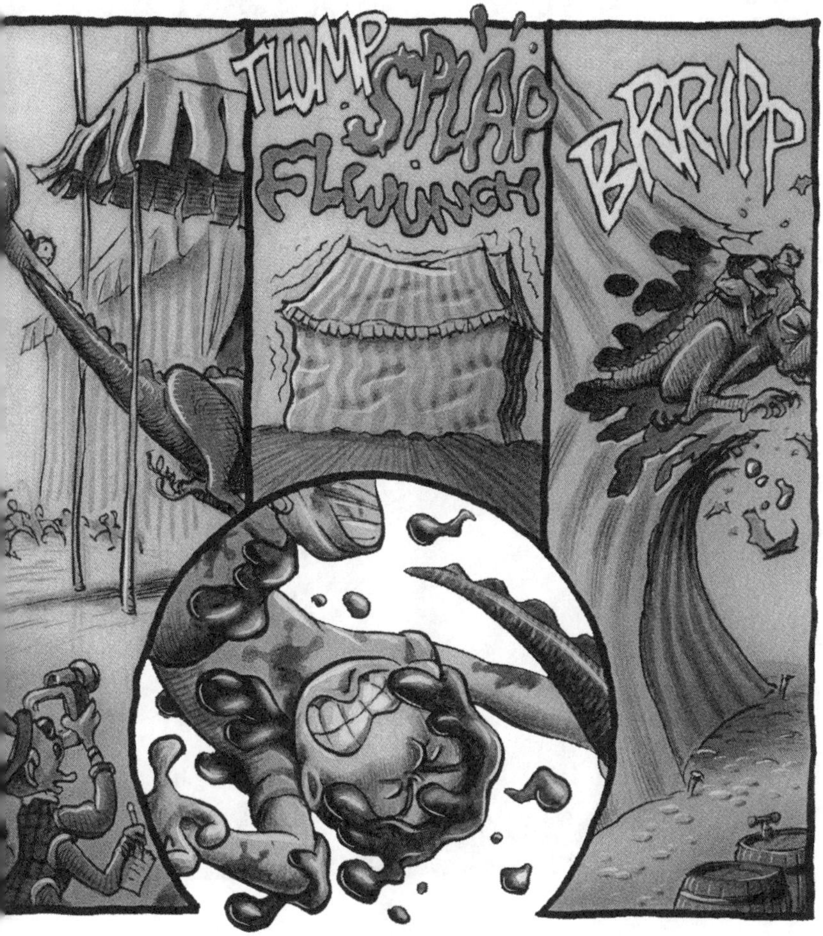
TLUMP
SPLAP
FLWUNCH
BRRIPP

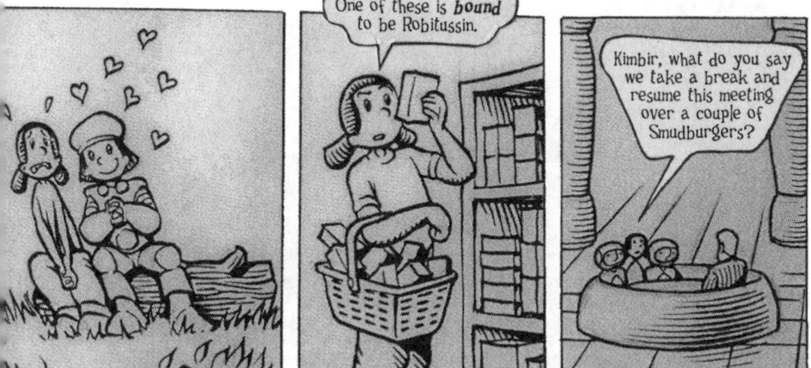
One of these is ***bound*** to be Robitussin.
Kimbir, what do you say we take a break and resume this meeting over a couple of Smudburgers?

URNING DOWN MARRIAGE PROPOSALS SHOPPING IN JAPAN CLINCHING DEALS IN OUTER SPACE

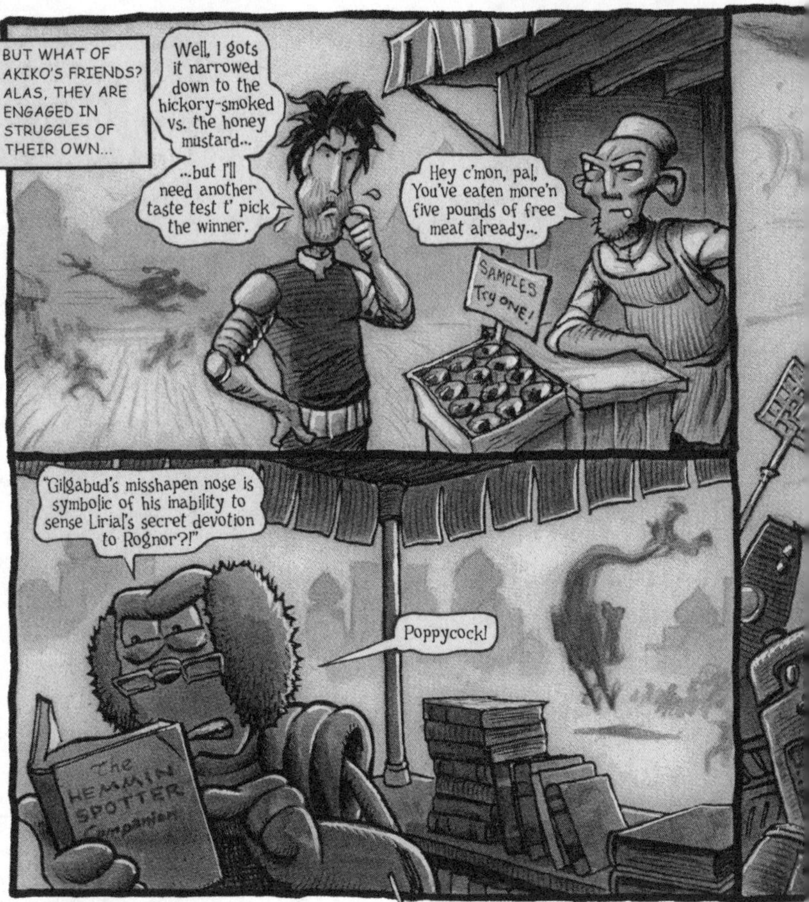
BUT WHAT OF AKIKO'S FRIENDS? ALAS, THEY ARE ENGAGED IN STRUGGLES OF THEIR OWN...
Well, I gots it narrowed down to the hickory-smoked vs. the honey mustard...
...but I'll need another taste test t' pick the winner.
Hey c'mon, pal, You've eaten more'n five pounds of free meat already...
SAMPLES Try ONE!
"Gilgabud's misshapen nose is symbolic of his inability to sense Lirial's secret devotion to Rognor?!"
Poppycock!
The HEMMIN SPOTTER Companion

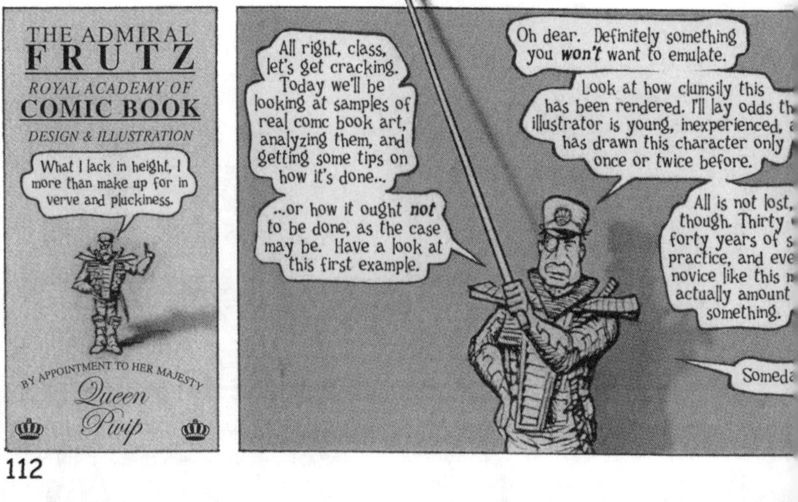
THE ADMIRAL FRUTZ
ROYAL ACADEMY OF
COMIC BOOK
DESIGN & ILLUSTRATION
What I lack in height, I more than make up for in verve and pluckiness.
BY APPOINTMENT TO HER MAJESTY
Queen Pwip
All right, class, let's get cracking. Today we'll be looking at samples of real comc book art, analyzing them, and getting some tips on how it's done...
...or how it ought *not* to be done, as the case may be. Have a look at this first example.
Oh dear. Definitely something you *won't* want to emulate.
Look at how clumsily this has been rendered. I'll lay odds th illustrator is young, inexperienced, has drawn this character only once or twice before.
All is not lost, though. Thirty forty years of s practice, and eve novice like this n actually amount something.
Someda

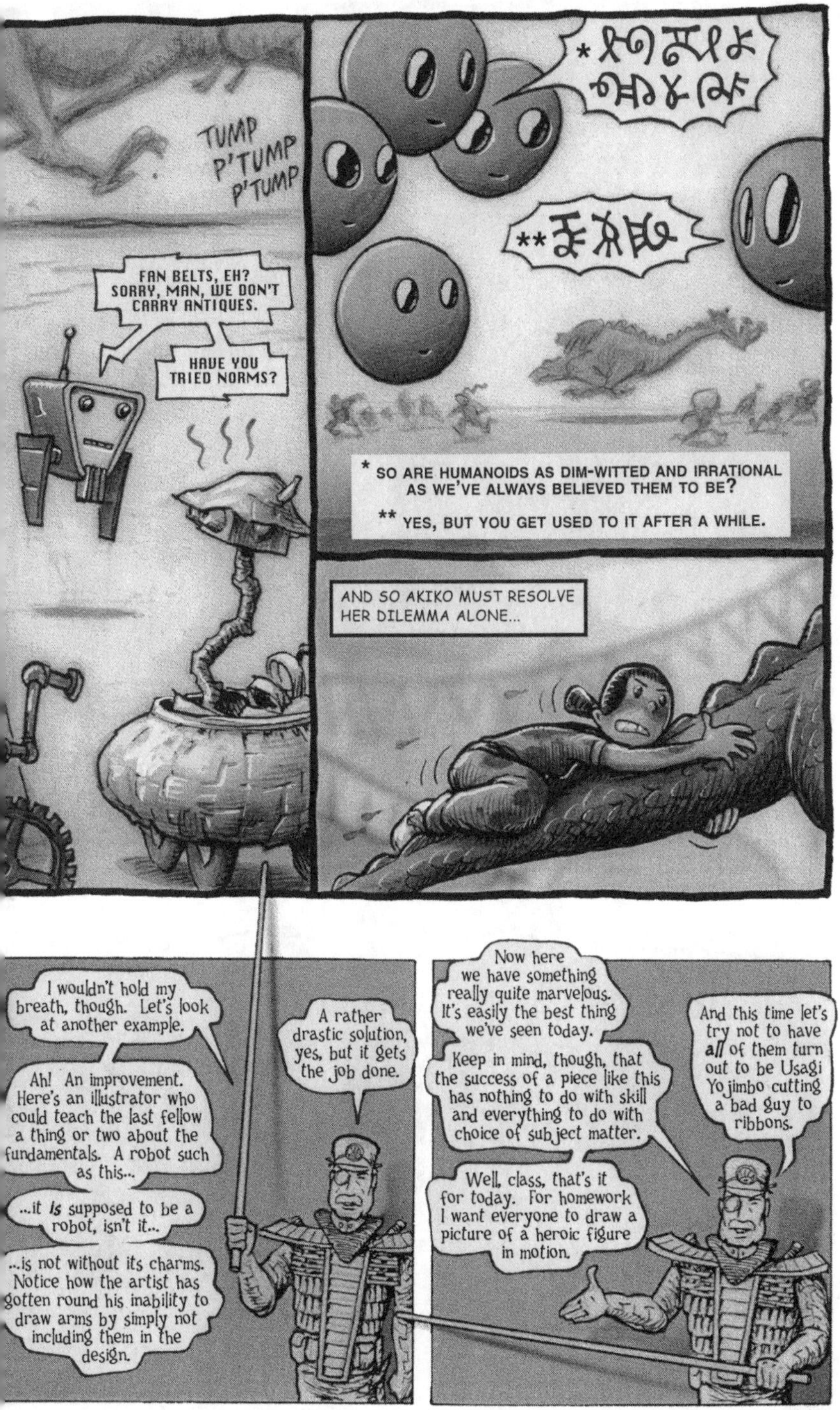
TUMP
P'TUMP
P'TUMP
FAN BELTS, EH? SORRY, MAN, WE DON'T CARRY ANTIQUES.
HAVE YOU TRIED NORMS?
* SO ARE HUMANOIDS AS DIM-WITTED AND IRRATIONAL AS WE'VE ALWAYS BELIEVED THEM TO BE?
** YES, BUT YOU GET USED TO IT AFTER A WHILE.
AND SO AKIKO MUST RESOLVE HER DILEMMA ALONE...
I wouldn't hold my breath, though. Let's look at another example.
Ah! An improvement. Here's an illustrator who could teach the last fellow a thing or two about the fundamentals. A robot such as this...
...it *is* supposed to be a robot, isn't it...
...is not without its charms. Notice how the artist has gotten round his inability to draw arms by simply not including them in the design.
A rather drastic solution, yes, but it gets the job done.
Now here we have something really quite marvelous. It's easily the best thing we've seen today.
Keep in mind, though, that the success of a piece like this has nothing to do with skill and everything to do with choice of subject matter.
Well, class, that's it for today. For homework I want everyone to draw a picture of a heroic figure in motion.
And this time let's try not to have *all* of them turn out to be Usagi Yojimbo cutting a bad guy to ribbons.

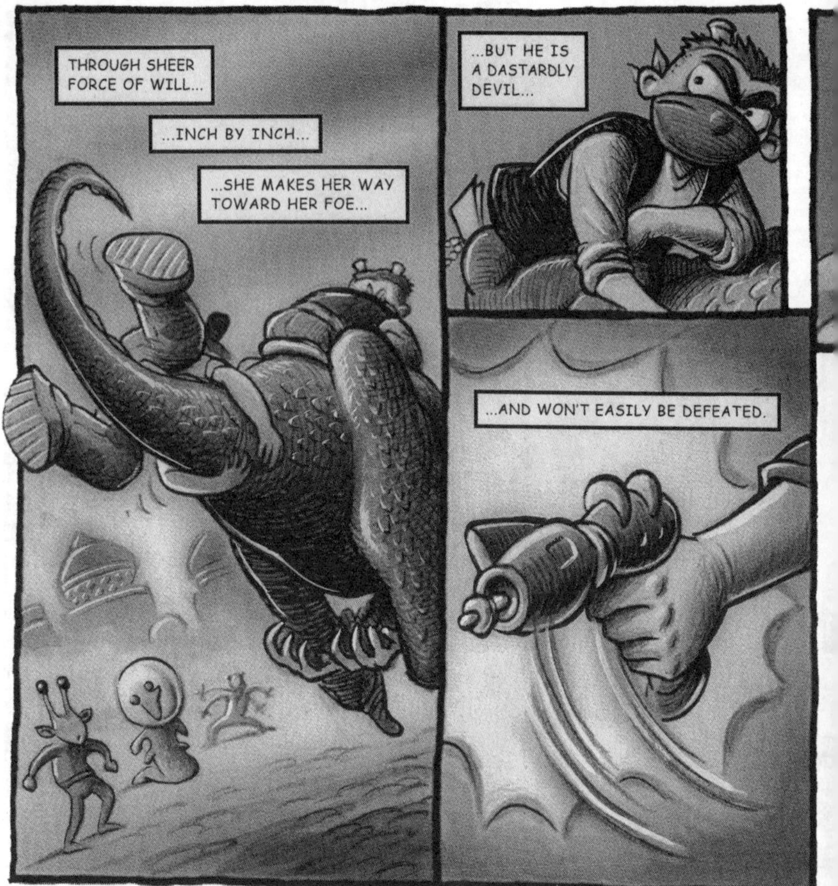
THROUGH SHEER FORCE OF WILL...
...INCH BY INCH...
...SHE MAKES HER WAY TOWARD HER FOE...
...BUT HE IS A DASTARDLY DEVIL...
...AND WON'T EASILY BE DEFEATED.

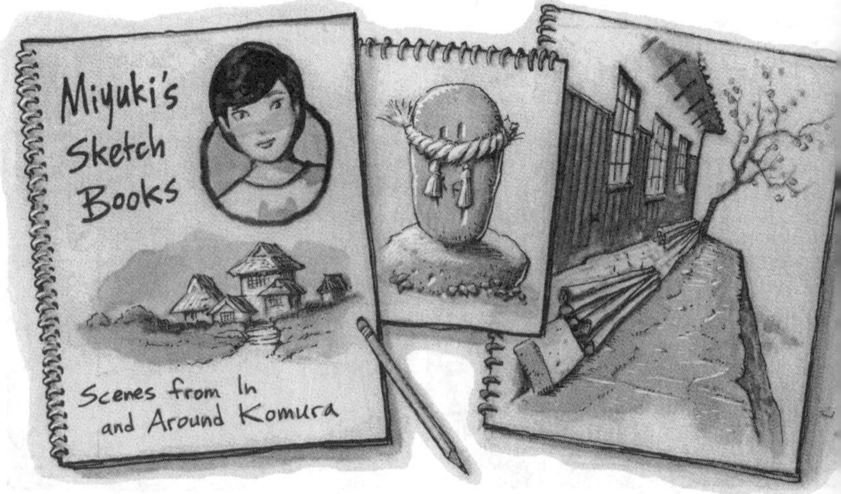
Miyuki's Sketch Books
Scenes from In and Around Komura

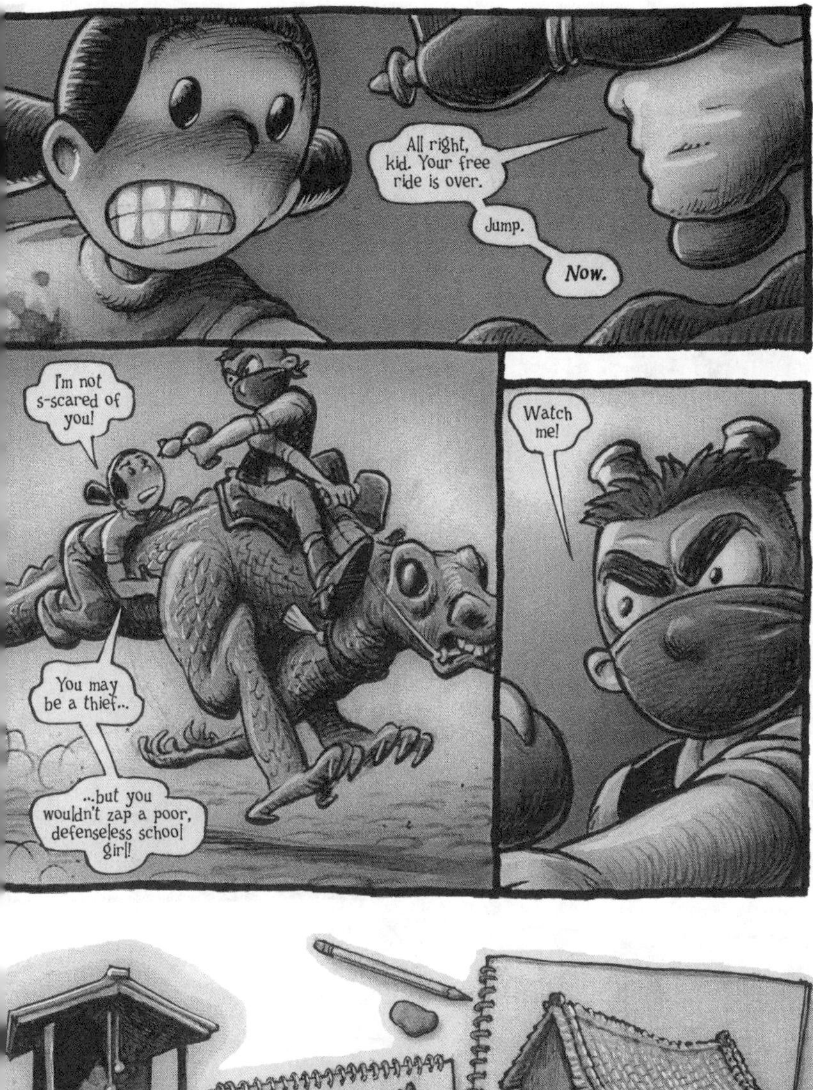
All right, kid. Your free ride is over.
Jump.
Now.
I'm not s-scared of you!
Watch me!
You may be a thief...
...but you wouldn't zap a poor, defenseless school girl!

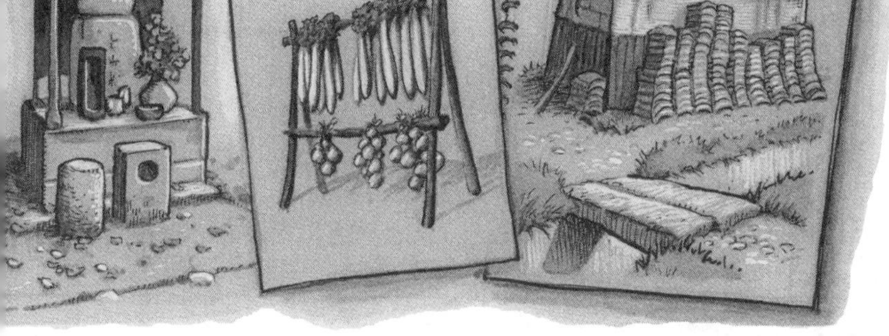

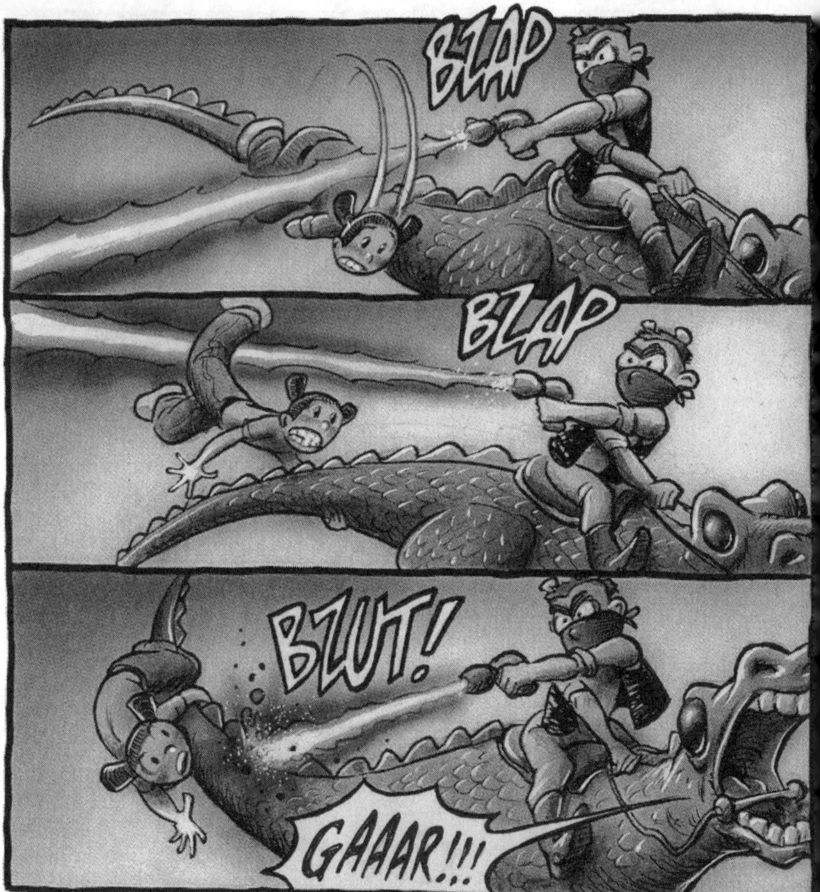
BZAP
BZAP
BZUT!
GAAAR!!!

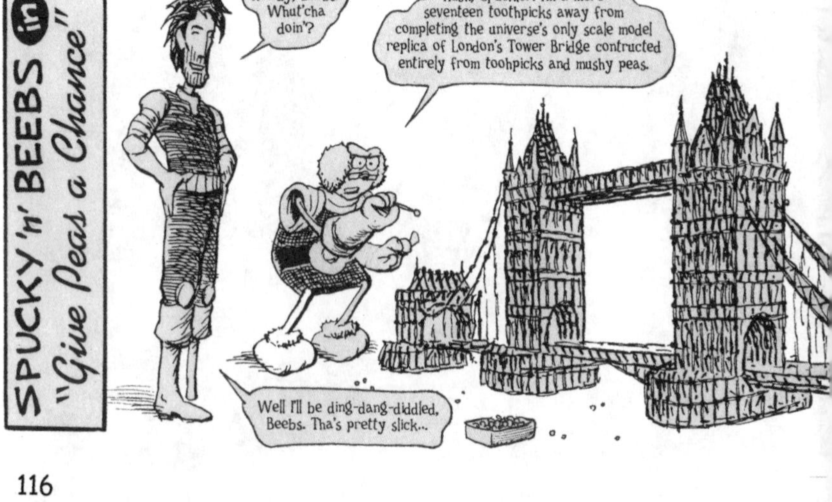
SPUCKY 'n' BEEBS in
"Give Peas a Chance"
Howdy, Beebs. Whut'cha doin'?
Hush, Spuckler. I'm a mere seventeen toothpicks away from completing the universe's only scale model replica of London's Tower Bridge contructed entirely from toohpicks and mushy peas.
Well I'll be ding-dang-diddled, Beebs. Tha's pretty slick...

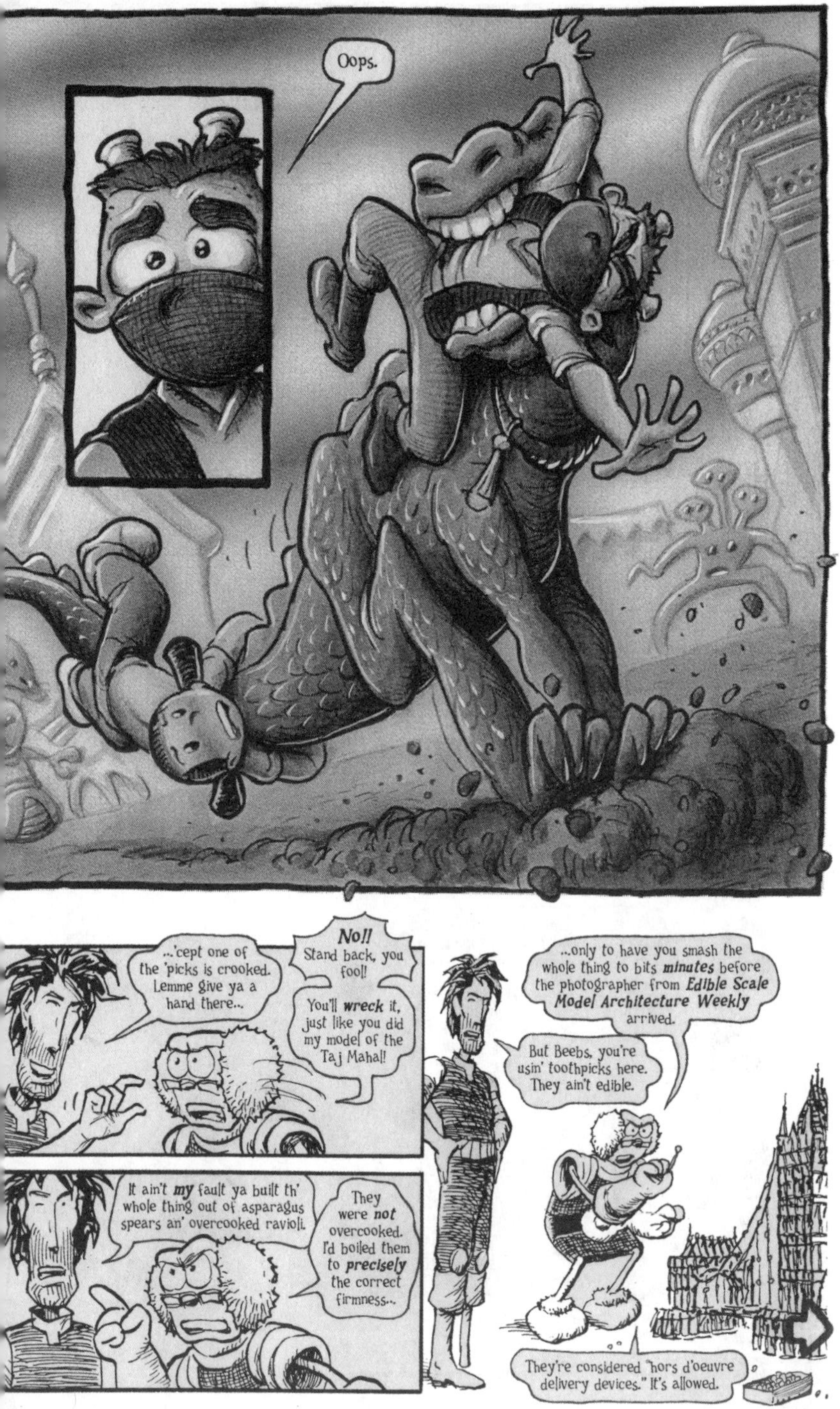
Oops.
...'cept one of the 'picks is crooked. Lemme give ya a hand there...
No!! Stand back, you fool!
You'll wreck it, just like you did my model of the Taj Mahal!
It ain't my fault ya built th' whole thing out of asparagus spears an' overcooked ravioli.
They were not overcooked. I'd boiled them to precisely the correct firmness...
...only to have you smash the whole thing to bits minutes before the photographer from Edible Scale Model Architecture Weekly arrived.
But Beebs, you're usin' toothpicks here. They ain't edible.
They're considered "hors d'oeuvre delivery devices." It's allowed.

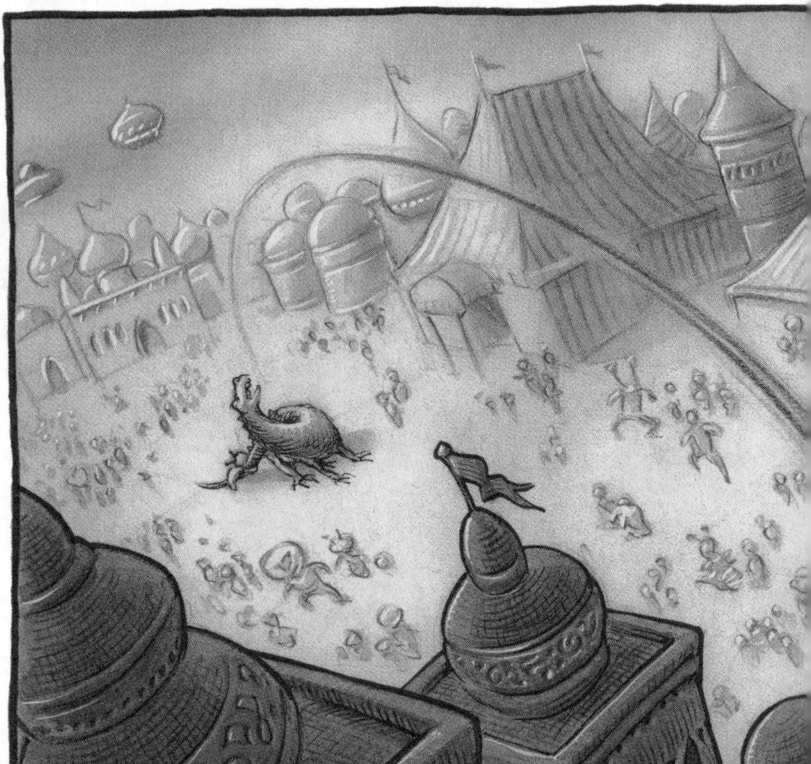

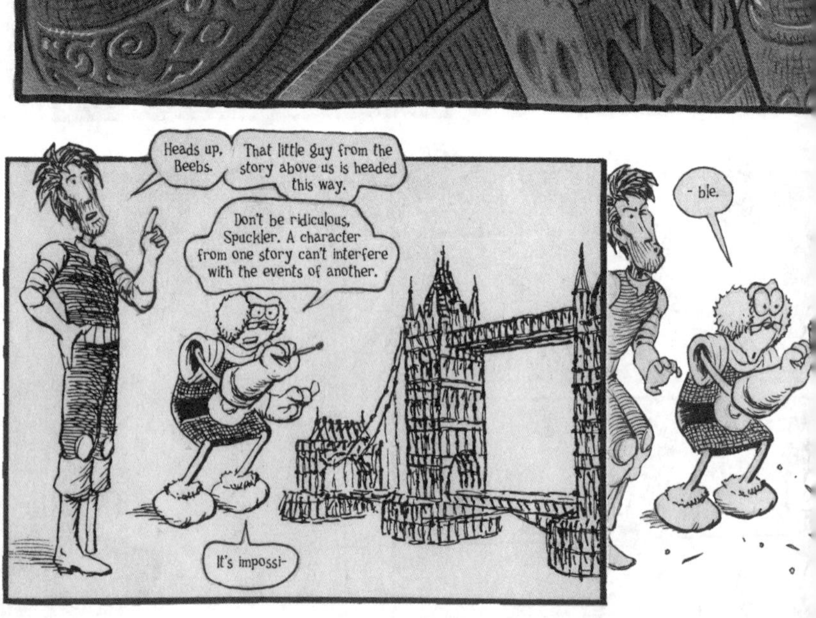
Heads up, Beebs.
That little guy from the story above us is headed this way.
Don't be ridiculous, Spuckler. A character from one story can't interfere with the events of another.
It's impossi-
- ble.

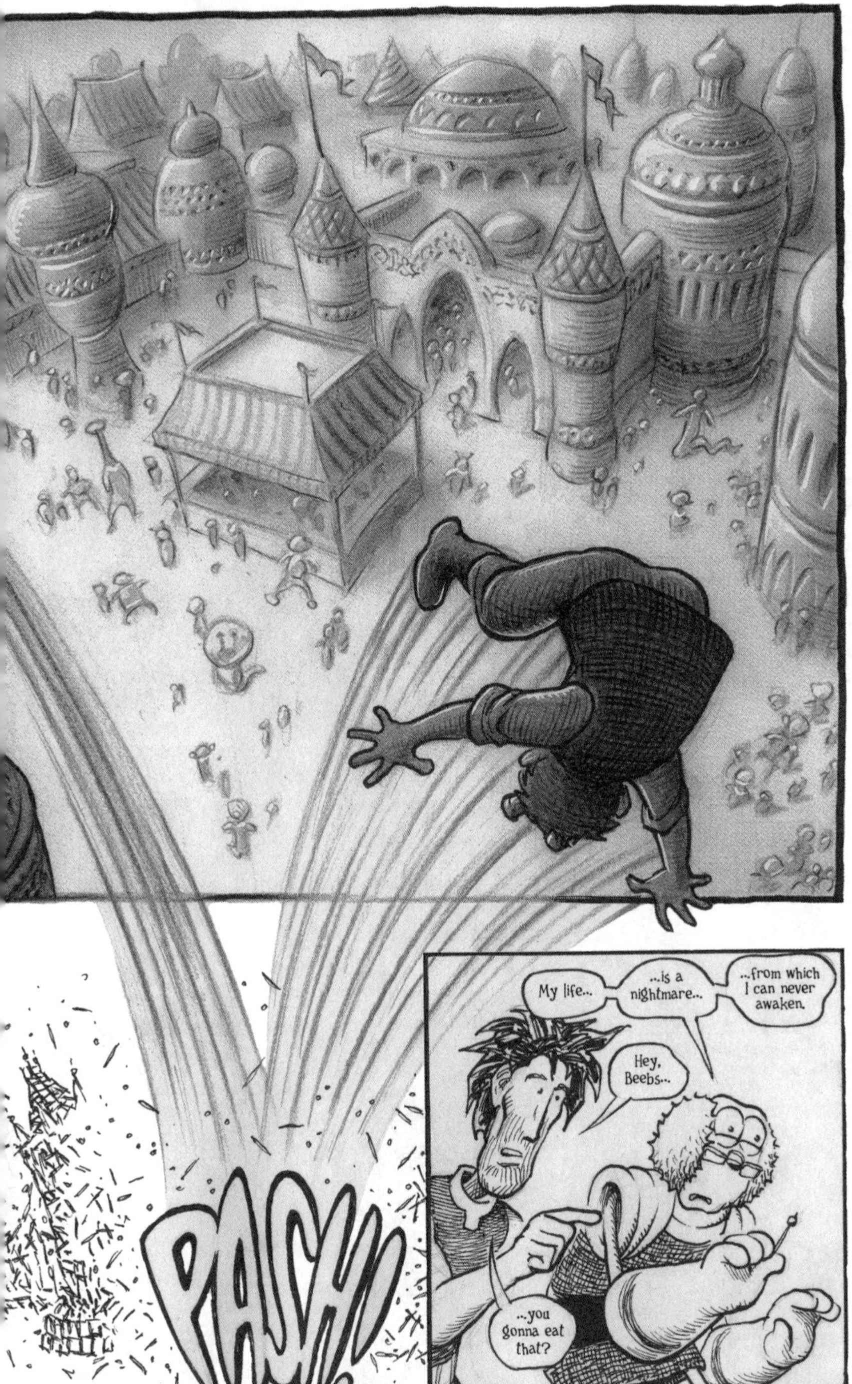
PACH!
My life...
...is a nightmare...
...from which I can never awaken.
Hey, Beebs...
...you gonna eat that?
THE END

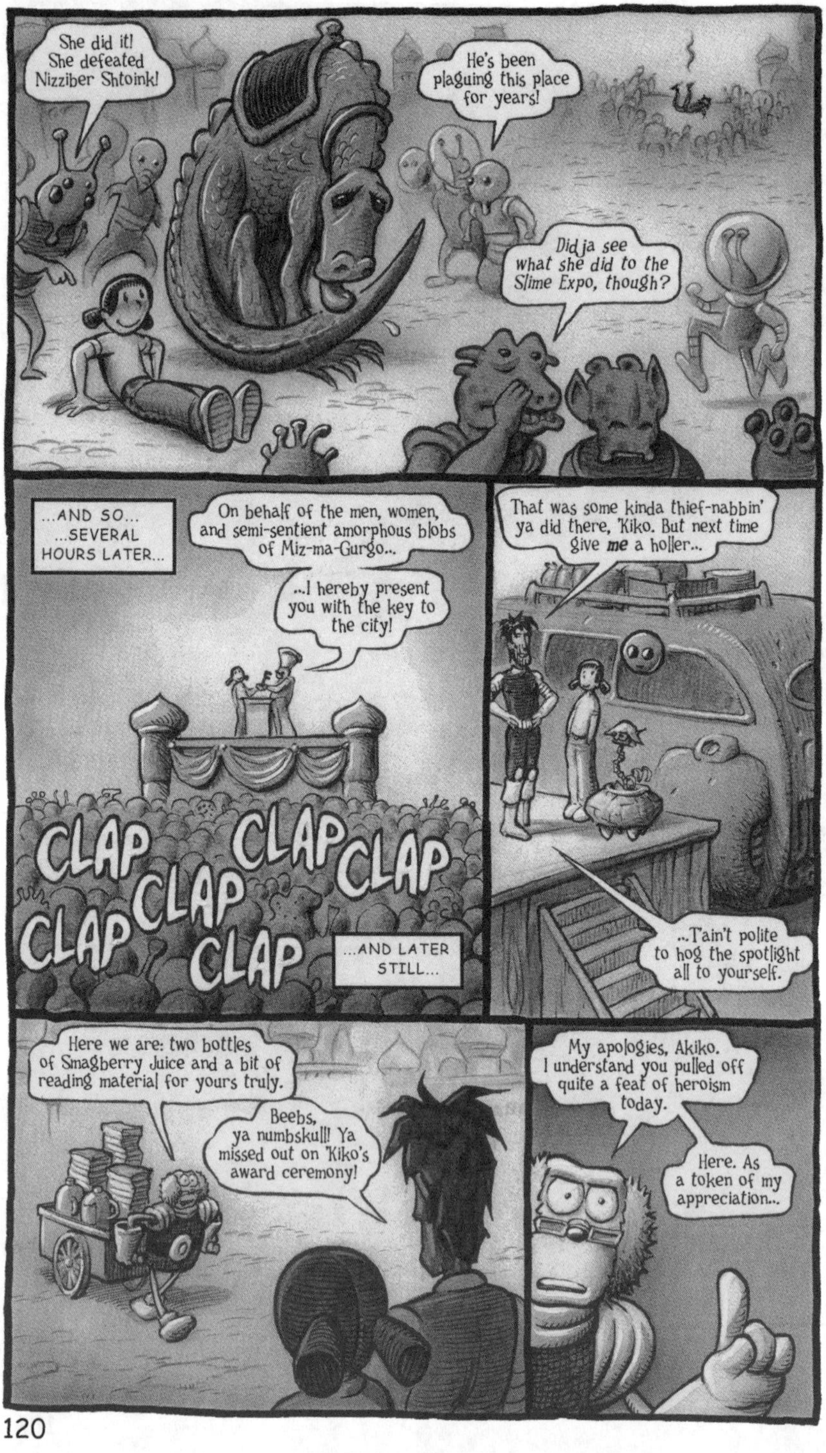

She did it! She defeated Nizziber Shtoink!
He's been plaguing this place for years!
Didja see what she did to the Slime Expo, though?
...AND SO... ...SEVERAL HOURS LATER...
On behalf of the men, women, and semi-sentient amorphous blobs of Miz-ma-Gurgo...
...I hereby present you with the key to the city!
CLAP CLAP CLAP CLAP CLAP CLAP
...AND LATER STILL...
That was some kinda thief-nabbin' ya did there, 'Kiko. But next time give *me* a holler...
...Tain't polite to hog the spotlight all to yourself.
Here we are: two bottles of Smagberry Juice and a bit of reading material for yours truly.
Beebs, ya numbskull! Ya missed out on 'Kiko's award ceremony!
My apologies, Akiko. I understand you pulled off quite a feat of heroism today.
Here. As a token of my appreciation...

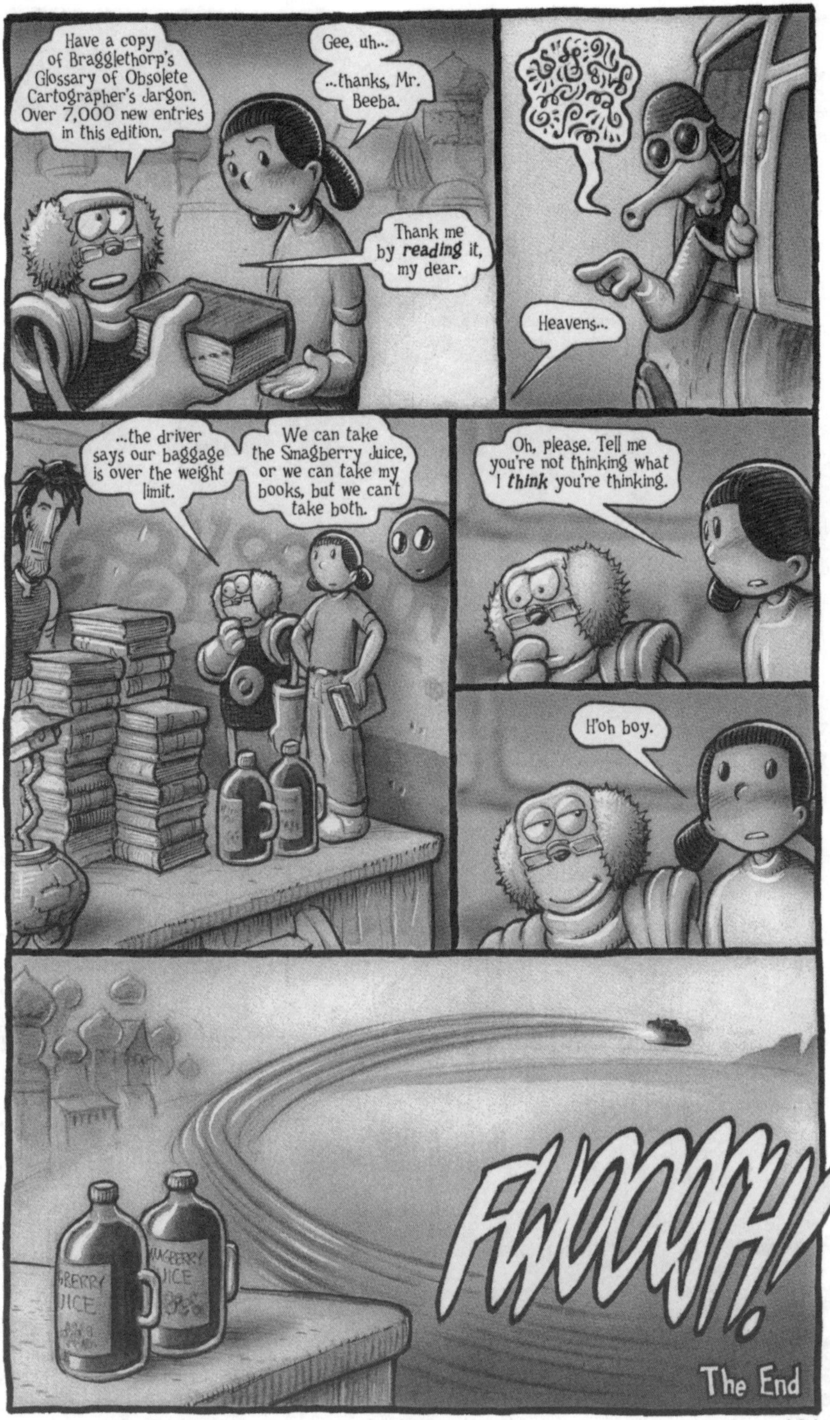
Have a copy of Bragglethorp's Glossary of Obsolete Cartographer's Jargon. Over 7,000 new entries in this edition.
Gee, uh...
...thanks, Mr. Beeba.
Thank me by *reading* it, my dear.
Heavens...
...the driver says our baggage is over the weight limit.
We can take the Smagberry Juice, or we can take my books, but we can't take both.
Oh, please. Tell me you're not thinking what I *think* you're thinking.
H'oh boy.
FWOOSH!
The End

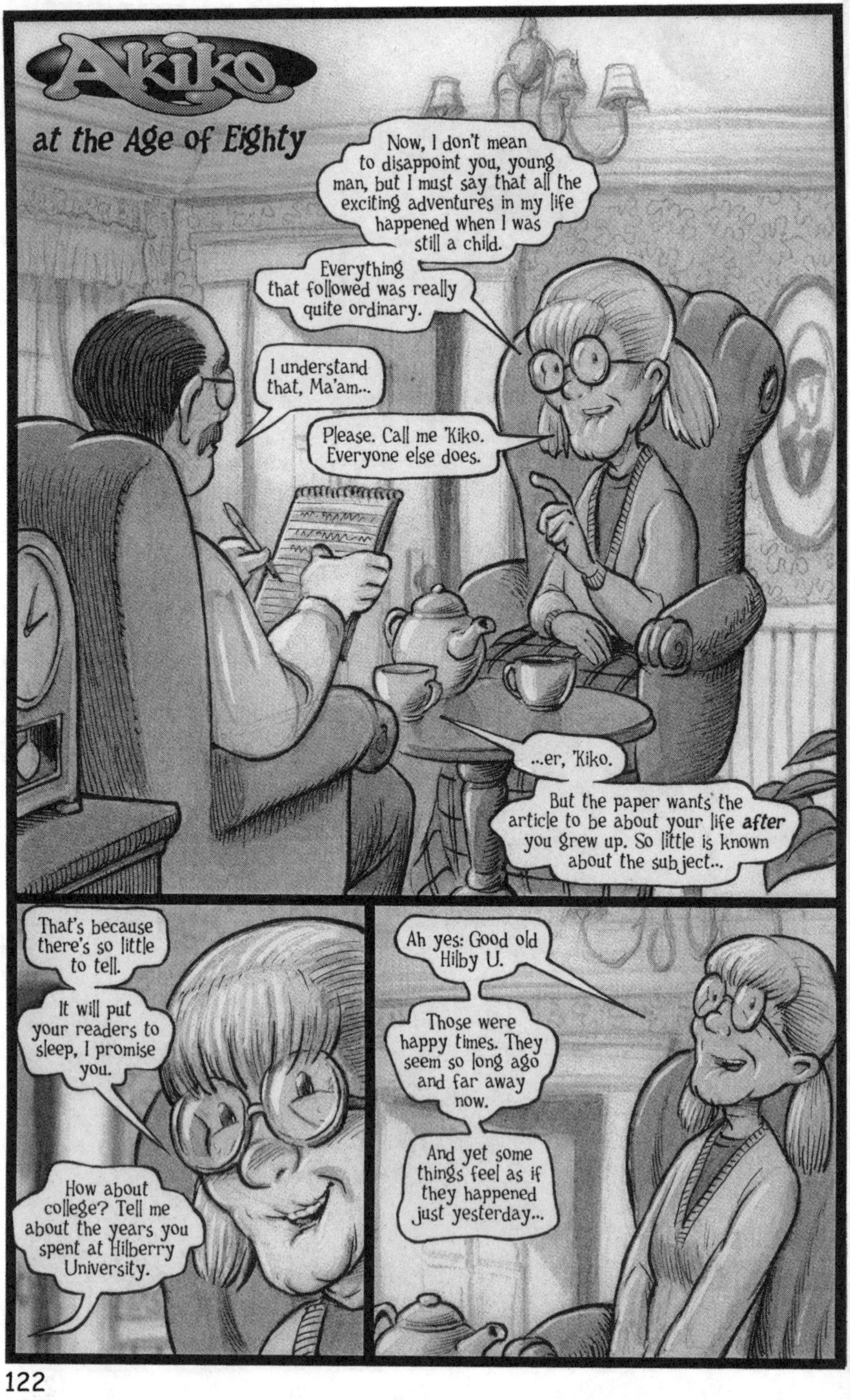
Akiko
at the Age of Eighty
Now, I don't mean to disappoint you, young man, but I must say that all the exciting adventures in my life happened when I was still a child.
Everything that followed was really quite ordinary.
I understand that, Ma'am...
Please. Call me 'Kiko. Everyone else does.
...er, 'Kiko.
But the paper wants the article to be about your life ***after*** you grew up. So little is known about the subject...
That's because there's so little to tell.
It will put your readers to sleep, I promise you.
How about college? Tell me about the years you spent at Hilberry University.
Ah yes: Good old Hilby U.
Those were happy times. They seem so long ago and far away now.
And yet some things feel as if they happened just yesterday...

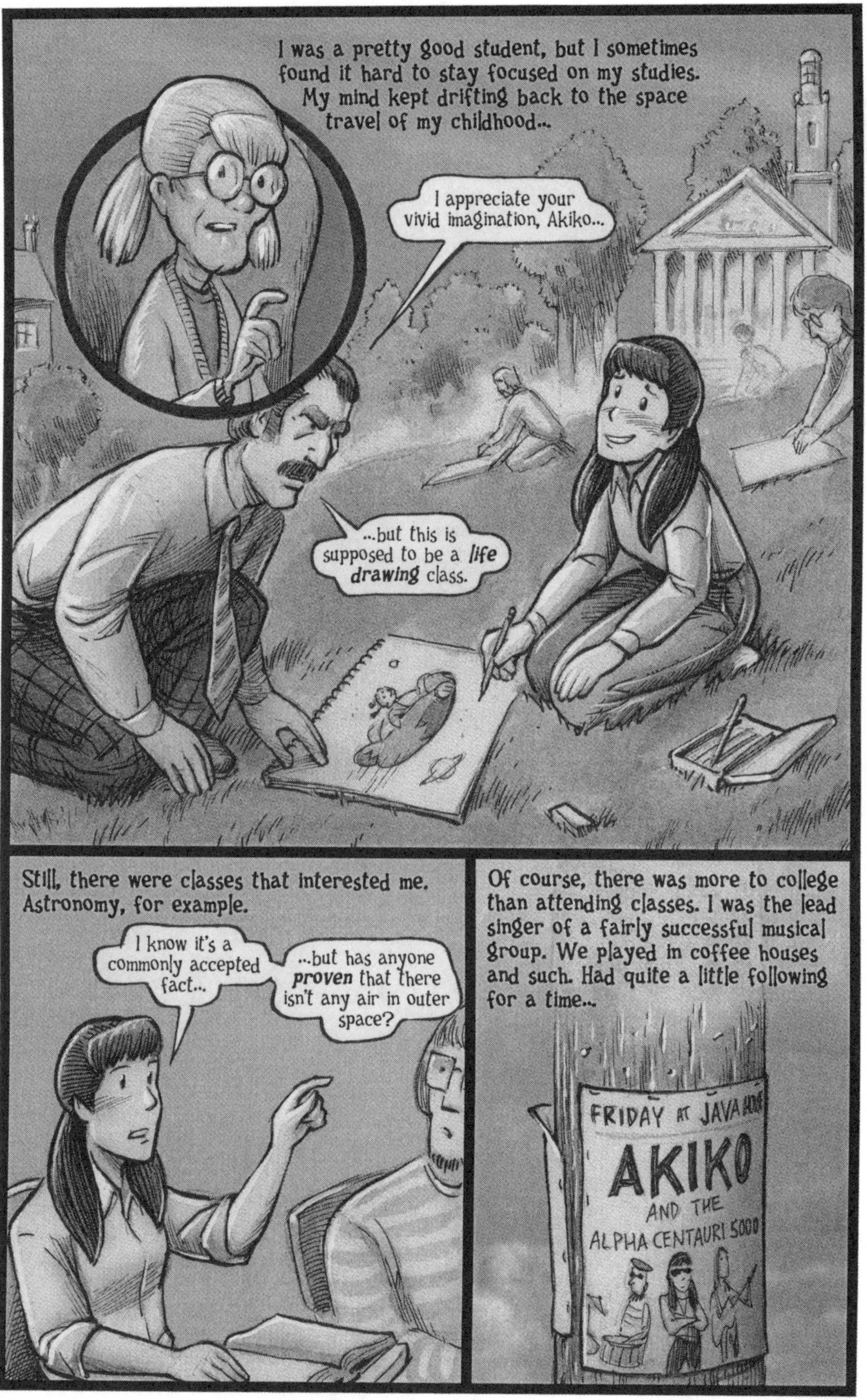
I was a pretty good student, but I sometimes found it hard to stay focused on my studies. My mind kept drifting back to the space travel of my childhood...
I appreciate your vivid imagination, Akiko...
...but this is supposed to be a *life drawing* class.
Still, there were classes that interested me. Astronomy, for example.
I know it's a commonly accepted fact...
...but has anyone *proven* that there isn't any air in outer space?
Of course, there was more to college than attending classes. I was the lead singer of a fairly successful musical group. We played in coffee houses and such. Had quite a little following for a time...
FRIDAY AT JAVA
AKIKO
AND THE
ALPHA CENTAURI 5000

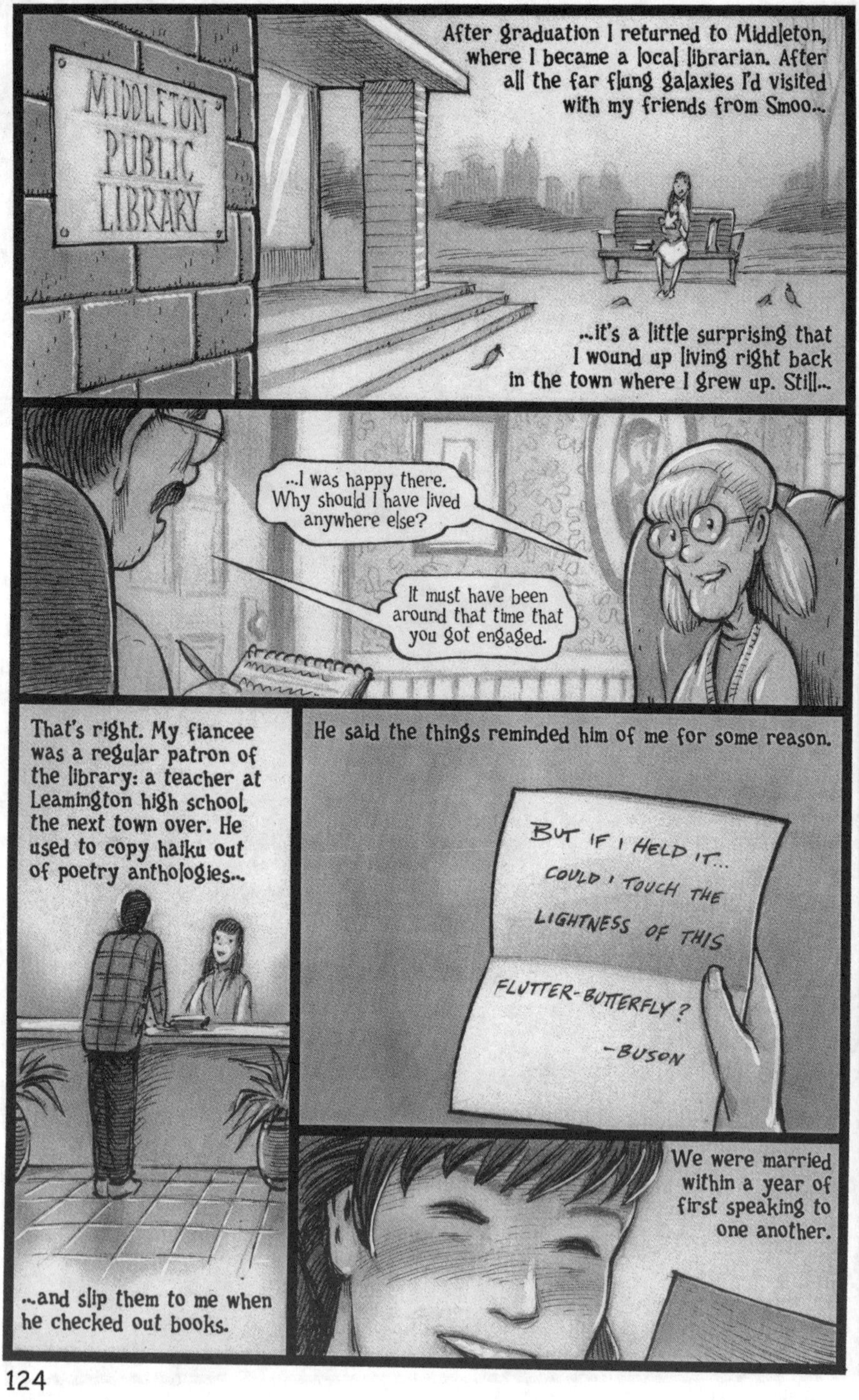
After graduation I returned to Middleton, where I became a local librarian. After all the far flung galaxies I'd visited with my friends from Smoo...
MIDDLETON PUBLIC LIBRARY
...it's a little surprising that I wound up living right back in the town where I grew up. Still...
...I was happy there. Why should I have lived anywhere else?
It must have been around that time that you got engaged.
That's right. My fiancee was a regular patron of the library: a teacher at Leamington high school, the next town over. He used to copy haiku out of poetry anthologies...
...and slip them to me when he checked out books.
He said the things reminded him of me for some reason.
BUT IF I HELD IT... COULD I TOUCH THE LIGHTNESS OF THIS FLUTTER-BUTTERFLY? —BUSON
We were married within a year of first speaking to one another.

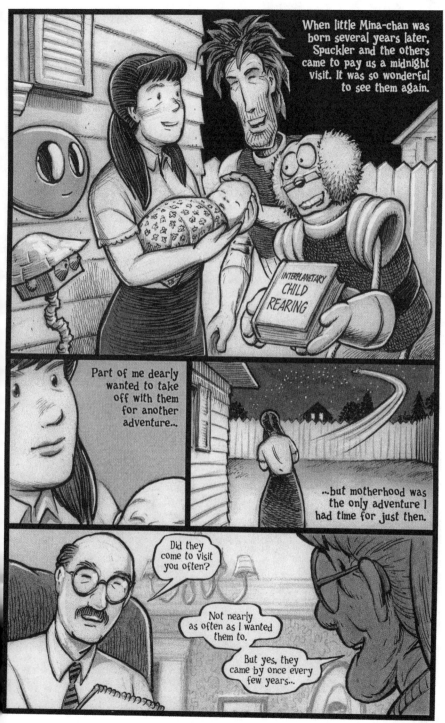

When little Mina-chan was born several years later, Spuckler and the others came to pay us a midnight visit. It was so wonderful to see them again.

Part of me dearly wanted to take off with them for another adventure...

...but motherhood was the only adventure I had time for just then.

INTERPLANETARY CHILD REARING

Did they come to visit you often?

Not nearly as often as I wanted them to.

But yes, they came by once every few years...

Once I arranged for them to join my family on a camping trip. Mina was eight or nine by then, nearly as old as I'd been when I made my first trip to Smoo.

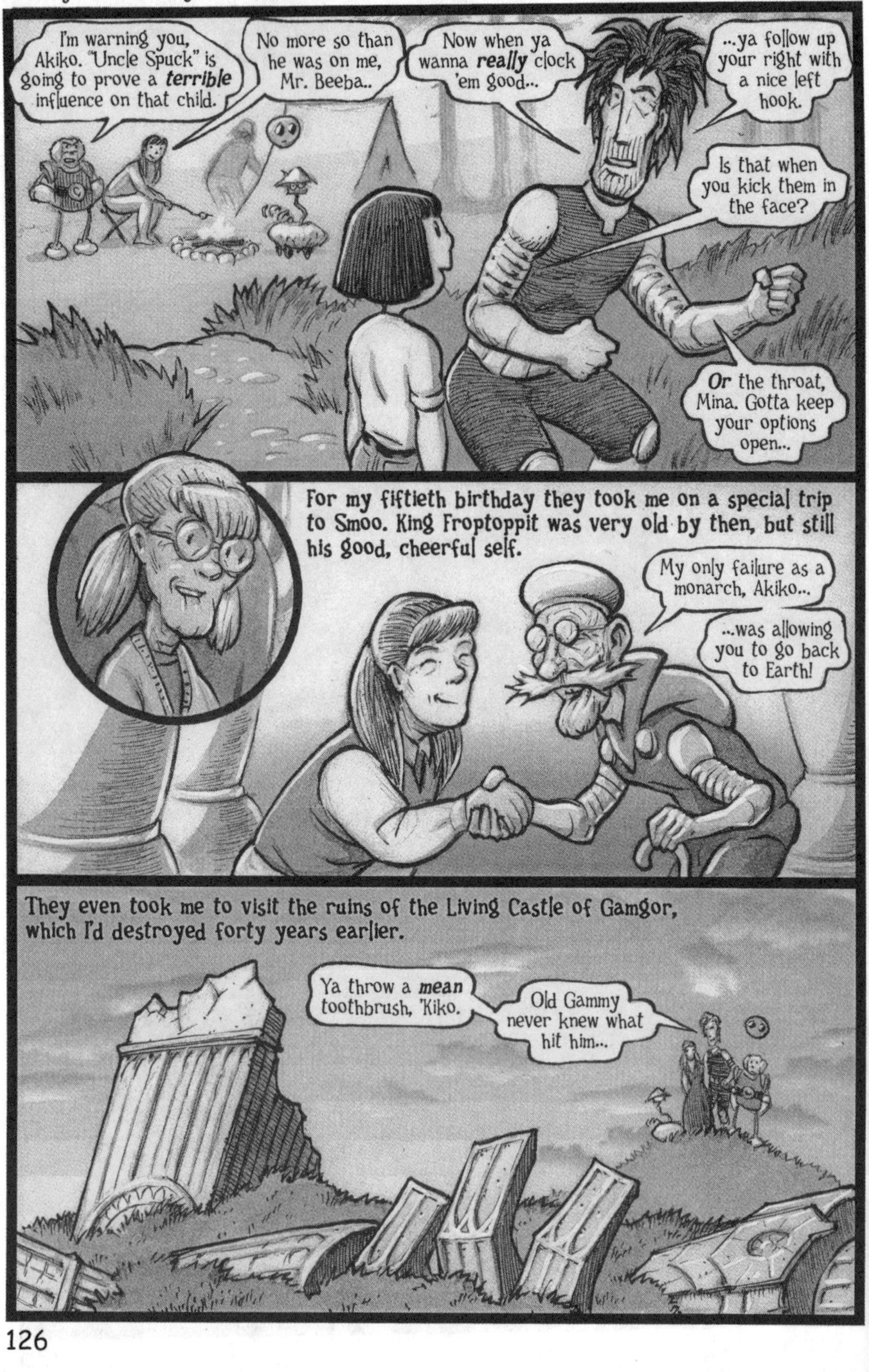
I'm warning you, Akiko. "Uncle Spuck" is going to prove a ***terrible*** influence on that child.
No more so than he was on me, Mr. Beeba..
Now when ya wanna ***really*** clock 'em good...
...ya follow up your right with a nice left hook.
Is that when you kick them in the face?
Or the throat, Mina. Gotta keep your options open...
For my fiftieth birthday they took me on a special trip to Smoo. King Froptoppit was very old by then, but still his good, cheerful self.
My only failure as a monarch, Akiko...
...was allowing you to go back to Earth!
They even took me to visit the ruins of the Living Castle of Gamgor, which I'd destroyed forty years earlier.
Ya throw a ***mean*** toothbrush, 'Kiko.
Old Gammy never knew what hit him...